CRACKED

THE FUTURE OF DAMS
IN A HOT, CHAOTIC WORLD

STEVEN HAWLEY

patagonia®

CRACKED THE FUTURE OF DAMS IN A HOT, CHAOTIC WORLD

Patagonia publishes a select list of titles on wilderness, wildlife, and outdoor sports that inspire and restore a connection to the natural world and encourage action to combat climate chaos.

© 2023 Steven Hawley

Published by Patagonia Works

Photograph copyrights held by the photographer as indicated in captions.

Every effort was made to recognize the tribes displaced from these lands by advancing societies. Please email books@patagonia.com to offer additions or corrections.

Hardcover Edition.

Printed in the USA on Roland Enviro 100 Satin FSC® certified 100 percent postconsumer-waste paper.

Editor – John Dutton
Photo Editor – Rich Crowder
Art Director/Designer – Christina Speed
Maps & Figures – Christina Speed
Project Manager – Sonia Moore
Photo Production – Taylor Norton
Production – Natausha Greenblott
Creative Director – Michael Leon
Publisher – Karla Olson

Hardcover ISBN 978-1-938340-77-2

E-Book ISBN 978-1-938340-78-9

Library of Congress Control Number 2022951013

ENVIRONMENTAL BENEFITS STATEMENT

Patagonia saved the following resources by printing on process chlorine free paper made with post-consumer recycled fiber versus paper made with virgin fiber. The cover wrap, end sheets, and text pages of this book all contain 100% post-consumer recycled fiber.

TREES	WATER	ENERGY	SOLID WASTE	GREENHOUSE GASES
282 FULLY GROWN	23,000 GALLONS	119 MILLION BTU's	1,000 POUNDS	121,400 POUNDS

This is based on the current requirement of 124,500 sheets (23,531 lbs) 28x40" 80# Rolland Enviro Satin Text 100% PCW/FSC.

Environmental impact estimates were made using the Environmental Paper Network Paper Calculator Version 4.0. For more information visit www.papercalculator.org.

1% FOR THE PLANET. MEMBER

FSC www.fsc.org
MIX
Paper from responsible sources
FSC® C002589

Cover photo: Denied access to habitat, a salmon lies dead below the Elwha Dam. The dam was removed in 2012, followed by the Glines Canyon Dam in 2014, bolstering the odds for a salmon revival. Lower Elwha Klallam ancestral lands, Washington. BEN KNIGHT

Front endsheet: After the main spillway for Oroville Dam was damaged, officials attempted to use the auxiliary spillway. Konkow and Enterprise Rancheria Estom Yumeka Maidu ancestral lands, California. DALE KOLKE / CALIFORNIA DEPARTMENT OF WATER RESOURCES

Title page: Fifty miles south of the United States-Mexico border, the Colorado River Delta and its once-rich estuary wetlands are now as parched as the surrounding Sonoran Desert. Cocopah ancestral lands. PETE MCBRIDE PHOTOGRAPHY

For K.,
with gratitude for your faith and patience:
all the love I can conjure in a single sentence.

Sediment transport happens. Dams make a feeble attempt to stop it, often at the cost of the dam itself. Completed in 1948, by 1964 the Matilija Dam was rendered useless due to sedimentation. Chumash ancestral lands, California. JIM MARTIN

Next spread: Hetch Hetchy Reservoir, impounded behind O'Shaughnessy Dam, provides water to 2.7 million residents and businesses in the San Francisco Bay Area. Southern Sierra Miwuk ancestral lands, California. CALIFORNIA DEPARTMENT OF WATER RESOURCES

FOREWORD

I've been giving voice to the needs of wild salmon and their rivers for four decades. My activism has felt futile in any kind of political sense, but even futile protests prevent impotent rage from reaching toxic levels, and occasionally dissident voices are heard on a level that defies expectation. My 1983 novel, *The River Why*, bewildered the New York and Boston publishers who rejected it by becoming a Northwest classic that continues to sell by the thousand though the love scene between its fisherman hero and a wild chinook salmon is far more tender than the love scene between the hero and the beautiful young woman he weds. The life of my protagonist helped inspire the creation of dozens of watchdog river and watershed councils, a trend that has since spread nationwide.

My all-time favorite activist project was in 2006, when with Patagonia the company's help, we launched thirteen river dories in a huge, fresh-harvested Washington wheat field. We peopled the boats with fly fishers, oarsmen, oarswomen, and fishing guides, and rowed our dories and cast our fly rods in the stubble. Our aim was to bring

The bathtub ring in Reservoir Powell. The Colorado River supplies water to forty million people, thirty million of whom may lose that water in the foreseeable future due to design flaws. Navajo, Hopi, and Southern Paiute ancestral lands, Arizona. JUSTIN SULLIVAN home, in a single image, the fact that the wild salmon and steelhead of the Rocky Mountain West and salmon-dependent orcas of the southern Salish Sea are being driven to extinction by four boondoggle dams on the lower Snake River.

The wheat field's owner welcomed us as friends because he had known and loved the free-flowing Snake and the farms and orchards that thrived in its riparian zone until they were inundated in the 1960s and '70s. Four hundred and fifty miles of slack water then began superheating the Columbia and Snake Rivers, stagnating the flow young salmon need to carry them to sea, and stuffing both rivers full of smolt-devouring predator species to negate the incomparable fecundity of a salmon refugia the size of Massachusetts laced with pristine high-elevation spawning rivers and streams. I wrote a prose poem entitled "Lost River" about the salmon tribes decimated by loss of culture, spirituality, wealth, and traditional fishing places. We produced a poster that became a Pacific Northwest icon and raised thousands of dollars for salmon activists.

It pains me to say that, sixteen years later, the wild salmon and steelhead of the interior West are in complete collapse, the salmon-dependent orcas of Southern Puget Sound are blinking out with them, and the bankrupt bureaucracies that wiped them out, Bonneville Power and the Army Corps of Engineers, have just been refunded by Washington State's "liberal" senators, an act akin to hiring meth cooks to run the nation's drug rehab programs.

But despite the blundering of malfeasant lobbyists and politicos, it thrills me to add that the most inarguably eloquent and beautifully illustrated testimonial against dams, Cracked, is poised to inspire tremendous change.

Steven Hawley has written, and Patagonia has brilliantly supported, an undamming book powerful beyond anything I thought possible in a time of cynicism, greed, and cave-troll politics. Cracked is itself a mass-breaching of the lies, corruption, and betrayals that have fueled an insane parade of dam-building by disembodied bureaucracies and totalitarian governments worldwide. This book from beginning to end is a tour de force. It affirms Nick Cave's thesis that a cynic is just an optimist with a crushed heart that can be mended and filled with hope once again. I know this because one such heart, as I read *Cracked*, was beating in me.

Steven's final chapter, "What Spirits Might Wear in 2050," is an apotheosis. Patagonia's multitude of photographs, charts, and maps are both beautiful and devastatingly powerful. And John Muir's, David Brower's, and Steven Hawley's climactic words carry so much river love that they left me singing the names of the Idaho and eastern Oregon rivers I've walked more than a thousand miles, not beside but, in (two dozen pairs of re-soled wading boots my evidence).

Steven and Patagonia have created a masterpiece that will fire generations to do for many rivers what Muir's long gaze and language are still doing for Yosemite's fair sister, Hetch Hetchy, and her iconic river, the Tuolumne. We possess, en masse, the power to restore world wonders the dam-building frenzy has temporarily stolen and defiled. Let the return of wonders begin with the energies set free in this river-lovers' bible. With calm clarity, this book shows us how to judge the value of a dam and begin removing the dangerous and valueless ones. This book reminds us that it is rivers, not reservoirs, that allow natural selection to select naturally and biodiversity to diversify.

This book sees the Earth as our sentient mother; the land, flora, and fauna as her body, clothes, and skin; the seas, lakes, and rivers as her organs, veins, and arteries; and reminds us that her breathing body is a holiness without which we cannot live. This book renews faith that the man, woman, or child who strives to defend Earth's holiness even in poverty or political impotence, and even against seemingly impossible odds, is not just a hero but an integral part of her, hence every bit as holy as she whom they seek to defend.

– *David James Duncan*

INTRODUCTION

This book was written with a reliance on one of the basic tenets of good faith in the written word; that interested readers may extrapolate to the universal from the examination of the specific. Your home water may not be depicted here, but the patterns of destruction that come with any dam-building regime are as recognizable as the American flag, and as reliable as the sunrise.

Really big dams, and the proliferation of millions of smaller ones, like so many other developments on the planet over the past three-quarters of a century, are an American invention. The American gospel of dams was · spreading to major watersheds worldwide as early as the 1950s. Those busy beavers at the United States Army Corps of Engineers were already globetrotting back then, promoting the virtues of megatons of concrete as a panacea for ills economic, agricultural, industrial, and hydrological. Their sales pitch, at home and abroad, was less than forthcoming about the inevitable risks and the colossal damage that would ensue.

The largest lake in Southeast Asia, Tonle Sap, was, until recently, filled by the seasonal swell of the Mekong River system, which would

Federal dams on the Snake River have drowned sites of great cultural significance. Confederated Tribes of the Colville Reservation ancestral lands, Washington. BEN HERNDON overrun the Tonle Sap River, pushing it backward in spring, filling the lake, and producing one of the world's most productive freshwater fishing grounds. Dams, beginning with eleven cement monsters on the Chinese side of the Mekong (where it is called the Lancang) began to reduce this annual event. Finally came a dam on the Tonle Sap River itself.

By 2019, inflows in the lake were a fraction of their former glory. The annual catch of fish from the lake had plummeted by 80 percent. Subsistence fishing accounts for a large fraction of available protein for millions of people who live along the Mekong. The possibility of starvation was also neglected as an outcome of dams when the idea was bought and sold here.

A countervailing worldwide phenomenon has been the reaction of ordinary people when their well-watered places on this little blue-green marvel of a planet are taken away from them—however temporarily. Australians mobilized recently to scrap a $350 million dam planned for the Mole River in New South Wales, while simultaneously facilitating the removal of small dams in the same region. South Africans removed dams in Kruger National Park. Japan got into the global swing of things with the removal of Arase Dam. France joined in by removing the Vezins Dam on the Sélune River in 2020, now the flagship of European river unplugging—in fact, in 2021, 239 dams, weirs, and other concrete causes of the sclerosis in Europe's rivers were removed.

The world over, the most exciting aspect of the global phenomenon of dam removal is its growing place among the many inspiring, spontaneous, democratic uprisings popping up everywhere. They proliferate because we are threatened as never before by the prospect of business as usual, sponsored by the myopic and greedy enterprises that define a certain deadly brand of capitalism, promoted and protected by many governments, both democratic and despotic. Dam removal should remind us that every act of resistance matters.

Andy Stone is an American who has traveled to Southeast Asia a dozen times to help organize resistance to dams. In 2009, he chanced into a meeting with the Rak Chiang Khong Conservation Group in rural

Laos. A small farm community was about to be displaced by dam construction. "I learned decades of history, heard dozens of stories," Stone says of his experience working in Laos. "They stopped an armed military land grab from displacing undocumented hill tribes. They strapped themselves to rocks to prevent channel blasting. They helped refugees reforest a watershed to avert violent eviction—and returned water to streams."

Of the many stories Stone told, one stands out in my mind. The matriarch of a village where he spent the bulk of his time was also lead rabble rouser, community organizer, and dissident. She earned money by selling brooms she made herself. She had, as a rural villager reliant on the bounty of the river, a million good reasons to oppose a dam that would ruin her and her people. The defiantly personal, however, remains most resonant: "I have never," she told Stone with a fierce grin on her face, "sold my labor."

Though I've never dipped a toe in the Mekong or any of its tributaries, I thought of her generous pride often when writing this book. I hope you'll think of her too.

Next spread: Las Vegas sprawl is reliant on Colorado River water. What will happen when the water runs out? Southern Paiute ancestral lands, Nevada. ALEX MACLEAN

WHAT WE TALK ABOUT WHEN WE TALK ABOUT DAMS

The only laser light show commissioned by the United States Bureau of Reclamation enjoyed quite a run. Though it did not feature Pink Floyd blasted at decibels sufficient to feel the bass notes rattle your skull, nor any acclaimed innovation in the world of psychedelic art, it was projected with sober intent onto the massive face of Grand Coulee Dam, in eastern Washington, most summer evenings from 1989 until 2013. The premise of the show—evolved from a peculiar genre of American Cold War–era advertising and Soviet-style propaganda that might be called Bad Disney—is that the Columbia River could suddenly speak.

I'd heard about this summer spectacle for years. Friends had described the Orwellian flavor of the scene, where spurious claims made over giant outdoor loudspeakers and a movie screen five hundred feet tall and a mile long were met with docile acceptance by nightly audiences. I made the long drive a decade ago to witness one of the final screenings. I'd heard that the Bureau of Reclamation (BuRec), one of a slate of select federal agencies that builds, manages, and distributes water and power from American dams, had belatedly come to the

Workers ride a pipe during the construction of Grand Coulee Dam. Early working conditions were so awful that employees walked off the job in droves. Confederated Tribes of the Colville Reservation ancestral lands, Washington. PUBLIC DOMAIN conclusion that the ideas projected onto the face of their flagship project were outdated. The show could not go on.

This movie featured the absurdity of a cartoon salmon leaping in mock celebration over the dam which in real life is threatening to drive the fish to extinction. Then, God-like, a menacing voice from behind the half-mile-wide monolith of concrete issued forth.

"Electricity! Hydroelectricity! Nonpolluting, inexpensive production of electric power from water. It may sound like a difficult concept for a river, but I understand all that involves me. ... You have done what I could not accomplish alone. Through your engineering skills you have diverted part of my course, and spread my waters over the land. You have created the missing link in the cycle of life: the rainfall nature could not provide. You have irrigated the land. You have made the desert bloom! I was once a raging torrent of raw energy and thundering rapids crashing headlong to the ocean, my potential energy spent carving the land in my blind race to the sea. Now my power is harnessed, and I am part of an efficient system that serves the people and the land!"

The agitprop ended with a smattering of applause; a hasty herding of children, chairs, and blankets; and a retreat to nearby RV parks where motor homes were plugged in at one of those neatly trimmed green-lawn sites with a picnic table and a fire pit cast in concrete. Where, presumably, parents comforted frightened children by pointing out salmon aren't cartoon monsters, and rivers don't speak, at least not in English.

Beyond the kitsch was the notion that the pre-dam wild river was a kind of sick, liquid Neanderthal, an angry irrational beast not yet fully evolved, a patient in need of a cure. The old river was a profligate energy waster, a reckless teenager; it took curves at high speeds, slashed at the soil, crashed into the ocean. It took an army of government engineers insisting on a nature contained in straight lines to make it calm, sane, predictable, profitable, productive, and amenable to the demands of civilization. To fully realize its potential, to provide a vital element missing in nature, the river had to quit being a river. Only in its transformation to a moving part in an efficient machine could water

Concrete cartoon: The Bureau of Reclamation tells its side of the story on the face of its largest dam. Confederated Tribes of the Colville Reservation ancestral lands, Washington. PETER ESSICK

evolve into a sentient being—one that as its highest calling serves human want and need. But that's not what happened.

During the first two decades of the twenty-first century, the whole messy truth about the legacy of last century's big dam-building frenzy has come to light. What started out as an arguably good government project has drifted oceans away from that original virtuous intent. The federal government plugged the nation's rivers in a misguided attempt to turn them into a revenue stream. Federal western water-control projects' main legacy will be one of needless ecological destruction, fostering a host of unnecessary injustices.

The more than ninety thousand dams on the American landscape can't reasonably be blamed for destroying the nation's entire biological inheritance. But they play, even for such gargantuan structures, an outsized role in that destruction. The pages that follow are a kind of "speed date" with the history of the past century of western American water control; it's dams, diversions, and canals; and, just as importantly, the politics that evolved from them, with a couple of prevalent themes to hold in mind.

First, when it was finally acknowledged that no combination of private capital, pioneer gumption, and military protection would tame the arid western United States, the federal government intervened with a water delivery program it promised would deliver a rising tide that would lift all boats. Dams would deliver water to families who wanted their own farms. Acreage limits, initially 160, topping out at 960 before being abandoned altogether (more on that later), were written into law christening the era of big dams. In doing so, the federal government attempted to defy, through engineering, technology, and a massive capital investment, the cold analysis that arid western landscapes were limited in potential for civilization-building. That analysis has proven correct. It appears, as I'll get to in the pages to come, that the costs of building and maintaining a sprawling water storage and delivery complex in arid country—growing increasingly more arid under the ravages of climate chaos—are well beyond the benefits furnished.

Next, despite law and policy that made it clear the federal investment in water storage and delivery should benefit working families on small farms, the intent of the law was systematically subverted, bent to serve those already with plenty rather than those in need. The pipes that deliver water are also bent, figuratively speaking, so that water runs "uphill toward money."

While there's nothing new in parsing yet another instantiation of the unscrupulously wealthy stealing the commons from an unsuspecting public, dams performed this service so well that soon enough every congressional district near a river in the western United States contained a critical mass of vocal boosters who wanted one.

When, in 1902, the Bureau of Reclamation was invented, a new cabal of powers turned their collective attention to dams. Making

... the costs of building and maintaining a sprawling water storage and delivery complex in arid country ... are well beyond the benefits furnished.

the desert bloom, it was uncritically assumed, was a giant leap for humankind, a project only a technologically advanced, eternally optimistic, fabulously wealthy, and powerful nation such as the United States could undertake. But it was short-sighted to assume that the total control of water—across a far-flung geography—was a bold leap for civilization.

Throughout human history, irrigation schemes and the formation of systems of government have had a symbiotic relationship. Any regime in any country that could harness water, especially where it was scarce, wielded an especially potent form of power—first over its environment, and later, over its people. The more complex the water system, the more centralized and concentrated seats of political and economic power tended to be. The regimes of antiquity tended to demonstrate, often in cruel and oppressive ways, the efficacy of centralized control, what might be identified in modern times as a combination of government

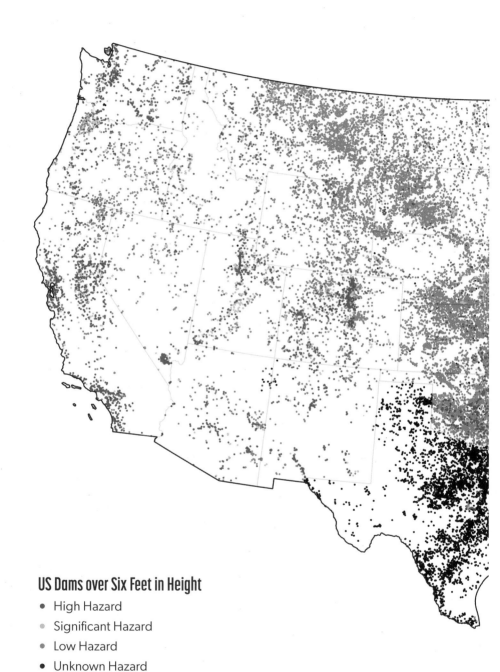

US Dams over Six Feet in Height

- High Hazard
- Significant Hazard
- Low Hazard
- Unknown Hazard

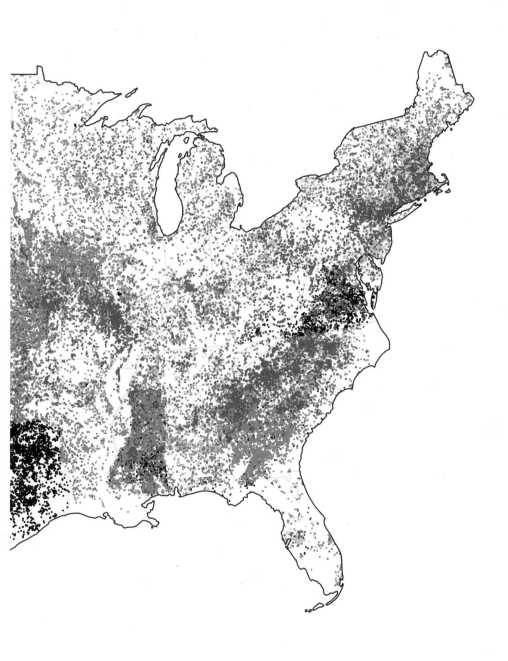

authority, expertise, financing, and administration. So whether you were conscripted into labor in late nineteenth-century Egypt, a fellah toiling alongside three hundred thousand others in the African sun on the Mahmoudiyah Canal, a slave hauling rock for the construction of the Roman aqueduct, or a Chinese peasant in the Han dynasty digging dikes and diversions to tame the Huang He River, the ultimate power and authority of the system under which you labored was as ugly, as hard, and as obvious as the callouses on your hands and feet. In pre-industrial times, water grew the glory of nations. Oligarchies ruled, built water storage and delivery systems, and generally made sure the benefits were delivered to them. America, high on the promises of the Enlightenment, in legal terms at least, set out to be different in this regard. But even the road to a well-watered hell is paved with good intentions.

Early laws governing rivers and streams on the East Coast of the United States were based on English riparian legal concepts, which held to a more egalitarian tradition of access and use. In the America of the late nineteenth century, Enlightenment-based intent was increasingly alienated from a starkly unenlightened reality.

As a massive, federalized water control effort was gaining steam, America had immersed itself in the extravagant excess of the Gilded Age. The term, coined by Mark Twain in 1873, refers to advances of the day in metallurgy that allowed a thin veneer of precious metal to wrap up a core of some considerably less valuable material. Twain thought it an apt metaphor for the state of his country. "What is the chief end of man?" queried Twain in 1871, riffing off a well-known religious line of inquiry from Protestant catechism. "To get rich. In what way? Dishonestly if we can; honestly if we must." It was an age of corruption in legislative bodies from the White House to Tammany Hall. It was the era when the term "political machine" was coined. Rampant fraud, theft, and abuse accompanied the rush to fulfill the vision of a nation stretching from sea to shining sea.

In the 1860s, under the auspices of the Homestead Act, an estimated eight million acres of public lands in California alone were turned over to private ownership. Like the Reclamation Act passed forty years later, the law was intended to put working farm families on land that could become theirs. In *Rivers of Empire*, historian Donald Worster describes what happened instead. "Most of the land came into the hands of a group of Sacramento and San Francisco 'appropriators' who lied, bribed, hired dummy entrymen, and manipulated laws to amass holdings of gargantuan size," writes Worster. "The outcome was that, by 1871, over 2,000 individuals owned more than 500 acres apiece, and 122 of them held an average of 71,983 acres ... In many cases, the land so amassed was merely held for speculation, the owner selling it for a good price later on, getting $2 to $10 or more for an acre that had cost him 60 cents or $1.25." Regulatory enforcement was lax, and much of the wealth intended for the average rural settler wound up benefiting the "investors" in the coastal cities.

Another popular turn of phrase then was "robber baron." These decades marked the rise of almost mythologically wealthy captains of industry—the Carnegies, the Rockefellers, Mellons, Vanderbilts, and Astors. They, and families like theirs, made their money in the rapid innovations of the day: the railroad, the telephone, refrigeration, the lightbulb. They made fortunes in the raw material for manufacture of such goods—steel, timber, petroleum, copper, gold, silver, iron. The new economy catalyzed rapid emigration from farm to city. It was a time of brutally abject poverty. Eleven million of the twelve million families in the United States lived on less than $1,200 a year; their per capita income was $380 annually.

The era marked a low ebb of human rights in America. Jim Crow law and policy relegated African Americans to another century of state-sanctioned racism. Native Americans in the West were relentlessly pursued and mercilessly slaughtered, the survivors relegated to islands of poor country on reservations. As the massive disparity of wealth polarized the country, America seemingly was becoming, simultaneously, more and less civilized. According to the Public Broadcasting Service, French prime minister Georges Clemenceau is said to have remarked, after a brief tour of the United States, that the nation had gone from a stage of barbarism to one of decadence—without achieving any civilization between the two.

The Emergence of the Corps of Engineers and the Bureau of Reclamation

The drive to dam every river emerged out of the Gilded Age spirit, and the mercenary mindset that went with it. Engineers, planners, and politicians promoted, and plenty of people accepted, the concept that rivers had to be sacrificed. It was for the good of the country, the argument went. But that turned out not to be true.

The historical context out of which America's dam-building craze arose created a system—rife with corruption, inequality, and racism—whereby the benefits of water control, just as had been true throughout history, accrued to a few while many paid the costs. Among the first to pay were migrant workers. Within forty years of its inception, federal dams created the demand—or as most large-scale farmers will acknowledge, the necessity—for "guest" workers in the United States. Yet this contradicts what was supposed to be a foundational mission of the Bureau of Reclamation—offering struggling families a path toward economic stability by putting them on their own farms and delivering the water to make them viable. BuRec was created to offer working families a way to improve their economic lot in life.

Later, dams were celebrated as a key asset in victories in both World War II and the Cold War. But this claim doesn't hold water either. Thoroughly damming the Columbia River appealed to America's post-war sense of pride, and its saber rattling at the Soviet Union. But it did so with a Soviet-style system of infrastructure development, a government-sponsored capitalism with a communist-style, military-flavored central planning element that utterly transformed much of the western United States. The mythology around dams—that they were built for the greater good of the nation, that they helped secure and promote "the American way of life"—owe their existence to the era in American history out of which the lust for water control was realized. Under the guise of equality and freedom for all, water, like many other American resources, began flowing uphill toward money.

The metastasizing inequality of civilization—the masses plunging toward a poverty-driven barbarism and the wealthy forming the gold-plated backbone of a new Consumers' Republic—prompted some critics, artists, and philosophers over the next century to consider with renewed scrutiny the freshly paved road which humankind was traveling in their new-fangled horseless carriages. This endeavor of social criticism persisted through the ensuing wars, genocides, economic roller coasters, and an expanding funhouse of technological discovery. Insightful observers wrote about the mindset necessary to create an economy and society where wealth was concentrated at the top. They scrutinized oppression in its various forms. They wrote about the obliteration of nature as a prerequisite to dominating other humans. Some of them applied these ideas to the rapid industrialization of the American landscape. An eco-crank, Edward Abbey, an erudite European dissident philosopher, Herbert Marcuse, and an early critic of technology, Lewis Mumford, had some ideas that shed light on the century's wild ride. Collectively, what they wrote explains a great deal about the motivation behind America's dam-building craze.

The quick-scan, philosophical critique of the turbo-charged, twentieth-century, man-versus-machine trope might read like this: the trouble with modern civilization and the technology on which it relies has been its tendency to displace the rational, intelligent, orderly, elegant, and life-affirming work of humankind. Art, music, culture, craft, kinship, spirituality, good food, booze, and fun and games are subsumed into a massively scaled, Earth-enveloping labyrinth of engineering, military, industrial, and technological works that sow the seeds of chaos and destruction, even as these forces foster the illusion of freedom in a regimented and increasingly restrictive modern life.

In *One-Dimensional Man*, German-American philosopher Herbert Marcuse described this problem: "a comfortable, smooth, reasonable, democratic unfreedom prevails in advanced industrial civilization, a token of technological progress." Marcuse was foremost among a group of Continental philosophers who emerged from the rubble of World War II with some questions about the direction civilization was heading and foretold of a crippling alienation from all forms of nature, including human nature, that would be a casualty of uncritical adoption of the latest forms of technology.

Scholar of modern cityscapes, the American Lewis Mumford argued against what he called "megamachines," power-centric inventions that tended to accumulate capital in various forms and foster a pursuit of growth and expansion for their own sake. He warned that this could eventually destroy all worthy human endeavors.

Later, desert philosopher Edward Abbey described this megamachine mindset of growth for the sake of growth as "a cancerous madness."

Marcuse, Mumford, Abbey, and their philosophical kin knew that modern technology would never be neutral in its effect on contemporary life. A profound rearrangement of family, social, professional, and personal life would be required to justify the size, cost, pace, and scale of building and maintaining this proverbial shining new city on a hill. Unquestioning adherence to technological and industrial boosterism would crash cultures and kill higher-order critical thought. If no one bothered to slow down and contemplate implications, conveniences like electricity, mass media, automobiles, and suburbia would run the risk of making us dumb, lazy, self-absorbed, sexually frustrated, and greedy, all the while creating a more violent, polluted, and ecologically and socially fragmented world.

Dams certainly don't bear all the blame for this increasingly desperate state of affairs. Yet western American water control was a key component in the development of uncritical acceptance of a technological fix for social ills in the marriage of private sector lobbying and government power, and the subsequent creation of public infrastructure with benefits that disproportionately flowed to the well-connected. But initially, the only problem dam boosters could perceive was that the endeavor to dam all the West's rivers kept running out of money.

Within a decade of its 1902 inception, BuRec had to be rescued with a $20 million loan from the Treasury Department. Insolvency came along with the inability of farmers to repay their share of project construction loans. By 1922, 60 percent of BuRec farmers were delinquent in their payments, and a measly 10 percent of the total costs had been paid off. The repayment schedule was doubled from ten to twenty years before World War I, and then again after the war from twenty to forty years, but this didn't help the agency's budget. Plunging commodity prices had tanked the farm economy, and by the late twenties, farmers were getting out. Water had made their land worth a little more than when they bought it, and the buyers were mostly long-term speculators who already saw the possibilities for profit in any big federal subsidy. But as Marc Reisner points out in *Cadillac Desert*, something more insidious was causing BuRec to go broke. Engineers within the agency began to view public works as ends in themselves: "stopping a wild river was a straightforward job, subjugable to logic, and the result was concrete, heroic, real: a dam. Enforcing repayment obligations and worrying about speculators was a cumbersome, troublesome time-consuming nuisance. Was the Bureau to abandon the most spellbinding effort of modern times—transforming the desert into a garden—just because a few big landowners were taking advantage of the program, just because some farmers couldn't pay back as much as Congress hoped?"

Conceived as a public service agency that would serve ordinary people, BuRec would rather quickly become strictly an engineering outfit, trapped in the hamster-wheel logic of building dams to build more dams. It abandoned the higher calling—economic opportunity for middle-class, rural Americans—of its original mission.

Initially, sticking strictly to engineering had its advantages. Hoover Dam was completed in five years for chump change: $49 million. Foreshadowing who would come to benefit most from future BuRec projects, at the time of Hoover's completion, the money doled out to private contractors had created what were at the time the six largest construction companies in the country. (One of them, Bechtel, is today one of the largest construction firms in the United States and feasts on a steady diet of fat government contracts. The sole contractor for Hoover was an entity called Six Companies, Inc.; two other spin-offs from that parent company are construction giants Morrison-Knudsen and Kaiser.)

Next spread: Built during the Depression at fire-sale prices, the construction of Hoover Dam launched what would become the largest construction firms in the United States. Southern Paiute ancestral lands, Nevada. CAROL M. HIGHSMITH (See note on page 321)

Low interest and Depression-era wages at Hoover Dam guaranteed nothing of the sort would ever be built that easily again. Inflation was making it harder with every passing year for BuRec to get even a dishonest cost-benefit analysis for a proposed dam to pass Congress for funding. But with Hoover, and soon Grand Coulee, generating scads of electricity, the federal dam builders hit on a grand idea: Why justify construction costs at all? New dams and irrigation projects would pay for themselves out of power revenues. These "cash register" dams became the rationale for a new generation of needless projects. The justification for each new dam was described by historian Donald Worster as a kind of "rationalized irrationality," a consideration only of means without regard to ends. "Electricity," wrote Worster, "became the very elixir of the bureaucratic life."

Engineers, politicians, and budding bureaucrats drank this punch. As Reisner put it, "For a dam, whether or not it made particularly good sense, whether or not it decimated a salmon fishery or drowned a gorgeous stretch of wild river, . . . was a Bonanza to the constituents of the Congressman in whose district it was located—especially the engineering and construction firms that became largely dependent on the government for work. The whole business was like a pyramid scheme—the many (the taxpayers) were paying to enrich the few—but most members of Congress figured that if they voted for everyone else's dams, someday *they* would get a dam, too."

Federal water management agencies began to exercise a kind of circular, internal logic: We need this dam to grow crops, to float barges, to harness power, to "become part of an efficient system that serves the people and the land," as the laser light show at Grand Coulee demonstrated. With a focus only on the most grandiose feats of engineering, they soon adopted the slogan "Total Use for Greater Wealth." The phrase meant what it said. In the short time span of the ensuing generation, almost every western river was killed off as a conveyance of nature's bounty, and reborn as a proclaimed moneymaker. If BuRec had its way, not a single drop of water on the continent would make it to the sea without turning a turbine, floating a barge, or watering a field. But the agency didn't get its way. Not because of reform, or any other sort of happy ending. It had competition.

By the 1930s, the United States Army Corps of Engineers, the engineering wing of the US Army, which had been building dams since before the Bureau of Reclamation existed, wanted more of the dam racket. And in at least one way, it was in a better position to do it. Any project the corps took on that could be justified as flood control would not have to be concerned with repayment to the Treasury.

Like the rest of the military's annual appropriation, Congress would simply decide to give the corps the money, no further questions asked. In addition to being fiscally less restrained, it eventually became more adept at partnering with influential, private interests who would benefit from corps-built dam projects. An early coup for the corps was at Pine Flat on the Kings River in the Sierra Foothills of California. In the 1880s, the Kings had been the battleground for a landmark water rights court case between two wealthy landowners. Noting that the same few families still controlled land in the area, the corps out-schmoozed, out-leveraged, and out-hustled BuRec, gaining appropriations for construction of the Pine Flat Dam in 1948.

The two agencies hated each other—until they fell in love on the Missouri. In 1940, the corps finished the Fort Peck Dam, creating a 140-mile-long swath of bass and walleye habitat. While the corps was plugging up the upper-Missouri, BuRec had set its sights on a suite of utterly budget-sucking projects throughout the river basin. All of them were losing money, but the losses might be covered by power revenues—generated by new dams. W. Glenn Sloan, a Montana BuRec engineer, was putting the finishing touches on his agency's plan when Lewis Pick, the corps regional director, had the misfortune of witnessing one of the Missouri's signature rampages in spring of 1943. He took the flood as a personal insult and demanded retribution in the form of a report that would punish the river for its insubordination with five monstrous dams.

Not to be outdone, BuRec finished its wish list of ninety dams. Whereupon the interagency pissing match began. The corps lobbied and testified against BuRec's plan. BuRec testified and lobbied against the corps' plan. President Roosevelt suggested in a letter to both parties that a regional, third-party agency like the Tennessee Valley Authority be created, in part to deal with the impasse. Neither side wanted to suffer the humiliation of having their bureaucratic wings clipped, so they met in the fall of 1944 to sort the whole thing out. In the span of a single day, BuRec and the corps consummated their relationship by screwing the American people out of a considerable chunk of their own land, water, and money.

BuRec and the corps reconciled their differences by promoting the buggered idea that all their proposed projects on the Missouri should be built, and then some, despite both agencies having earlier testified that the benefits of one agency's plan would be cancelled out by the other. The price tag in 1944 dollars: a cool $2 billion.

The consequences were brutal: The best winter cattle range and some of the best waterfowl habitat in the country—along with a good measure of BuRec's and the corps' credibility—went out the window. The corps took a singularly sadistic approach to making sure any reparations to Fort Berthold Native Americans went unmet with the construction of the Garrison Dam, which, after completion in 1953, flooded the ground where the Mandan, Hidatsa, and Arikara people had lived for

There are no monetary reparations that could adequately compensate for the half-century of torment the three tribes suffered.

thousands of years. The three tribes, seeing the handwriting on the wall at a time when Native American legal rights had bottomed out, asked only for land equal in acreage to what they would lose, plus grazing and timber rights. That was too much for the corps. Instead, the tribes got $33 an acre for the fertile river-bottom land they lost (plus another $7.5 million for immediate needs). It took fifty years—the three tribes fighting the United States every step of the way—but eventually, a settlement that at least began a move toward economic justice was made. The land, however, is still drowned.

There are no monetary reparations that could adequately compensate for the half-century of torment the three tribes suffered. In *Coyote*

George Gillette, of the Fort Berthold Tribe, weeps after signing the 1948 contract selling 155,000 acres of their reservation back to the US government for the Garrison Dam and Reservoir project. "… the future does not look good." AP IMAGES

Warrior, writer Paul VanDevelder quotes Phyllis Cross, whose home in Elbowoods, North Dakota, was buried beneath the slack water behind Garrison Dam. She described the ensuing existential darkness that engulfed her community this way: "Our thinking failed us because suddenly our landmarks, our social and physical landmarks, the framework for everything we were, was gone. Our identity derived from our villages. Those were destroyed. ... When everything was gone, there was no one waiting to help us put the world back in order. ... How do you bury the past when your identity is trapped in its lasting effects? What do you call your life as a community, as a people, when despair is the only emotion you can trust?" A national dam-building program that was intended to help people victimized them instead. And some of the people that did benefit had begun to amass great wealth, partially by acting like credit criminals.

The Modern Gilded Age

Further out west, another of BuRec's flagship projects demonstrates the economic and ecological injustice inherent in far-flung irrigation schemes. The Central Valley Project (CVP) in California waters three million acres. Built in the decades coinciding with the apex of BuRec's powers, the project takes water from rivers as far north as southern Oregon and sends it as far south as within an easy hop to the Mexican border. According to a 2004[1] report by the Environmental Working Group, around sixty-eight hundred farms receive its water, which is subsidized to the tune of $416 million annually. This works out to an average of about $61,000 per year per farm. But the average is misleading. Scrutinizing who gets the water, as well as the money that follows, indicates just how well BuRec's dams operate to transfer public wealth into private hands. The top 5 percent of CVP water recipients get nearly half of the water, amounting to an average per-farm subsidy of more than half a million dollars. The top ten farms received subsidized water valued at between $1.7 million and $4.2 million each in handouts.

CVP farmers also get generously subsidized rates for the electricity to pump water. BuRec charges the same rate for power all over the

---

[1] In those years, it became increasingly difficult to get accurate numbers on debts owed by individual irrigation districts to the Bureau of Reclamation, a gray area that was exploited more recently when, as described later in this chapter, legislation wholly transferring ownership of federal irrigation works to at least two individual irrigation districts—without an estimate of the value of this property, nor an audit of money still owed by the irrigation districts for these assets—was passed by Congress.

project. Irrigation districts that use the most power therefore get the most subsidy. The average electricity welfare benefit is pegged at around $100,000 per year, but as George Orwell suggested in his allegorical *Animal Farm*, "all animals are equal, but some animals are more equal than others." In some years, nine water districts got better than $1 million per year in power subsidies. A few of these most equal animals belong to the Westlands Water District near Fresno, California, the largest and by far the most controversial irrigation district in the country. Formed in 1952, it was carved out of scrub brush west of Fresno. Its six hundred thousand acres included major holdings by corporate entities not generally associated with family farming: Southern Pacific Railroad, Standard Oil, and the now defunct Connecticut conglomerate Bangor Punta, whose many companies included at least one bucolic interest—sugar plantations in Cuba.

Westlands was formed amidst a push in the Golden State to loosen the acreage restriction that came along with BuRec projects. Powerful interests wanted the state to build its own irrigation works. They got what they wanted. In 1959, a referendum was approved, allocating a $1.75 billion down payment. The measure was barely approved by voters, passing by one hundred seventy thousand votes out of six million cast. Urban citizens paid the bulk of the cost, while land developers and agribusiness interests took the lion's share of benefits. Before approval, independent economists had calculated the project would yield fifty cents of benefits for every dollar of cost. Unfettered from the acreage limit requirements of BuRec projects, the biggest beneficiaries of this boondoggle were landowners in Kern and Kings Counties, the hard-working farmers at Chevron (owner of thirty-eight thousand acres in state water project territory), Tejon Ranch (nearly thirty-six thousand acres, owned by the *Los Angeles Times*), Getty Oil, and Shell Oil (owners of thirty-five thousand and thirty-two thousand acres, respectively). Clearly on a winning streak, wealthy interests began lobbying state and federal officials to get the water turned on at Westlands. Congress obligingly approved construction of San Luis Creek Dam in 1960. A joint venture of BuRec and the State of California, federal subscribers

Next spread: The Westlands Water District's western edge borders the parched Diablo Range in California's Central Valley. Not so parched are the heavily watered and subsidized patrons of Westlands. Yokuts ancestral lands. DAMON WINTER / *NEW YORK TIMES*

of water from this project would be stuck with the federal acreage limit; state users would not. Landowners on the federal side of the project holding acreage in excess of the federal limit would have ten years to sell—ostensibly to family farmers who were in line to buy.

In 1975, a group of Senators came to visit Westlands after fielding a litany of complaints regarding non-compliance with the federal acreage policy. What they found—farmers denied project land acquisition despite waiting in line with approved credit to purchase federally irrigated lands that had to be sold to stay within acreage limits—convinced President Carter's Interior Secretary Cecil Andrus to suspend BuRec's land transfer program, pending an investigation. A different investigation, led by an NGO called National Land for People, found that Westland owners were playing a shell game. Project lands were being reorganized into a maze of corporate holdings, with ownership traced far outside the zip codes of project locations. People in Japan, the Caribbean, and Mexico were all apparently resident Westlands farmers.

Watering Westlands, that is, the endeavor of simply getting water there, cost the American taxpayer $3.3 billion. Yet when water deliveries began, farm owners were getting water at $7.50 an acre-foot, a price not nearly sufficient to recover construction costs, and barely enough to cover annual operation and maintenance. Two economists, Philip LeVeen and George Goldman, calculated the subsidy to Westlands landowners was $2,200 per acre.

Westlands was—and is—so thirsty that when demand spikes, giant pumps near Tracy, California, are turned on, reorienting currents in the Sacramento-San Joaquin Delta, confusing migrating salmon. Winter Chinook were listed under the Endangered Species Act in 1989. Delta smelt, three-inch fish that form a critical link in the Delta's food chain, were listed in 1993. Westlands was not only killing fish—but also birds.

In the early 1980s, waterfowl at the Kesterson National Wildlife Refuge, downstream of the Westlands District, started dying. The reason was poor drainage of soils in the San Joaquin River Valley that was overlooked when the grand plans for Westland were hatched.

Selenium, and other toxic minerals, concentrated on project land as the consequence of irrigation practices. In the 1970s, a partial drainage ditch was dug, but due to cost and engineering complications, the project was halted. Where the ditch project ran out of money and political will, a dozen settling ponds were built. The terminus of the abandoned drain from Westlands was declared a wildlife refuge—the Kesterson National Wildlife Refuge.

To finish the big ditch all the way to San Francisco Bay might cost as much as $5 billion. Better to leverage the elite political connections of some of Westlands' patrons, hire a truckload of lobbyists and lawyers, delay and obfuscate, and wait until the right political climate came along to plant the seeds of a more advantageous solution. As those first birds were going belly-up at Kesterson, none of the shills for Westlands could imagine how well this strategy would work out.

After riding out the political turbulence from these ecological catastrophes in the 1990s and suffering the insult of a 1992 law that dedicated flows for fish and wildlife in the Delta, Westlands' water-hoarding patrons found the twenty-first century much more amenable to their cause. In 2002, President George W. Bush's White House let stand a ruling by a Fresno federal court that unwound the intent of that 1992 law. In 2005, Bush's Secretary of the Interior, Gale Norton, amidst a growing scandal over her and some of her federal colleagues' cozy relationship with oil and gas executives, quietly appointed David Bernhardt as attorney for the Department of the Interior. He became the top lawyer and ethics officer at the agency overseeing the health and welfare of federal land and water. Bernhardt, an ethics czar untroubled by the seamy revelations within the Interior Department, instead returned at the end of the Bush administration to private practice as an attorney and lobbyist for extractive industry, representing clients that the Department, his former employer, was supposed to regulate.

In 2011, lobbying and lawyering on behalf of one of these clients, the Westlands Water District, Bernhardt filed suit against the Bureau of Reclamation, claiming it was solely responsible for the construction costs of completing the ditch that would drain Westlands.

Westlands' lawsuit over their abandoned drainage ditch coincided with the start of an intense lobbying effort, of which Bernhardt was also part. Between 2012 and 2015, Westlands would spend $2.3 million lobbying Congress, and another $576,000 lobbying the California State Legislature. Behind closed doors, Westlands and BuRec started bargaining. In 2015, the stunning details of the deal that was struck became public. Westlands came out smelling like a well-fertilized and watered rose.

What cost American taxpayers $3.3 billion to construct is now owned by the well-monied and watered patrons of Westlands.

Its debt of roughly $350 million owed to the federal government, covering the district's share of the cost of the Central Valley Project, was zeroed out. Furthermore, the agreement transferred ownership of federally funded water infrastructure to the district—for free. No appraisal, no compensation. What cost American taxpayers $3.3 billion to construct is now owned by the well-monied and watered patrons of Westlands. Best of all, if you are one of those patrons, Westlands' water allocation is now guaranteed for delivery in perpetuity—come hell or high water, whether the rest of the state's farmers get any water from anywhere at all, or whether anyone in Los Angeles gets a shower. Its non-reviewable, non-negotiable water right is good for up to eight hundred ninety-five thousand acre-feet of water a year—one and half times the annual water budget of Los Angeles. The trade-off, if you can call it that with a straight face, is a transfer of the responsibility to finally build that drainage ditch, or otherwise dispose of toxic agricultural run-off in the district. But there's not much in the way of accountability for this burden, only a set of benchmarks for the goal of cleaner water on the downstream end of Westlands, not now, but at some future date.

It gets worse. Bernhardt wasn't done working for his client, even if he had to break the law to do it. Bernhardt rejoined the Interior

Department under the Trump administration in 2017, just as Congress was voting to approve the sweetheart deal of which he was a key architect. According to a 2019 article in the *New York Times*, Bernhardt leaned on at least one federal official to further loosen the requirement that some portion of the Delta's water be left for its aquatic inhabitants. When confronted with the allegation, Bernhardt said he had "verbal permission" from an Interior Department official to pursue the move.

Meanwhile, Congress was voting on the bill that gives away Westlands infrastructure and the Delta's water to Westlands' patrons. It passed, but in a feeble attempt at including some form of accountability in approving the transaction, language was inserted in the bill that would have created a five-year moratorium on the likes of Bernhardt going to work for the federal government on projects for which they'd lobbied. The language was stripped from the bill, and Westlands' grand bargain became law with no conditions attached. For his service to Westlands, Bernhardt wasn't sanctioned or punished. He was promoted to Interior Secretary in 2019, and immediately became the subject of several ethics investigations.

As crooked as the Interior was during the Bush and Trump administrations, what happened at Westlands can't be blamed solely on party politics. The deal to hand over federal assets and free water forever was negotiated by Obama administration officials working on BuRec's behalf. That Westlands officials were successful owes much to a culture of cronyism and entitlement nurtured by BuRec irrigation districts over decades. But water flowing uphill toward money comes with costs.

In an era of climate chaos and aridification in the West, perhaps the most obvious costs are ecological. But the damage isn't limited to the environment. Fresno County, where the majority of Westlands' lavishly irrigated acres lie, is one of the poorest in the nation. Farming one's way out of poverty—ostensibly the original intention and mission of the Bureau of Reclamation—will be a lot more difficult for those on the bottom rungs of the economic ladder, now that Westlands has tied up the lion's share of land and water, in service of those who already had plenty.

In addition to environmental destruction—extirpated salmon runs, toxic farm runoff, depleted rivers, streams, and aquifers—another gargantuan externalized cost of grandiose irrigation schemes is labor. In dreaming up nifty new ways to make the desert bloom, in creating the conditions necessary to transform scarce western water into "total use for greater wealth," and in subverting the intention to lift poor and middle-class farmers into some modicum of economic stability, dams, or more accurately, dam politics, have created poverty. Demographics in Fresno County, as in counties hosting other large BuRec projects, tell the tale. Some, but not all farm owners would get rich. Workers, by contrast, would always remain on the margins, politically and economically. They would go unpaid or paid too little. They would get few if any benefits, despite paying taxes like any other US worker. Still, others, including some of the most conservative, patriotic citizens in the nation, would be indiscriminately sickened, exposed to deadly toxins in the name of national security.

The Staggering Human Cost of Making the Desert Bloom

The Columbia Basin Project in central Washington state delivers water from the Columbia River to 671,000 acres of farmland on the Columbia Plateau. Water from Lake Roosevelt pooled behind Grand Coulee Dam gets pumped uphill to the twenty-seven-mile-long Banks Lake. From there, the water flows via a series of gravity-fed canals. Outlets for unused water empty back into the Columbia River above Richland and Pasco, better than a hundred miles south. The project includes more than three hundred miles of main canals, two thousand miles of laterals, and thirty-five hundred miles of drainpipes. The wealth that this feat of engineering has produced is also impressive. Yet the dollar amounts don't tell the whole story. In the world of modern federal water control, the benefits are enjoyed by a few, the considerable costs borne by many. And the beneficiaries of this system have thus far proven to be credit criminals, neglecting to pay what was agreed upon as their fair share.

Social, fiscal, and environmental troubles mount behind Grand Coulee Dam on the Columbia River in eastern Washington. According to BuRec, the yearly value of the Columbia Basin Project is $1.27 billion in irrigated crops, more than $500 million in power production, $206 million in flood damage prevention, and $50 million in recreation: a grand total of $1.84 billion. Each year, water (in amounts exceeding the entire flow of the Colorado River) is sprinkled on the otherwise dry plateau of eastern Washington. Yet the cost of making the desert bloom here runs into a considerable black hole, which is apparently the way BuRec likes it: due to insufficient data collected by the agency, it is impossible to determine exactly how much debt has accrued. But reasonable estimates have been made.

According to a 2014 study by the US Government Accountability Office, the Columbia Basin Project pumps 2.5 million acre-feet of river water for delivery to 2,050 farms. By 2012, $685 million had been allocated for the construction of irrigated agriculture, which was earmarked as a loan that project farmers would have to pay back. But the Bureau

... the World Commission on Dams ... concluded that real costs of dams have rarely been accurately estimated and were not likely to ever be fully recouped. The price of social and environmental damages were in many cases far too high, and in almost every case never fully considered.

expects that $495 million of this cost will be paid for by "other sources." The specifics on these other sources are difficult to track down, but it has been generally assumed that some opaque arrangement of taxpayer and electricity ratepayer money is covering this amount—nearly half a billion dollars. Of the remaining $190 million left to be repaid by the irrigators, only $60 million has been paid at the time of this writing.

In the year 2000, the World Commission on Dams (WCD) included Grand Coulee as one of several case studies on the effects of big water control projects. This report was key in causing the World Bank, among other financiers, to rethink their support of big dam construction. It concluded that real costs of dams have rarely been accurately estimated and were not likely to ever be fully recouped. The price of social and environmental damages was in many cases far too high, and in almost every case never fully considered. The WCD report noted that the original intent of Grand Coulee irrigation was to put eighty thousand people on ten thousand economically self-sufficient farms. Today about six thousand people reside on 2,050 farms. For their water alone they are annually subsidized by regional electricity ratepayers for $58 million. The report also noted that the original plan to have farmers pay back 50 percent of the construction costs of the project has been downgraded to 10 to 15 percent.

A few farmers benefit, but workers always pay. Wherever federal irrigation projects exist, these workers make possible the dam-enabled, federally sponsored empire of industrial agriculture. In places like the Columbia Basin, this is largely because of an oversight. No engineer or bureaucrat ever gave much thought to what kind of labor force would perform the considerable work that goes along with making the desert bloom. The solution became perhaps the largest externalized cost of big dams.

Beginning in 1942, with World War II exacerbating a dam-induced farm labor shortage, the US-backed Bracero Program sponsored 4.5 million Mexican "guest" workers to cross the border into America. Many of them wound up in eastern Washington, working fields emerging out of the Columbia Basin Project. Even with the official migrant-labor Bracero Program, American farms still hired many undocumented workers. A mass deportation operation removed at least three hundred thousand undocumented workers in the summer of 1954 alone.

The Bracero Program ended in 1964, amidst vocal protests over unpaid wages, unsafe work conditions, and retribution against workers that reported violations. Irrigated agriculture, of course, did not stop that year. The need for cheap seasonal employees grew, as did the obvious concurrent need for some kind of sane immigration policy.

In the absence of the latter, the United States continues with the heir of the Bracero Program, the H-2A guest worker visa program. Like

Bracero, migrant workers are granted entry into the United States, but without any path toward permanent citizenship. According to statistics compiled by the Center for Public Integrity, since 1997, there has been a fourteen-fold increase of H-2A jobs, driven in part by the increasingly locked-down southern border. And, as of 2020, it has put in a state of limbo almost two hundred eighty thousand workers inside the country. As was the case in the Bracero era, a culture of fear—of losing a job, of not having a guest worker visa renewed, or of otherwise being deported—acts as a powerful disincentive to report workplace violations.

The inherent injustice of the H-2A program was exacerbated by policies of the Trump administration. In the final days of the Trump presidency, the administration announced new rules for the H-2A program. A wage freeze, and a suite of other provisions friendly to farm owners, and hostile to farm workers, was part of the package. Amid a toxic culture of hostility toward immigrants, H-2A jobs increased 155 percent in the Trump years, as intensified border security increasingly made guest worker visas the most viable avenue into the United States. Even as demand for guest workers rose, so too did evidence that many of the oppressive conditions that have been a constant companion of industrial-scale irrigated agriculture have not been adequately addressed.

Washington State ranks third in the nation in the number of H-2A workers hired. The "Inland Empire," the state's lavishly watered midsection, accounts for one-third of the state's $9 billion farm economy. Gebbers Farms near Brewster, Washington, isn't part of the Columbia Basin Project, but gets some of its water from the Greater Wenatchee Irrigation District. A family-owned business that farms on over thirteen thousand acres, Gebbers Farms is one of the world's largest cherry growers. It employs forty-five hundred souls, with over two thousand guest workers. The family business generates revenue of about $13 million a year. Former guest workers told the *Seattle Times* that a guest worker can earn $15,000 working Gebbers' orchards on a six-month contract.

In July of 2020, two of Gebbers Farms guest workers died of COVID-19. Juan Carlos Santiago Rincón, a thirty-seven-year-old from Querétaro, Mexico, died July 8. On July 31, sixty-three-year-old Earl

Edwards, a Jamaican citizen, died as well. While the Washington State Department of Labor and Industries investigated, a third Gebbers Farms employee, Francisco Montiel, died of COVID-19, after working for Gebbers Farms for almost thirty years.

On August 4, 2020, Gebbers Farms was cited for twenty-four violations of state labor practices, twelve for the condition of workers' housing, and twelve for unsafe modes of worker transportation. The fine, the second largest in Washington State history, came to a little more than $2 million. The nature of the violations, investigators found, warranted the hefty fines. "Gebbers made it very apparent to investigators that they had no intention of following the rules as written," said Labor and Industries Director Joel Sacks in a press release from his department. In an interview with the *Seattle Times* from his home in Mexico, former eleven-year Gebbers Farms employee Ernesto Dimas described the working conditions that made him realize a season's wages were not worth his life. Workers quarters were cramped, with men coughing and sneezing in bunks laid out too close to one another. Daily body temperature checks were inaccurately recorded by a fellow contract worker. "It was like we were disposable," Dimas said. "Like we didn't matter."

Gebbers disagreed. The company appealed the fine. A compromise was reached. Gebbers would invest an amount equal to the fine in the well-being of its workers and the health of the community, with $1.4 million going to improve housing and transportation on the farm, and the remainder going into a fund to improve local health care as well as workers' access to it. While such investments are perhaps more constructive than a fine, labor activists pointed out that although the compromise would benefit workers, such leniency benefitted Gebbers Farms even more, essentially incentivizing an investment in company infrastructure.

Hydropower is Colonialist Power

Making certain groups of people feel invisible, like they don't matter, or actually making them physically disappear, is not without precedent in the short, brutal history of federal water control in the Columbia Basin.

Every Indian tribe with a multiple-millennium history of salmon at the center of their spiritual, cultural, and economic existence also has a story of being thoroughly ignored by federal planners who co-opted control of the river for radically different purposes. But the profound violation of human rights isn't limited to First Nations or migrant workers. The dams, their defenders like to claim, serve multiple purposes. One of those purposes, in the years following the construction of Grand Coulee, was to split the atom—unleashing the most destructive weapon ever known. The power (electrical and otherwise) to accomplish this feat came from the big dam that doubles, on warm summer nights, as the world's largest movie screen.

Hydropower Splits the Atom

In December 1942, a year after the United States entered World War II, United States Army Corps of Engineers Lieutenant Colonel Frank Matthias took a driving tour through the western American desert on a quest to find a place far from the vestiges of civilization, but also near a lot of water. In addition to his superiors at the corps, executives from the DuPont Corporation were kept up to speed on Matthias's search. Assigned to the New Deal–spawned Tennessee Valley Authority in the 1930s, the Lieutenant Colonel knew a downtrodden agricultural community when he saw one. What he saw in Franklin County in southeastern Washington State caused him to report that the area looked prime to build a top-secret plutonium factory. With haste, the struggling farmers and ranchers of the area, along with citizens of the hamlets of White Bluffs and Hanford, were peacefully and officially displaced—subject to a quick, US government–sponsored exodus. Poles and wires from the massive, recently completed Grand Coulee Dam were strung, and a year later, in 1943, the site, which would become known as the Hanford Nuclear Reservation, was electrified.

As the race to build the atom bomb commenced, early Hanford reflected the same approach to the problem of labor that had been applied to the construction of Grand Coulee Dam in the previous decade. Hastily constructed barracks, a hodge-podge assembly of grocery store, bar, theater, and an attendant black market for gambling, pros-titution, drugs, and violent crime plagued early attempts. Most of the motley collection of workers didn't understand the work they were do-ing—they were told they didn't need to understand it, and if they did understand they needed to keep their mouths shut about it.

To address a labor shortage, as was the case with farm work, Mexican and African American workers were hired—only after being subject to security screenings and an interview process not applied to whites. Separate living quarters—in the case of Mexican workers—were repur-posed out of dilapidated barracks sixty miles away from the Hanford job site, the shuttle bus cost deducted from their pay. About the only thing in the early days of Hanford that was "equal opportunity" was general unhappiness. The oppressive secrecy, coupled with scorching hot summers, Siberian winters, and an eternal westerly gale that blew dust incessantly, prompted morale to evaporate like a bowl of whiskey in a hot wind. Military commanders reported heavy drinking. In her book *Plutopia*, historian Kate Brown writes about what DuPont police found in 1943 and 1944 at Hanford: "217 employees on the lam from the law and 50 draft dodgers [...] 4 suicides, 5 murders, 69 sex cases, 88 cases of bootlegging, 177 robberies, 1,124 burglaries, and 3,156 charges for intoxication."

Thousands of men were employed at Hanford, but working condi-tions were so bleak that in the summer of 1944, 750 to 850 workers were walking off the job each day. As they boarded buses to Spokane or Pendleton or Portland, they took with them with alarming frequency the risk of divulging nuclear secrets. In the technological race to split the atom, the government had an age-old labor problem. The DuPont Corporation had a solution.

Rather than fence-in the nuclear reservation, giving Hanford the feng shui of a bleak federal prison, DuPont executives proposed building the country's first "model community." In 1946, General Electric took over the Hanford contract from DuPont because they were deemed more worthy of the task of developing civilian, medical, and scientific benefits from nuclear power. The Hanford facility left the jurisdiction of

Squalid living conditions at early twentieth-century federal projects led planners to conceive of building lavish suburbs in the desert for nuclear workers. Wanapum Band of Priest Rapids ancestral lands, Washington. 2006.134.3, WASHINGTON STATE HISTORICAL SOCIETY, TACOMA, WA

Construction Camp

the Department of Defense and came under the umbrella of the newly formed Atomic Energy Commission. Technicians, engineers, security agents, and their families, along with wage workers who were deemed worthy, would be housed in G.E.-built homes that defied war-time conceptions of luxury. Fully furnished houses with three or four bedrooms (unheard of in that day, except for the very wealthiest families) on large lots, maintained by a Big Brother-ish Department of Village Services. Good schools, conducting classes in brand-new buildings. First-class recreational programs and facilities. The government would own the whole thing, G.E. would design and manage it, from the layout of bedrooms and bathrooms to the city streets. The town would be a no-free-enterprise zone. Everything in this nuclear Potemkin village was government-owned, and G.E.-run.

General Electric drew up the plans for the city, including a master economic plan, with zero input from the public or future residents: the whole project was classified as a state secret. Hanford workers would enjoy sweetheart deals on rent. Government ownership, coupled with corporate management, would allow the town to appear as if it were a testament to the virtue of private enterprise. It would also allow G.E. to closely monitor high-ranking Hanford employees. Whistle-blowers and labor organizers would be culled from the Hanford community. Latinos and African Americans would not be welcome. G.E.'s rent policy was a pioneer of the post-war housing industry practice of "red-lining"— drawing lines around neighborhoods inside of which it was agreed by rent screeners and mortgage lenders that potential buyers other than the right kind of whites would not qualify.

Richland, Washington, a short drive east from the Hanford Nuclear Reservation, became this General Electric–planned town. It was a successful venture—beyond even the wildest wet dreams of the most ambitious G.E. executive. As Kate Brown describes it *Plutopia*, Richland started out as a model community that ensured people of color and low-paid wage workers stayed on the outskirts. The model was so exceptional that Richland now appears unexceptional. Richland is the invention of the modern suburb.

DuPont's profits were tied to extravagant cost overruns in the construction of Richland. Each company had a "cost plus" contract with the federal government, which meant the more money they spent, the higher company profits would rise. When complaints by watchdogs inside or out of the government arose, they were quelled by patriotic outcries highlighting the perils of war, and later, the Cold War threat of Soviet-inspired communism. Designating Richland as a "critical defense area" helped foster immunity to these kinds of accusations.

After the end of World War II, the Soviet Union started making plutonium for its own weapons program. G.E. and other defense contractors used the occasion to lay the groundwork for what would become America's permanent war economy. There would be no "winding down" of operations at Hanford, as some budget hawks and peaceniks had hoped. Plutonium would be made there until 1989. National defense would become a well-known rationale not only for expanding Hanford's plutonium operation, but also for building more dams on the Columbia, indeed on every major river in the West. Military spending and associated federal infrastructure, including dams, would become a major factor in the mass post-war migration of Americans to the arid West, where, with the help of advertising and mass media, Marlboro men, wide-open spaces, and stunning vistas became synonymous with a fetishized version of American freedom.

Cities like Richland were replicated in Texas, Idaho, California, and New Mexico.

White people liked living in Richland. The manicured lawns, the dependable jobs and generous wages and salaries, the uniformly WASP-y neighbors, the good schools, all lent a rosy sense for some that the pinnacle of American civilization had been reached. Early journalistic profiles of Richland proclaimed it to be the kind of town to which other places would aspire. G.E. latched onto these glowing reviews, and realized they'd created prototype consumers for their wares, an advertiser's dream of a captive audience in a decent, but isolated, town filled with citizens with a little disposable income.

Richland was the initial proving ground for "the American way of life," a turn of phrase promoted by the G.E.-led National Association of Manufacturers as early as the 1940s. It helped reduce more complex ideas about democratic freedom to the notion that America was better than Russia and everywhere else because of the volume and variety of things to be bought and sold in the United States of America. Thus, the quality of American freedom became equated with the quantity of American consumerism.

If there was any more than passing thought given to the contradiction that a prototype modern capitalist city, supposedly a crowning achievement of the free-market system, was wholly owned by the United States government, closely monitored by the military, and controlled by a single corporation that reaped all the profit from the town, not much was heard about it in the public sphere. Perhaps Richland residents had other worries on their minds.

Children in Richland during the 1940s and '50s recall the clink of glass bottles placed in what could be mistaken for a milk delivery box ensconced on front porches in the town. The empty bottles were delivered for parents to fill with their urine. G.E. and the federal government were using Richland's nuclear workers as guinea pigs, trying to figure out the insidious pathways by which radioactive isotopes worm their way deep inside living organisms, increasing in concentration at every step up the food chain. Piss-testing parents should have been one way to protect these workers, as knowledge about the dangers of radioactivity became better known. But protecting families was not government or company protocol.

The nascent body of scientific discovery around nuclear radiation was used instead to devise an experiment in which these same workers, along with thousands of others across a broad swath of the United States, were deliberately poisoned.

Ionizing radiation occurs when unstable atoms release energy as their nuclei break down. One form of such radiation, detectable as a smokestack-borne by-product of plutonium processing facilities, is Iodine-131. Scientists had figured out that measuring volumes of

Iodine-131 could be used to estimate the amount of plutonium being manufactured by the Soviets. To calculate the ratio of the yield of plutonium to the volume of Iodine-131, which American spies had confirmed was spewing from smokestacks at Russian plutonium factories, a baseline had to be established at an observable plutonium manufacturing facility. Grand Coulee Dam–powered Hanford was certainly observable.

To establish this baseline, G.E. scientists coordinated with the US Air Force to conduct an ill-advised experiment, dubbed "The Green Run," on December 2 and 3 of 1949. It exceeded their own estimates of how much poison they would pump into the air above Hanford by almost three times. Eleven thousand curies of Iodine-131 billowed from Hanford smokestacks into the atmosphere and across a seventy-five-thousand-square mile area, roughly from The Dalles, Oregon, to Spokane, Washington. G.E. scientists had estimated the release would be limited to those directly downwind of Hanford. They also guessed wrongly that these unfortunate souls would be exposed to four thousand curies of radiation, still an astronomical dose.

By comparison, when the Three Mile Island nuclear plant accident occurred in 1979, only fifteen curies of Iodine-131 were released, and thousands were evacuated. Those downwind of Hanford were afforded no such warning. To make matters worse, the weather on those dark days in December of 1949, fickle in the winters of the inland Pacific Northwest, served up wildly shifting winds, dropping temperatures, and an inversion that kept radiation close to the ground. Managing scientists monitored as the cloud of radiation, chased by Air Force planes, shifted with the wind to pass over parts of Richland, where Hanford-employed families were sleeping. In the days that followed, vegetation in the downwind city of Kennewick registered Iodine-131 at levels a thousand times beyond the risk limit of the day.

The Green Run wasn't the only radiation exposure the residents of the Pacific Northwest suffered. Over forty years, more than seven hundred thousand curies were unleashed. Within the boundaries of the Hanford site, toxic and radioactive liquids were routinely dumped into open pits. Other waste was sequestered in 177 tanks that today belch and burp a toxic brew of nuclear waste with the potential to create nuclear disasters both sudden and violent, as well as geologically paced and virtually undetectable. Iodine-129, for example, has a half-life of 15.7 million years, and has been found in the groundwater beneath Hanford, some of which seeps its way toward the Columbia River. It's at least an even bet that traces of the Hanford experiment will be evident after humans have gone the way of the dinosaurs.

It was power from the Grand Coulee Dam that produced the working ingredient—plutonium, manufactured at Hanford—in the bomb dropped on Nagasaki. While a cogent argument might be made for the necessity of that atrocity, what followed in the years after at Hanford is clouded with considerably more ambiguity, moral and otherwise.

In the meantime, "downwinders"—the name given to the thousands of people suffering cancers, autoimmune diseases, heart problems, and other disabilities—have been thoroughly disabused of the notion that their country would stand behind the sacrifices they unwittingly made. The airborne exposures were eventually made public through

... a report released by the federal government confirmed that ... the US government knowingly and ... willfully released radiation throughout a vast swath of territory in the Pacific Northwest.

the heroic efforts of activists and journalists. But legal action on behalf of red-blooded, patriotic, rural downwinders, many of them veterans, was vigorously contested in the courts by the US government.

In 1990, a report released by the federal government confirmed that from the time Hanford began producing plutonium, and for four decades thereafter, the US government knowingly and on more than one occasion willfully released radiation throughout a vast swath of territory in the Pacific Northwest. On the heels of the federal report, more than five thousand people who lived downwind or downriver of

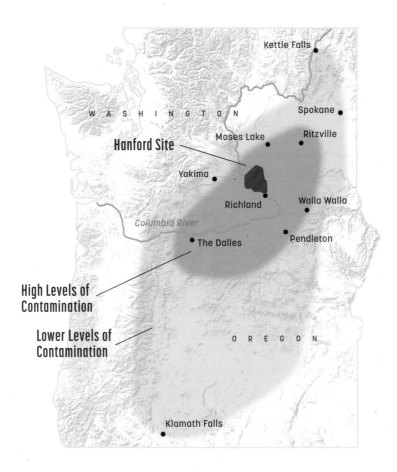

Dubbed "The Green Run," Iodine-131 was deliberately released on unwitting residents around the Hanford site.

Hanford filed personal injury claims against the United States. Jury trials did not commence for another fifteen years after these cases were filed. By 2005, the plaintiffs had been whittled down to six "bellwethers," victims of Hanford whose cases were deemed representative of all five thousand originally filed. Finally, in 2015, paltry settlements were made with some, but not all, of these six representatives.

The corporations contracted to operate Hanford—DuPont, General Electric, Nuclear Industries, Inc., Atlantic Richfield, and Rockwell International—were indemnified against any liability. American taxpayers footed the bill for the $80 million price tag of defending these corporations. Money can buy a wickedly effective legal defense. To give just one example, despite findings from other hotspots where above-ground nuclear testing took place—Hiroshima, Nagasaki, the Marshall Islands Test Site, and the Nevada Test Site—that thyroid cancer rates rise predictably in the wake of exposure to Iodine-131, no correlative conclusion was drawn for Hanford downwinders.

Worse, Hanford is now one of the world's nastiest nuclear messes. Cleanup and subsequent monitoring efforts will persist for centuries. The budget request for 2020 for cleanup efforts at Hanford: $2.1 billion. The total cost has been loosely estimated at $120 billion, a price tag that equals the revenue stream of more than 120 years of Grand Coulee Dam electricity sales at today's prices.

The New Grand Coulee Cartoon

In its relentless zeal to convince the public that damming rivers is a public good, BuRec still has a cartoon to show you, projected onto the face of Grand Coulee on summer nights. Neil Diamond is out, as are some of the more racially and ecologically indefensible tropes. But the sense I got in the summer of 2019 from watching the updated version was something like talking to the head of a company or organization that learns the new buzzwords to demonstrate social or ecological progress but changes nothing of consequence in the company's behavior or processes. Nonetheless, hope springs eternal, even in the face of imprecise metaphors. It is still not out of the realm of possibility for the American people to fix federal water control—which would start with an honest reckoning of current and historical facts.

The broader history the talking river at Grand Coulee glosses over reads something like this: Within a decade of its christening, a virtuous government project hailed as the technological savior of the American middle class became the dynamo for a secret military experiment that repeatedly and intentionally poisoned American citizens with radioactive isotopes. A "model community," designed and controlled by General Electric, helped germinate in the average citizen's mind the belief that "the American way of life" depends at least as much on purchasing power as it does human liberty.

At the same time, the grand scale of Grand Coulee's irrigation works created a commensurate need for workers, who arrived not from the American middle class but as imported laborers, who were quickly and thoroughly exploited as wage slaves. As this happened, wealthy beneficiaries of subsidized irrigation launched a decades-long campaign to divorce these public works projects from most of the intended public good. One of the end results was the wholesale giveaway of public assets for private gain at the country's largest irrigation district.

Dams are dirty. They are factories sitting in the middle of our rivers that pollute and warm water. In the case of the federal Columbia Basin dams, they have wiped out a world treasure. One of the world's richest marine ecosystems, once the world's top producer of Chinook salmon, has been transformed into a series of slack-water impoundments. All of the West Coast's once-prolific runs of Pacific salmon have been utterly decimated by dams.

That is the start of the non-cartoon version of the role of giant federal water control projects in the American West. Without the balm of Bad Disney, the dim outlines of a discernible pattern can be made out: an aggression against a wild river is ultimately an aggression against people. Despite this reality, as is the case with war, there are still many who will tell you it's worth it. If its future looks brighter to some than its past, that may only be a mirage, a hallucination of plenitude in what will soon be a drier, hotter, less hospitable West. Shrinking rivers and reservoirs, cracking once-fertile soil gone alkaline under a relentless hot sun, are looking disturbingly more likely than the schlock of a talking dam that strangled to death a gem of a living river.

WHAT'S MISSING HERE: THE SNAKE RIVER DAMS

Carrie Chapman Nightwalker Schuster sits in a lawn chair in the shade, close to the reservoir's shore to beat the August heat. The grass has been lavishly watered, and recently mowed, the rhythmic *tsh-tsh-tsh* of sprinklers engage in a muted call and response with the intermittent breeze in the cottonwoods. Evenly spaced trees are accented with asphalt. A looped road leads motor homes to their cement parking pads. Some children shriek as they chase around the outside of the cinderblock bathrooms. Floating docks bracket the double boat ramp. Mourning doves carry on a hushed conversation in their low whistles.

Schuster is a Palouse tribal elder. The green grass at her feet belongs to the US Army Corps of Engineers. But some of the land at the bottom of the reservoir once belonged to her family.

She surveys the campground. She's wearing a long red gown decorated with dentalium shells, ceremonial attire she feels compelled to wear when visiting this place—her drowned childhood home. Her hair is short and graying, but her countenance reflects the spark of someone younger. She's quick to smile and has an infectious laugh. "You can feel

The Selway River in Idaho is just one of the many pristine spawning habitats that would be available for anadromous fish if the four dams on the lower Snake River came out. Nimiipuu ancestral lands. GEORGE OSTERTAG / ALAMY the power of this place still, even with the dam," she says, eyes closed. "I can feel it coming up through the ground. You can feel it more clearly in the spring, when we take our first bite of the year's salmon, and we sing. It sounds like the world is waking up."

Though all appears neat and orderly, Fishhook Park, a forty-minute drive from the eastern Washington city of Pasco, is as close as you can get without scuba gear to an underwater crime scene. When the gates closed on Ice Harbor Dam here in 1962, the impounded waters of the Snake River flooded Schuster's ancestral family home. They lived here since time immemorial. Their land was stolen from them by the United States Army in the mid-nineteenth century. Schuster's family purchased a sliver of their territory back, only to lose it again when the army, this time citing eminent domain, removed them from their land again as the gates on Ice Harbor closed.

Ice Harbor and three other dams were completed on the lower Snake River from 1961 through 1975. They choked off the migratory corridor to the best remaining salmon habitat in the Lower 48 states: 4.4 million acres of wilderness in Idaho, eastern Washington, and Oregon, harboring thousands of miles of mountain streams that historically produced millions of salmon. Half of all the salmon in the Columbia Basin once derived from the Columbia River's longest tributary, the Snake.

At the very heart of this grand territory were—and are—Schuster's people. They know one another well by trade, by culture, by intermarriage, and by a shared language, Sahaptin. But they know each other best by their love for the big river. They are Klickitat, Kittitas, Cayuse, Nez Percé, Yakama, Wanapum, Palouse, Lower Snake, Walla Walla, and Umatilla people, among others. They also share a common struggle to restore their river and its fish. Many neighboring tribes signed treaties with the United States in the mid-1850s. And while the Palouse people are named in an 1855 treaty, they never singed any treaties with the US federal government, a point that has become a source of pride for Schuster. "I can speak my mind," she tells me, "and not worry about raising the ire of some politician scheming to take away my so-called rights." She notes that access to treaty-reserved rights have been limited since the day the

In dedicating Lower Granite Dam, then Idaho Governor Cecil Andrus said: "I want to point out that the costs of this system have been horrendous both in dollars and in costs to our natural resources." Confederated Tribes of the Colville Reservation ancestral lands, Washington. MASON TRINCA

0 4

1855 treaty was signed. "Our right to take fish from this river is a treaty right for some," she says. "But since that practice is a part of our history, our culture, our religion, that makes it a basic human right as well."

Over the course of the afternoon at Fishhook Park, bitter memories are interspersed with sweeter ones. There were the salmon they caught, some in excess of a hundred pounds. Ten-foot-long sturgeon that would appear at the end of a fisherman's line like some prehistoric, razor-backed beast. And a canoe of their own, to travel up- and down-river as far as a child pleased. She also recalls vividly her grandfather's singing as he made his annual rounds in his own canoe, tending the graves of relatives out on the islands. "Mytilla [her grandfather] was a medicine man," says Schuster. "It was a very solemn duty, tending the graves each spring. We were not allowed to accompany him. But we could hear him singing. When he started singing, you could hear his song just vibrate up and down the canyon walls."

"I had the most glorious life a child could ever live here," she recalls, speaking slowly. "On the day we had to leave, my mother had been packing and packing and packing. And finally the police came. Before

... we began to realize the way that [the dam] was going to impact our lives ... they started digging up our dead.

this, we knew something important was going on, because my mother and her father were gone to Portland, to Seattle, to Walla Walla, to try to get the army to reconsider the dam. Well, the reality finally hit me: I was going to have to leave here. I would never again sleep on the banks of the Snake. Never again wake up to the sound of the falls nearby." A quiver in her voice does not deter her from her story. "My mother begged for more time. And when that wasn't granted to her, she gave the police officer a piece of her mind. That's how hard my mother fought, up until that last day."

The months leading up to the exile from ancestral lands were a trauma in themselves. "We were not told that one of the agreements the Corps of Engineers entered into was with the archaeology departments at the University of Washington and Washington State," Schuster says. "And I think the way we found out, was when we began to realize the way that [the dam] was going to impact our lives. Because they started digging up our dead."

"One day we saw the archaeologists, led by Dr. [Richard] Daugherty, digging out on the islands. They had this amphibious vehicle that they were using to get to and from out there. At this point my mother's eyes were going bad, and she couldn't quite make out what was being dug out of the earth. So, I was her eyes," Schuster says. "'They're taking a canoe!' I told her. It was then we knew that they were stealing my mother's grandfather, my great-grandfather."

The Palouse were buried in canoes. The deceased would be placed in a fetal position in one half of the canoe; the other half was cut to form a lid. After Schuster's great-grandfather's canoe was extracted from its resting place, Daugherty drove along the shore, the wooden form of the vessel strapped to the rear of the vehicle, appearing dilapidated, dripping with plaster where a cast of the deceased passenger had already been taken. Their grandfather's bones, it occurred to them with horrific shock, had been removed from the burial canoe. "My mother and grandfather tried to wave him down. They yelled. But he would not stop. He drove right past without looking at them."

Thirty years later, Schuster's family received an apology from Washington State University. But the remains of her great-grandfather have never been returned. "We lost our humanity that day, the right to the dignity of the safekeeping of our elders," says Schuster. "We had not figured out that dam building could be so culturally invasive. Our elders were dehumanized. They became mere specimens, there for the pleasure of anthropology departments—for students to make their doctorate degrees on us as a people." The invasive violence of colonization continues into the present.

After bloody conflicts that lasted roughly from 1855 to 1890, smaller, non-treaty bands of Indigenous people like the Snake River Palouse were simply removed to existing reservations, or ignored entirely, left to matriculate into the white world with no ties to language, family, the river, or any other link or reference to past existence. Into the twenty-first century, the result for some, including Schuster's son, Jesse, was a life on the streets battling chemical dependency. Jesse got clean and became a rising star in the fight to restore the river, only to succumb to heart failure in May of 2020 at the age of forty-two.

The diaspora of her family and clan put their language and culture—the very lives of her people—on a path to extinction. She and her mother dedicated their lives to making sure this didn't happen. "In the modern world, young people, especially, are constantly asked to blindly accept what adults offer as the truth. I wasn't created that way," says Schuster, "to be an easy follower. I think the Lord made me that way so I would ask the right questions to the right people."

One of the questions Schuster is asking these days is whether the dam that drowned her home more than half a century ago should continue to exist. It was the dams, she notes, that gave archaeologists a free pass to plunder her family's graves. It was the dams that made plenty of white people rich while impoverishing the Palouse. But it's the future and not the past that most concerns Schuster. "We really want to see the quality of the water restored. I used to drink from the Snake River," she says. "This river is home to a startling variety of fish—not just salmon. And they're being destroyed. What's destroying them are the dams. They need to come down."

We Need to Fulfill Our Treaty Obligations

A few years after Carrie Schuster's family grave was robbed, a similar theft from another burial canoe—hastily excavated before the site was drowned by another dam—recovered a Jefferson Medal, a commemorative coin the Lewis and Clark expedition gave to tribes they encountered on their journey. The betrayal signified by its removal from the burial site, essentially revoking an American symbol of goodwill, verified what tribes along the Columbia have long told each other about the symbolism of that coin.

Cruel irony: the Indian peace medal, similar to the ones Lewis and Clark distributed on their journey westward in 1805–1806. PUBLIC DOMAIN

They say there are two faces to the American coin of diplomacy. One side promises that the United States would uphold agreements made in treaties negotiated with the continent's first citizens. On the other side lies the historical reality that few of the promises made in the 370 treaties the United States signed with Indigenous Nations have been kept in their original form.

Federal tribal trust responsibility includes, but is not limited to, treaty obligations. Its central thrust recognizes a federal duty to protect tribal lands, resources, and the native way of life from the intrusions of the majority society. Each federal agency is bound by this trust responsibility. Yet each federal agency with a responsibility to uphold the bounty of natural systems—a right guaranteed to them—has failed to fulfill this obligation. The failure is especially egregious where salmon runs are a part of treaty rights.

The treaty tribes are entitled to a fair share of the salmon harvest from all streams in their ceded areas. Declines in the salmon productivity of the river, due to subsequent human action, have not changed this entitlement.

Today, the Columbia Basin tribes have lost almost all the once-abundant salmon they protected in their treaties with the United States. The farther upriver one goes, the greater the losses that have occurred.

By the turn of the twenty-first century, tribal salmon harvests were less than 1 percent of precontact levels.

In 2021, the Nez Percé Department of Fish and Wildlife published the results of a study that predicted salmon have less than twenty years to survive unless significant improvement to habitat is made. The biggest bang for the buck to improve salmon's odds is dam removal.

In spite of the clear obligation spelled out in treaties, a host of pertinent federal laws mandating salmon recovery, and an extinction clock ticking toward midnight, taking out dams on the Snake River has been met with furious resistance. A congressman from Idaho, and separately, a retired Corps of Engineers executive, offer compelling evidence that the dam huggers are wrong. Dams could be removed, no one would suffer economic injury, and in fact most parties could come out in better shape. But the mythology derived from the political power of these dams is proving difficult to overcome.

The Political Power of Federal Hydropower

When Idaho Representative Mike Simpson gave a high-profile speech in Boise in early 2019, calling on the region to solve its long-standing salmon crisis, including taking a hard look at Snake River dam removal, Indigenous tribes of the Pacific Northwest aligned behind Simpson's call, as did a broad coalition of conservation groups. Building consensus around removing four federal dams, even with the help of a sitting congressman, is no mean feat.

Columbia River dams have played a starring role in manufacturing vast fortunes for corporate America, with companies like Alcoa, Weyerhaeuser, Boeing, and Google all profiting handsomely from cheap hydropower. Dams created wealth out of water for European immigrants who arrived to farm newly irrigated land, and in subsequent generations, made millions for corporate agriculture ventures.

Salmon politics in Washington State are complicated by the fact that the state receives all the irrigation benefits and the lion's share of the hydropower benefits from dams along the Columbia and its tributaries. Regardless of political party affiliation, since the mid-twentieth century, the conventional wisdom in Washington State politics has been to express undying loyalty to status quo hydropower operations. In keeping with tradition, Washington Governor Jay Inslee, along with Senators Maria Cantwell and Patty Murray, came out against Representative Simpson's salmon recovery plan, the Columbia Basin Initiative, promising they would release a more comprehensive plan of their own.

In June of 2022, Governor Inslee and Senator Murray released their draft report. It's short on specifics and reads more like a feasibility report completed by middling graduate students in public policy. Most of the information in it was gleaned from previously published reports, including a five-year, $80 million report ordered by a federal court and completed by the Army Corps of Engineers in 2020. That report also concluded that dam removal would be the most effective option for salmon recovery, but balked at endorsing the option, claiming it was too expensive. Federal laws outlining species recovery do not burden agencies with balancing the risk of extinction against cost.

The Murray/Inslee report is slightly more optimistic, but still wrong. The gist of the Washington politicians' report is that dam removal is feasible, but wildly expensive: somewhere between $10 billion and $27 billion for removing the dams and replacing the services they provided. For comparison's sake, the cost of removing two dams on the Elwha River in northwestern Washington State was $60 million. Removal plus ecological restoration, plus the National Park Service's generous $150 million purchase of a water treatment plant for the nearby city of Port Angeles brought the grand total for freeing the Elwha to $351 million. The cost floor of the Murray/Inslee plan is almost thirty times that amount.

Removing Snake River dams would be a simpler task than what occurred on the Elwha. The former feature an earthen berm for half to two-thirds of each dam's length that would be simpler and cheaper to bulldoze than chipping away at concrete. Dam huggers defending the Snake River rightly point out these dams produce benefits beyond flood control or irrigation, including 940 megawatts of electricity every year. But what's this worth? One answer, from a high-ranking, thirty-year veteran of the US Army Corps of Engineers, which owns and operates

the Snake River dams, has its genesis back at the start of Elwha dam removals. The short answer: not nearly as much as the whole region has been fooled into believing.

When Jim Waddell got far enough along in his distinguished career with the US Army Corps of Engineers that he could see the finish line, he bought a few acres overlooking the Strait of Juan de Fuca near Port Angeles, Washington. An engineer by training, he designed the place himself. Most of the top floor is dedicated to a lifelong hobby: the construction and painting of models of planes, trains, and cars. The mind that can focus for hours on intricate painting with a brush the size of a toothpick understands the fullest implications of the adage that the devil is in the details. One wall of the upstairs model room is dedicated to details of a different sort. Though he officially retired from the corps, at four of their projects, he sees unfinished business. "I'm not strictly a dam breaching advocate," says Waddell. "I'm a passionate advocate of the truth."

In 2011, at a symposium on dam removal that took place at Peninsula College in Port Angeles, just as nearby Elwha River dams were about to be demolished, a portion of the program was dedicated to a discussion about Snake River dam removal. Waddell was there. "I was listening to folks saying, 'We need to do this for the sake of the fish, but these dams provide so much in terms of benefits to the region, it might take fifteen years to get them down.' Well, it has taken almost fifteen years, but not for the reasons any of those people mentioned."

In a rare moment of impulsiveness that evening back in 2011, he took to the microphone at the front of the room and caused several hundred jaws to drop with his testimony. The dams, he told the crowd, are not only fish-killers, they are money-losers. The region could save money and salmon by taking them out now.

What Waddell spoke about that evening; he'd already known for a decade. In the late 1990s, he was stationed in the US Army Corps of Engineers Walla Walla District. The district was in the midst of a years-long, multimillion-dollar study, which he was tasked with reviewing. "Some of the key numbers just didn't add up," he recalls, "so I started asking where they came from. A lot of them came from a model

Gary Dorr sings a prayer at a sacred ancestral site on the lower Snake River. Confederated Tribes of the Colville Reservation ancestral lands, Washington. BEN HERNDON derived from the Bonneville Power Administration (BPA) [the federal power authority that markets and sells electricity from the dams]. So I said, 'Let's see the model.' And I was told, 'You can't see it, it's proprietary.' So, what they were using was essentially this black box that no one else could see into. It spits out a number, and the corps and the rest of the region just blindly accept it."

He pulls down a massive black three-ring binder, the rings of which are the diameter of a softball. To fight back against the numbers spit out of the black box, Waddell tells me, you have to know where to look. Federal budget agency oversight is a part of Waddell's career skill set. "You'll hear policy people at BPA and other agencies say, 'We don't have this or that number,' but my experience has been you can find any number you're looking for. The accountants keep track of all this stuff, and they keep track of it beautifully."

For years, Waddell has been building paper trails he knows offer a full accounting of the cost of the lower Snake River dams. He spends an hour meticulously explaining his math and has the documents to back it up. He shows generation data from each of the four dams. Columns and rows of costs coded so that only the most determined forensic accountant could figure out what the numbers mean. Fish mitigation expenditures. "When you add it all up, from 2009 to about 2019, these dams were losing $40 to $50 million a year," Waddell sums up.

"In the red or the black," Waddell acknowledges, "is less important than right or wrong. Back when I was at Walla Walla, I thought, 'Well these guys are just being sloppy with the numbers.' But I really discovered the truth when I went back and started doing my homework. What I found was that basic assumptions they were making were wrong. So, they weren't off by a few million dollars. It was hundreds of millions."

So how did the basic assumptions get so skewed? The BPA was created as a response to the Great Depression. The law that created it, passed in 1937, mandates that power be sold at cost to public utility districts throughout the Pacific Northwest. During the Second World War, dams on the Columbia were the dynamos that powered a huge part of the American war machine. As a reward, through the 1980s, the aluminum industry thrived on below cost electricity rates, a war-time emergency arrangement that was supposed to end with combat operations in 1945, but didn't.

Other businesses got in on the racket including Boeing—which powered its growth on hydropower—along with major timber corporations and other industrial, technical, and agricultural producers. In 2007, Google signed a contract with Wasco's People's Utility District (PUD) in The Dalles, Oregon—a sweetheart deal that guaranteed power cheaper than what anyone else in the area gets, plus a fifteen-year tax holiday. Facebook and Apple have built data centers nearby, capitalizing on the same sweetheart deals.

As a result, the BPA, created as part of the Depression-era New Deal to be self-financing through revenue from power sales, has racked up massive debt. The BPA is obliged to sell power at no more than what it costs to produce and deliver it. Accountants, policy experts, and politicians turned a blind eye to the numbers: If one segment of your customer base gets power at cost, and another gets power below cost, the result will be debt. Lots of it. More dams were built. More debt accrued. Relief came in the 1970s, when a network of power lines extended to Southern California and facilitated Columbia Basin hydropower delivery on the open "spot" market for electricity, at rates two to three times the at-cost rate. It was a windfall, but a temporary one.

Never mind that Columbia River salmon and the people who depend on them were paying the price for the delivery of cheap hydropower for corporate customers and Southern Californians.

In 2009, when California's ambitious renewable policy began to pay dividends for the Golden State, obviating much of the need for utilities there to buy power from the BPA, debt again became an issue. Over the ensuing decade, the BPA burned through almost a billion dollars in cash reserves, and its total debt swelled to nearly $14.5 billion.

Each year, the BPA writes a check to the federal treasury to service this debt. This annual payout hovers around a billion dollars. In terms of cash outlay, debt obligations outweigh the much-touted cost of salmon recovery by roughly threefold.

Debt is a horrific taskmaster. Creating enough top-line revenue to meet debt payments means running the river to maximize hydropower production. Saving salmon has always been a sideline. Perversely, the BPA pays the bill for salmon recovery, but it also holds the purse strings to funding for state and tribal fish and wildlife agencies. This has created one of the BPA's most obvious, but seldom-recognized conflicts of interest: Saving salmon goes counter to the mission of maximizing revenue. It also runs counter to the development of renewable energy sources that would reduce the region's dependence on hydropower. The BPA has to pay off the bank, and it is doing so on the backs of the once-prolific salmon runs.

Just as perversely, the BPA enjoys the protection and enhancement of this strange arrangement, funded by its own ratepayers. Lobbying organizations, subsidized by contributions from the BPA's public and corporate utility clients, unleashed a multimillion-dollar disinformation campaign, ultimately bankrolled out of the revenue stream provided by virtually everyone paying a monthly power bill in the region. The campaign aimed at cementing the role of dams in the regional economy and denying the cost to the health of the river and its fish.

The website of one of these hydropower lobbies, Northwest RiverPartners, reads, "A decade-by-decade comparison shows significant increases in the total number of returning adult salmon for both the Columbia and Snake Rivers since the first federal dams were built." The statement is true only if your map of the Columbia Basin ends at the first dam, some 130 miles from the ocean, at Bonneville. Idaho's salmon returns, four hundred miles and seven more dams upstream, and which once accounted for half of all the fish in the Columbia Basin, have tanked. In the pre-dam era, there were, on average, two million spring Chinook salmon that came out of the Snake River Basin. In 2020, there were eighty-five hundred. In what was once one of the most productive tributaries, the aptly named Middle Fork Salmon River, there were 322.

All this is perplexing and demoralizing to a self-described passionate advocate of the truth. "The whole region suffers from a bias that says all the dams create a system of energy and you can't dismantle any

part of it without it costing an absurd amount of money," Waddell says.
"It's a bias brought on by accepted incompetence."

What Waddell is describing, it seems to me, is a kind of region-wide,
energy policy Stockholm syndrome. The absurdity of the Bonneville
Power Administration has not yet fully dawned on policymakers in the
Pacific Northwest: a governmental power marketing authority disguis-
ing its debt-ridden incompetence in the vernacular of a corporation
hell-bent on profit, backed by the unchecked powers of a federal agency
that created its clout by losing billions of dollars of ratepayer money.

Despite the entrenched politics, Waddell isn't giving up. I ask him
what compelled him to stand up and take the mic at the Elwha symposium all those years ago. "I guess you could say it was my environmental
ethic," he says. "When I was head of the Office of Strategic Initiatives
for the corps, we were up to our necks in the whole controversy around
Kennewick Man.[2] The Umatilla were not happy with us. My orders
were, 'Fix this relationship.'"

Waddell designed a program he hoped would fulfill his duty. "I started
out by reading a few books and talking to a couple of consultants, and it
all just struck me as bullshit. I knew we needed something different." In
working with the Umatilla, Waddell created something altogether novel,
and at least for a short while, effective. "I didn't want anything performa-
tive, and I didn't want anything that a bunch of government people could
show up to and check a box and say, 'Okay great, now we have a good relationship with the Indians.'" The Umatilla helped Waddell and thirty other
corps employees set up their tipis at a lake high in the Blue Mountains
in eastern Oregon. What took place there, according to Waddell, was a
rare moment of genuine empathy and understanding. It changed his life.

---

[2] Kennewick Man is an eighty-five-hundred-year-old skeleton discovered in the Columbia
River near the city of Kennewick in 1996. Scientists with a rather dim view of the long cultural and biological history of the Columbia Basin claimed that the remains could not have
belonged to any of the Columbia River tribes because of the level of marine-derived nutrients in his bones. For at least ten thousand years, Pacific Northwest tribes have been
catching and eating salmon. The Umatilla and Colville People insisted Kennewick Man
was one of their ancient relations. In 2015, DNA tests proved them correct. In 2017, the remains of the ancient fisherman were repatriated in accordance with tribal burial traditions.

"Part of what happened to me was spiritual, and I don't talk about that with just anyone," he says. "But the realization that I have—we all have—an environmental ethic, is because we are a part of nature, not separate from it. That means, among many other things, that economy and ecology are really two sides of the same coin. We shouldn't consider the well-being of one without equally considering the other."

Project 5311: How the Nimiipuu Came to Adopt Solar Power

Applied to the world of electricity production, dams on the Snake and Columbia Rivers have unfairly weighted that economy-ecology coin against salmon recovery. It has been, for salmon and those who depend on them, an unwinnable, heads-I-win-tails-you-lose flip of the coin. The Nez Percé, whose homelands in eastern Oregon and north-central Idaho encompass some of the wildest rivers and vertiginous, rugged, stunning, and gorgeous mountains anywhere, have a plan that just might make the toss of that coin an even chance.

In 2019, the Nimiipuu (the name the Nez Percé call themselves) installed their first few solar panels. The project was the result of many years of planning. Tribal Executive Director Jesse Leighton recalls what their initial goals entailed. "We weren't initially thinking big," he says. "We'd never really audited what the Tribe is paying for electricity. Like any major operation, we have different departments, schools, health center, casino, administrative buildings. Turns out when you add all that up, we were paying a million dollars a year in power bills."

At the same time, the battle with the Bonneville Power Administration over salmon restoration wore on. In 2007, a federal judge handed the BPA and its sister agencies a rebuke. Their salmon recovery plan was inadequate, the judge ruled. The courts rejected the federal plan to save the salmon as inadequate several times throughout the first two decades of the twenty-first century. A revised plan, created in cooperation between the federal defendants (the agencies) and the plaintiffs (several tribes and the states of Washington and Oregon) was ordered. What happened instead was a case study in the BPA's conflict of interest. As negotiations over the revised plan were underway, funding for fish

Some fifty-five hundred miles of salmon spawning habitat would be opened up in the dam-choked Columbia River Basin if the four dams on the lower Snake River were removed.

and wildlife projects was redirected. Suddenly, bull trout restoration in the Kootenai River Valley in Montana was getting a lot of attention. But salmon recovery money got scarce. The BPA used the pretext of the negotiations to offer the plaintiffs a deal: money for fish and wildlife programs in exchange for backing out of the lawsuit that created the order to revise a salmon recovery plan. Accepting the BPA's terms meant going along with whatever the feds construed as meaningful salmon recovery. And a gag order: no mention of Snake River dam removal.

Since the 1990s, a convincing body of scientific literature has thoroughly documented the various ways in which hatchery fish are a danger to wild salmon. The most destruction occurs where hatchery and wild fish reproduce. The resulting genetic fitness of their offspring is compromised, and these traits that translate to fewer surviving fish are passed along to every ensuing generation of descendants. Despite this knowledge, over the past twenty years, federal fisheries managers in the Columbia Basin have dumped $2.2 billion into hatchery production. The cost of a single returning adult hatchery fish to taxpayers ranges from $250 to $650 per fish. Worse, the hatchery fix has presided over a steep decline in salmon populations. In the early 1980s, Pacific Northwest policy makers set a goal to increase the number of returning salmon from two and a half million salmon per year to five million. The recovery plan leaned heavily on hatchery production, and the results are stunning: instead of doubling returning adult salmon, hatcheries and status quo hydropower operations cut the number in half, to just over a million adults per year, in a system that just ten human generations ago produced ten to thirty million fish annually—for free, with no help from any hatchery.

Eventually, several tribes, two states, the Army Corps, and the Bureau of Reclamation signed an agreement with the BPA. Dubbed the Fish Accords, the original agreement lasted until 2018. It was touted by the BPA as the thing that would finally get the fish on the road to recovery. Instead, salmon numbers dipped to all-time lows. "The BPA spent $17 billion on salmon recovery and nothing's changed," says Leighton. "They know they did something wrong. We think we could do it right, for maybe a third of the cost. But we need to do something more than just argue about it."

As more solar panels went up around Lapwai, Idaho, Leighton and other Nimiipuu leaders began to see bigger possibilities. Much bigger. "Someone pulled a BPA study from 2016 that stated they would need 5,311 megawatts of power to replace what would be lost if the Snake River dams were to come out," recalls Leighton. "We started looking at what it would take to do that. And that's when the light really went on. We wouldn't be able to build that much energy on our own. But working with other tribes, we might."

Like so much of the BPA's accounting, the 5,311 number is padded. In reality, the four Snake River dams average a little under 900 megawatts of production annually. "But if we build 5,311," says Leighton, "we could talk about taking out other dams beyond the ones on the Snake."

Project 5311 would be the planet's largest Virtual Power Plant (VPP). A VPP is a network of decentralized renewable energy generators—hundreds or even thousands of them, coupled with storage, and controlled with software. Elon Musk and Tesla famously rescued wildfire-ravaged Australia with the initial building blocks of what is currently the largest VPP in the world, a network that could eventually serve fifty thousand households and generate around 250 megawatts of interconnected power. The potential for bigger networks is tantalizingly close. California has more than fifteen thousand megawatts of solar power capacity. A fraction of that is backed by battery storage, and an even smaller fraction of that is networked to create a VPP. Retrofitting all the panel capacity with battery storage and communications technology that stitches it all together will take years. But if you follow a blueprint to

The cost of a single returning adult hatchery fish to taxpayers ranges from $250 to $650 per fish. Worse, the hatchery fix has presided over a steep decline in salmon populations.

install panels, add storage, and network everything from the start, the work could be done more cheaply and quickly. "We think for $6 or $7 billion, we could build it," says Leighton. "It sounds like a lot, but it's not even half of what the BPA has spent on salmon recovery that isn't working. We rolled this out [in May of 2022] at the Reservation Economic Summit, and the positive response was really something. Not only from our neighboring western tribes but from all over the country. And if you look at where reserve lands are in the West, we could really build the resilient grid of the future. And it's great for tribes everywhere to really

lock arms and work together on something big like this, rather than independently like we do on most other things."

In the meantime, the Nimiipuu are working to transform their own infrastructure. About eight hundred panels have gone up around the reservation on various public buildings. "The next phase is homes. Every home on the reservation, we're looking to put up panels with storage. The low-hanging fruit for us is energy independence, which we think we can achieve in the next few years," says Leighton.

By the looks of things, the Nimiipuu have a good head start. Tuck Miller works for RevoluSun, a Boise-based energy company contracted with the Nimiipuu to help bring their solar vision to fruition. Miller guides me through the grounds of a water treatment station in Lapwai, which the tribe identified as a key piece of infrastructure. "When you're planning these systems, the water treatment plant is really the first thing to consider, because if that quits working, lots of other things do too," he says. Adjacent to the main building is a nondescript structure the size and rectangular shape of a steel shipping container. It's battery storage for the 150 solar panels installed next to it. "Everything you see here, the panels, the switch gear, the conduit, the inverters, the vaults, the megapack, were installed by tribal members," Miller says. "We have twenty to twenty-five people working here. We were told by some outsiders this couldn't be done. But I'll tell you what. I came here to teach solar, but I'm the student. I'm sixty-three and I've learned more working [here] than in my sixty-one years prior. We white people, we think we know about energy. But ours is a narrow view." He describes what he's learned about the landscape. "Lapwai, you know what that means? Valley of the Butterflies. This was once a rich prairie. Now pretty much everything you see on the hills is an invasive weed. On those hillsides were bighorn sheep. In the woods were elk and moose. In the tall grass there were sharp-tail grouse. The salmon are just the last in a long line of things that are disappearing."

Between the racks of solar panels, Miller and his crew have planted a garden. Agrovoltaics—using the shade provided by ground-mount solar panels to enhance the growth of plants—is another aspect of the program. On a hot June afternoon, the crew harvests greens to deliver to the

Nimiipuu Energy was built to render the lower Snake River dams obsolete. Solar energy and battery technology provides tools in the struggle for energy independence and the eventual removal of salmon-killing dams. Nimiipuu ancestral lands, Idaho. AARON BREN elder center nearby. After the hot sweaty labor, Miller circles up the crew. He asks them if they could recount for me a small ceremony they under-took at the Hatwai substation one fall morning on the western border of Nimiipuu reserved land—not far from where the Clearwater River's flow slackens. It's not lost on anyone that the primary river energy that was for thousands of years a conduit for salmon has been transformed, becoming a conduit for electricity that powers air conditioners as far away as Los Angeles. A tallish, younger man named Redwing recounts the story. "We went there and put a spear into the ground with a feather on it, and said a prayer, that the work we're doing will help bring us more salmon," he says. "We have a saying on the crew, that every solar panel we install equals one more salmon that can come back."

Talk turns to salmon fishing and the politics of salmon fishing, and it isn't until that conversation has played out that I luck into talking to a trio of women on the crew. They tell me it was a half dozen women that were the original hires in the tribe's solar program. I ask if their pioneering career choice has somehow inspired the younger generation, and what advice they might give to a young girl interested in doing the jobs they have. Jerri, a quiet, slightly built, middle-aged woman, the lead electrician of the entire crew, and who can explain as well as anyone how inverters and optimizers work, responded in a vein beyond mere career advice. "Nothing is too big to battle," she began. "Our rights are our rights, and we need to stand up for them. Work hard at it, stick with it, you can overcome anything. If we bring our salmon back, then maybe we can bring the elk back like they used to be. Maybe we can bring the buffalo back out on the prairie. Maybe we can bring our roots back."

The New Medicine

The Nimiipuu are looking at the big picture of the future of energy in the American West, in part to maintain, and where necessary rekindle, the life-giving rituals of the past. The swift, powerful rivers of the Nimiipuu homeland possess their own kind of energy, which might figuratively recharge a more metaphysical kind of battery. To experience this requires the right kind of watercraft.

On a gray Wednesday in November, adjacent the parking lot of the health services building in Lapwai, Idaho, "the people" are working to make their river once again a living memory. A first step in this deliberately painstaking journey begins with simple hand tools, deployed to help recognize the shape of the past as well as a possible future in the grain of a recently felled Douglas fir. It's the work of peeling back layers of years, creating a venerable form of a vessel that might navigate a free-running river. Metaphorically, it will ply the river of time just as nimbly. To both remember and pursue the promise the river holds, the Nimiipuu are building traditional canoes again, vessels they hope will help in their campaign to undam the Snake River and return it to some semblance of its wilder days as a salmon superhighway.

"I don't know why we stopped building canoes," says Elliot Moffatt, a Nimiipuu gentleman with graying hair and a wicked sense of humor. "I guess you could say I've had a tribal canoe for years. Except it's one manufactured by Coleman." Moffatt, along with his friend and fellow Nimiipuu Julian Matthews, was instrumental in starting Nimiipuu Protecting the Environment, a nonprofit entity that operates outside the functions of the tribal government to advocate for the health of tribal land and water. The nonprofit has another ally in tribal citizen Gary Dorr. He was one of the legal minds, and a constant presence, during the 2016 Standing Rock protests over the route of the now defunct Keystone oil pipeline. "The Keystone pipeline was set to cross Nebraska where it would impede tribal treaty rights. So, I was an intervenor in their case," he says.

Dorr, bespectacled, with a braided ponytail and built lean like the elite long-distance runner he once was, is working a drawknife on the stern section of the canoe hull under construction. "You make your prayer and stick to it," he says of his streak of raising hell against the most powerful industry in the world. "Same way we found this tree," he says of the Doug fir that's being transformed into a canoe. "It's just one of those things you go around praying with. You go into the woods with your eyes open. The tree will lead you to itself." He takes a break from the drawknife to greet a group of school children who've come to learn

Next spread: Gary Woodcock paddles through the locks of Lower Granite Dam on the Snake River in a Salish dugout canoe. Confederated Tribes of the Colville Reservation ancestral lands, Washington. BEN HERNDON

about the canoe and work a little on shaping it. There's a prayer Dorr leads before the kids are allowed to pick up a tool. His words invoke what is holy, but also serve—as children's prayers often do—to remind them to be safe, in this instance, around heavy, sharp objects. The pragmatic and the sacred are not separate concerns.

The kids' hour of canoe-building is done, and Dorr returns to the drawknife. "This boat will be christened *The New Medicine*," says Dorr. "It's a smaller canoe. But we've made four trips up the Selway River. Walking in the forest. Some big cedars up there we've prayed with. We'd like to bring one down, carve it into a full-sized canoe. These canoes, they were as important to our culture as horses or salmon. They were our telephone, our delivery truck, our bus. Not just us, but lots of other tribes. You saw this at Standing Rock. Lots of tribes paddled into camp on the river, in canoes they carved themselves."

A fire glowing in a portable steel firepan sits about forty feet away from the sawhorses that cradle the future *The New Medicine*. A rhythmic hollow bass note syncopation beats along as the gloaming fades into night. As darkness falls, with the scent of campfire smoke wafting through the air and our backs turned to the health center building, it seems it could be any century of the last ten. The Doug fir that's being transformed into watercraft, it occurs to me, was a seedling eighty to a hundred years ago, when the river ran wild. A scientist would probably be able to find chemical traces of salmon-derived nutrients in the fibers of *The New Medicine*.

A few stars poke through broken clouds as the full dark of night envelops the tiny river town. Someone returns from a truck with a half dozen work lights, quiet, lightweight, plastic lanterns powered by LED bulbs. The old ways are certainly worth practicing. But the new lights are good to have. The fire flickers, but purely for aesthetics. "When you paddle one of our canoes out on the water," says Matthews, "they say every pull of the paddle is a prayer. You have to work together to navigate, to get safely to shore. That's why we think this'll be such a great thing to teach our kids."

Soon enough, everyone takes a break to sit around the fire. Louise Simpson, a tribal elder, tells the story of a young hunter in the old days who shot a bear after being told not to. Upon inspecting the kill, which came to rest on a downed log, the young hunter saw, much to his dismay and sorrow, it was a man. The hunter had killed a departed human spirit, traveling in the form of a bear.

The group reacts with a silence that is somehow comforting rather than awkward. The story implies, it seems to me, that great care should be taken with every human action. Listening is as vital as doing. Prayer in the Nimiipuu way, I get the impression, is at least one part learning to hear better. "What you sense in a canoe is the river so close underneath you," Dorr says. "You hear the water against the hull, you feel it lifting or sinking you. You get to know the water, intimately. Which makes [you] more likely to care for and protect it."

The distances between stories, facts, and beliefs can be navigated in myriad ways. Soon, at least part of that distance will be paddled once again in a traditional Nimiipuu canoe. *The New Medicine*, in turn, will be another kind of prayer for salmon's second coming. I don't say this or anything else that I'm thinking as we sit around the fire. I don't need to tell them about Schuster's buried childhood home in the reservoir behind Ice Harbor Dam. Or about her grandfather making his own prayerful rounds each spring on the snowmelt-swollen river, in a boat similar to the one being built under the lights, or how, at least to an outsider's perspective, a new canoe, built in this old way, can seem like the beginning of some wonderful things coming full circle. I keep my thoughts to myself, a prerequisite, perhaps, to better listening.

On the long, night drive home, as the road winds past the Tucannon River—another Snake River tributary once teeming with salmon, but now nearly barren—I pull over and try to imagine, at the onset of winter, the spring song Carrie Chapman Nightwalker Schuster described to me, sung on a bright spring morning after that first bite of the first salmon of the year. I listen for that song, a chorus of falling water, the trace of what the river once was, and could be again.

INTERLUDE: GETTING THE GARDEN BACK

I'm watching clean, cold water rush by, scribbling in a notebook as a way of reminding myself that the growing "free-the-rivers" movement is meant to inspire, encourage, and perhaps edify anyone who's interested in a healthy future for the planet. Free-river advocates are part of what writer Paul Hawken in Blessed Unrest describes as the civil society movement. Over one million groups—from the smallest nonprofit to major international NGOs—are all doing their level best to preserve or create wilderness, peace, justice, clean air and water, healthy food, access to health care, gender equity, and the atmosphere surrounding our planet that supports life. Tearing down old dams and preventing new ones deserves recognition among these worthwhile causes. A hard-won return to a free-flowing river does as much, or more than anything else, to quickly and dramatically restore faith in the cycles of nature, including human nature, in an age when loss of faith in nature happens all too quickly. This joyous outcome occurs because a river restored isn't preserving a mere remnant of a wilderness, a greenspace in a city, or a rare fish in the sea. A healthy river revitalizes whole systems. Fixing a river fixes a host of problems. It solves those problems, instead of mitigating for one particular kind of trouble. The work of moving water is done quickly and quietly, and for free, instilling a belief in its witnesses that this kind of endless return on investment can and should be done anywhere and everywhere.

— Steven Hawley, river journal entry,
October 2012, on the first anniversary
of the removal of Condit Dam

In the fall of 2011, sitting on that same rock where a year later, cool clean water would be rushing by, it smelled bad. Sewer bad. So bad you had to hold your nose in between the grins, high fives, and seemingly endless cups of beer. When Pacific Power, Condit Dam's owner, blew the bottom out of Condit Dam on the White Salmon, a century's worth of sludge, ash, oars, tires, logs, aluminum cans, bottles, diapers, rods, reels, wrappers, and mud—almost three million cubic yards of it—was transported downstream in a matter of hours. Some of it parked on the banks of the White Salmon River, heaped like dump trucks of instant pudding. Some of it stopped just outside the river's mouth, in the slack water of the Columbia, forming an island from which appreciative kitesurfers now launch. But on that day, it all looked and smelled awful. Privately, some wondered how fast or even if the river would begin to look like a healthy river again. Pretty damn fast, as it turns out.

One year to the day after that temporary public health nuisance had locals holding their noses, and not a hundred yards upstream from the former location of Condit Dam, Chinook salmon spawned in clear water over a clean riverbed of gravel. This bears repeating: fish finned and prodded and performed their courtship dance—all within a hundred yards upstream of where the dam stood the year before. The river "bed" then consisted of a forty-foot-deep layer of muck. A fish would have needed seismic equipment and a stout drill rig to find anything

resembling the loose cobbles salmon need to reproduce. In a single year, the river—at no cost to taxpayers, utility companies, Superfund budgets, state departments of fish and wildlife, or lottery commissions—cleaned itself up and made itself presentable for its namesake fish.

When I come to sit on this rock, I eventually come to think of another prophecy that's come true. Before Condit Dam was taken out, federal officials presided over what became a meeting of peeved White Salmon anglers, angry men who demanded to know why they should suffer the injustice of the loss of their flatwater fishing at the river's mouth. After one surly white fisherman had vented, an old Yakama Indian man stood and spoke. He said, "My family has lived at the mouth of the White Salmon for hundreds of years. Where you guys like to fish from your boats, we used to have our house and a big garden. I, for one, am looking forward to having that little piece of land back."

That man's anticipation came to pass. A five-acre plot of fine alluvial soil has settled out on the west bank of the river, just the way the old man remembered it. He got his garden back. That's all any of us could ever ask.

PREVIOUS SPREAD: The White Salmon River is as lush a garden as anyone could want. Yakama ancestral lands, Washington. BILIOUS / ALAMY

In 2011, the Condit Dam was removed from the White Salmon River. The river came back to life as fish returned to spawning grounds and ecosystems recovered. Yakama ancestral lands, Washington. WILLIAM MCAULIFFE / COURTESY OF PACIFICORP

THE FUTURE OF THE COLORADO: A RECKONING

In late December of 2021, a downslope windstorm descended on Colorado's Front Range near Boulder. It fanned the flames of an unprecedented firestorm, with winds roaring through the unincorporated towns of Louisville and Superior. A thousand buildings were destroyed. Fire season, traditionally May to September, has become a year-round menace. The first fire of 2021 was contained on January 16 of that year. The first fire of 2022, the aforementioned Boulder Fire, was started at the end of 2021.

In recent years, the entire Colorado Basin, 100 percent of it, has experienced drought. In 80 percent of the basin, the drought is severe. It's also unprecedented in duration. A paper in *Nature* places the current dry spell, which began in 2000, as among the worst of the last twelve hundred years.

According to a journal article in *Water Resources Research*, the first fourteen years of the twenty-first century saw the average flow of the Colorado River reduced almost 20 percent compared to flows in the twentieth century. The authors, Brad Udall, of Colorado State University,

Transmission towers near the Glen Canyon Dam, Arizona. As severe drought grips the western United States, water levels at Reservoir Powell have dropped to their lowest levels ever. Navajo, Hopi, and Southern Paiute ancestral lands. JUSTIN SULLIVAN / GETTY IMAGES

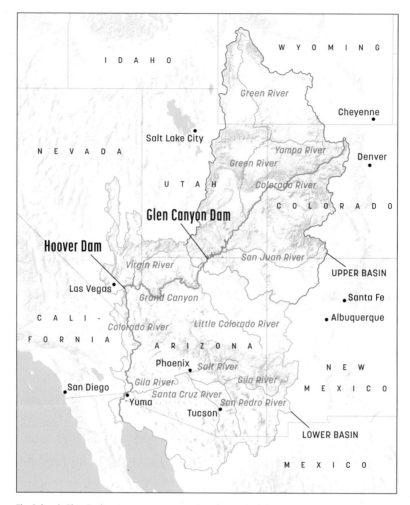

The Colorado River Basin covers seven states and Mexico and is divided into the upper and lower basin for water allocation purposes.

and Jonathan Overpeck, of the University of Michigan, forecast rising air temperatures and continued flow reduction. "It is imperative that decision-makers begin to consider seriously the policy implications of potential large-scale future flow declines," they wrote.

In 2020, the state of Arizona hauled 2.4 million gallons of water to backcountry catchments where wildlife could access a drink. Seeps, creeks springs, ponds, and other natural watering holes for creatures great and small have mostly dried up, including freshwater springs in Grand Canyon upon which Hopi people rely for irrigation and ceremonial purposes, and recreational boaters for water resupply.

In the summer of 2021, Reservoir Mead, impounded behind Hoover Dam, drained to its lowest level since the spring of 1937, when the reservoir was being filled after construction was completed. The surface of the reservoir dipped below 1,075 feet above sea level, triggering the first ever cuts in water deliveries. First to lose out: the state of Arizona, which, under the terms of a 2007 drought agreement, gives up five hundred thousand acre-feet of water. This represents the vast majority of surface irrigation in the state. Cuts to the Central Arizona Project canal—that delivers water to Phoenix and Tucson—are also part of the bargain.

In the upper basin, Reservoir Powell also dipped to its lowest level since the 1980s when it was last considered full. Reservoirs Mead and Powell ended the year at 31 and 27 percent of capacity, respectively. BuRec managers at Reservoir Powell announced in January of 2022 that they would withhold three hundred fifty thousand acre-feet that would normally flow into Reservoir Mead, to prevent triggering a low-water emergency at Powell. At the time the announcement was made, the elevation of Powell was 3,536 feet, just eleven feet above the trigger point of 3,525. At 3,490 feet, it's no longer safe to generate electricity at the Glen Canyon Dam, which creates Reservoir Powell.

Since 2000, Reservoir Powell's surface has dropped by a 140 feet. In 2021, it dropped fifty feet.

Farther upstream, deliveries to farmers from impoundments behind the Dolores and McPhee Dams were reduced to just 5 to 10 percent of their standard water allotment. Crop yields shrunk by 95 percent. Releases of water out of McPhee were reduced to ten cubic feet per second. River water warmed to above seventy degrees.

What the intensifying drought forebodes for the water storage and delivery system of the Colorado is anything but good news. The data points to the urgent need for a new way of thinking about water

2000

distribution in the basin. The policy- and decision-makers dither, still hoping and praying it will rain and snow more. In the summer of 2021, Spencer Cox, the governor of Utah, beseeched his fellow citizens to pray for precipitation. While both prayer and policy lags behind the drought, science reveals that the physical processes that are making all that water disappear are only going to intensify.

Evaporation, the Colorado Basin's Second Largest Water Consumer

Evaporation from reservoirs consumes more water than the cities for which dams provide water. A 2008 United Nations report on world water use revealed that somewhere between 1960 and 1970, evaporation

2022

from dam-created reservoirs began to exceed municipal and industrial consumption of water. Annually, about 170 cubic kilometers of water now evaporate from water held behind dams each year. Losses in desert locales have proven to be especially costly. Nasser Reservoir, plugged by the Aswan High Dam on the Nile River in Egypt, loses eleven cubic kilometers of water each year, enough to meet the residential and commercial water needs of all of Africa.

Two-thirds of India is arid or semi-arid; 5.6 cubic kilometers of dam water are lost to heat every year. Losses from reservoirs there, in keeping with the pattern revealed by the UN study, exceed commercial, industrial, and residential uses combined.

The incredible shrinking Mead. Reservoir Mead on July 7, 2000 (left), and on July 3, 2022 (right). Mead has lost more than two-thirds of it's capacity since the turn of the century. Southern Paiute ancestral lands, Arizona. NASA EARTH OBSERVATORY

Globally, the inexorable work of evaporation will exacerbate water troubles. A billion people now live where freshwater supply is short. That number is expected to double by 2050. Where snow accumulates in mountains, earlier runoff and longer growing seasons will complicate irrigation schemes and threaten already meager in-stream flows. Glacier-dependent regions of South America and Asia will see water supplies disappear, along with glaciers. River flows will decrease, droughts will last longer, and mean average temperatures will rise, which means that a growing percentage of the fetid slack water behind every dam will only evaporate more. How much more? The future, of course, is a road that lies in darkness. But recent research in the arid American West suggests the severity of the problem may be far worse than any politician has noticed or admitted.

Science tells us the Colorado Basin is already bearing the brunt of reservoir and climate change–induced water shortages in the United States. Each year, Reservoirs Powell and Mead lose a shocking volume of water to the process of cloud-making: approximately five to six times the annual water usage of Denver. More than a million acre-feet of water goes up in vapor, enough to meet the water needs of three million households in arid Colorado. Some long-standing estimates peg the loss at around 10 percent of the river's flow. At that rate, which may be a costly underestimate, reservoir evaporation is the second largest water "user" behind agriculture, surpassing municipal use.

The evaporation problem has been acknowledged and dismissed by water managers, major consumers, water lawyers, and lobbyists for quite a few years now. The standard line is that evaporation loss is simply the cost of doing business; if you want a modern civilization in the desert, reservoirs are required, and so is the standard 10 percent evaporation tax on that water stored behind dams. Science hints that this conventional wisdom is wrong; that if a sober-eyed, data-driven look at the true cost of evaporative loss ever made its way into the hands of conscientious policymakers, changes to the way water is stored, especially in arid places, would be forthcoming. For at least one scientist fascinated by water vapor, a more accurate estimate of the cost of evaporation has been a long time coming.

The impasse between information and action, between science and policy, has been much on the mind of Robert L. Grossman, one of the founding faculty members of the University of Colorado Boulder's atmospheric sciences department. Like many others in the University of Colorado Boulder community, the winter wildfire displaced him from his Front Range home temporarily. He misses, he tells me from his cabin in Norwood, the leisurely morning cup of coffee studying clouds.

He's retired, but he used to study clouds for a living and has a solid grasp of the processes that translate water into the vaporous masses that coast over the Front Range on a daily basis. "My view from my house is looking south down the Front Range," says Grossman, describing his place in the hills above Boulder. "One thing I noticed … was that there was, no matter the weather, nearly always a large cloud that came out of a particular gap in the mountains. The interesting thing, I keyed in on right away, is that this was frequently a really big cloud, low, dense, lots of water vapor. Why are clouds there when there are no others around? Another thing I figured out immediately was that this cloud comes out of the valley that sequesters Gross Reservoir."

Denver Water, the public water utility that provides running water for 1.3 million people in the greater Denver Metro area, confirmed plans in late 2021 to expand Gross Reservoir, about a half-hour drive west of Denver, by raising the height of the dam that created it by 131 feet, which would triple its capacity. Gross is fed its water by a twenty-four-mile-long pipe that takes water from the mountains on the other side of the Continental Divide.

About two hundred thousand trees that currently provide some modicum of cooling for the surrounding hills around the reservoir will be cut to make room for the bigger bathtub. Local conservation groups oppose the project. Gary Wockner, the executive director of Save the Colorado, describes the ecological impact of the proposed expansion this way: "It's bad for fish and wildlife. It takes water from the mountains on the other side of the Continental Divide. It also turns the area around the reservoir into a denuded wasteland."

Denver Water's response to critics of the expansion comes down to this: climate change is here, and Denver is still one of the fastest-growing cities in the country. Demand will outstrip supply very soon without more storage.

From a science perspective, Grossman thinks there's a better reason for thinking twice about the Gross expansion. Even before plans to expand the reservoir were confirmed, Grossman was dismayed to find the state's water plan didn't mention evaporation at all. He wrote a nine-page comment to Denver Water outlining his concerns. "I told them, 'Look what's happening here. Dust on snow, which may be a consequence of over-grazing and ag [agriculture] activity to our south and west. Rain on snow, warmer temps, water supply uncertainties due to variable snowpack from year to year. Evaporation is an irreversible loss to your system. And you don't even know what that number is.' Their answer was, 'We're looking into it.' I won't be around to see it, but I'd bet that by 2050, if they move forward with this project, there could be a bathtub ring around the reservoir as dramatic as the one you can see today at Lake Mead. Like every reservoir," says Grossman, "Gross is an evaporation machine."

Like most scientists, Grossman is painfully aware that climate change has arrived, and concurs with the predictions about the complexities and potential hardships of less water in a more populated world. But he thinks current predictions about the water shortages of the future are likely underestimated, in part because the method by which evaporation loss in reservoirs is calculated remains terribly inadequate.

At hundreds of sites monitored by the Bureau of Reclamation, a crude methodology for calculating evaporation is still used, even though it might not finish in the running at a high school science fair. The "pan evaporation method" relies on a standard-sized wading pool, twelve feet in diameter and eighteen inches deep, to accurately gauge evaporative loss from reservoirs with variable depths, altitudes, vegetative cover, wind speed and direction, and exposure to sunlight. Baseline data at these sites was established by agency scientists, who compiled data from 1956 to 1970, amalgamated the results, and calculated standardized evaporation coefficients that are still in use today. "They were meticulous, but they were wrong," Grossman says. "There's just no way you could account for the complexity. I've studied maps of Lake Powell and Lake Mead until my eyes bled," Grossman says. "The complexity is so enormous, with the various arms, what you really have isn't a giant reservoir but a chain of reservoirs. Lake Powell is two hundred miles long, and to calculate evaporation there, they have one pan. At Lake Mead, the pan is actually nowhere near the surface of the lake; it's at Boulder City, at a [BuRec] facility there."

That the data set from an office parking lot in Boulder City might not accurately represent evaporation rates several miles away at Lake Mead, but that it's nonetheless the official manner of record keeping, is a perplexing mystery to Grossman. "Engineers have been paying attention to evaporation rates for a long time," he says. "People have mostly forgotten that David Brower's evaporation argument back in the 1950s was a part of what beat the dam at Echo Park."

Grossman tells the story of how, as a graduate student in the early 1960s, he worked for BuRec one summer on Hefner Reservoir in Oklahoma, where an early version of some sophisticated equipment that could collect atmospheric data was being tested. This information, along with a method of evaporative loss calculation dubbed "eddy correlation" that Grossman helped develop, would give a more accurate picture of how much water was lost. "Reclamation pulled the plug on that one," Grossman recalls. "I'm not sure why. I watched that technology go into use all over the world. Not to be antagonistic to these folks, but that instrument finally showed up on Lake Powell in 2010. You get the feeling that at least early on, there was some unspoken policy that river managers would be better off the fewer facts they had." The lack of adherence to sound, scientific principles troubles Grossman.

"Even with the current program, the lack of understanding of physics is astounding. You look at the data sets taken at many pan stations, and you see they quit recording at the end of October when the pan

Next spread: The bathtub ring of light minerals at Reservoir Mead shows the high-water mark of the reservoir, which has since shrunk to its lowest point since it was first filled in the 1930s. Southern Paiute ancestral lands, Arizona. AP IMAGES / JOHN LOCHER

freezes. They assume the evaporation rate goes to zero. That's not true! I have photos of Blue Mesa [a Reservoir in western Colorado] one day in the winter of 2016," recalls Grossman. "It's eight degrees Fahrenheit, but the lake hadn't frozen over yet. And the water is violently evaporating. Steam devils coming off the surface, swirling clouds. Of course, reservoirs store heat throughout the summer, and release it in massive quantities as air temps cool in the fall and winter. Evaporation happens year-round. There are some winter days when more evaporation takes place than on many summer days." The interaction between air and water, Grossman contends, deserves more scientific attention. Some of his colleagues have taken heed.

Peter Blanken is a geography professor at the University of Colorado Boulder and shares a keen interest in evaporation. He got started studying evaporation on the Great Lakes. "What initially fascinated me was that here was the source of 20 percent of the world's surface freshwater, and we know very little about their surfaces as they interact with the atmosphere. We know more about the surface of Mars than we do about surface water–atmosphere interactions around the globe." Blanken has become increasingly curious about bodies of water to his west. "It really became clear to me that we are on to a major issue, a major crisis I suppose you could call it, facing western water supplies." Two things initially piqued Blanken's interest about evaporation in western reservoirs: the inadequacy of reliance on the pan evaporation method, and the subsequent likelihood of underestimates of current losses. "I think if you look at some updated methods, we could be losing 20 to 25 percent of the allocated flow of the Colorado Basin to evaporation. And this number will likely get bigger. The atmospheric demand will increase as temperatures rise." Blanken sympathizes with the dilemma faced by those tasked with the enormously complex work of balancing water in an area as vast as the Colorado Basin. "There's momentum to address what's happening here, but there's also inertia. When you ask, 'How much water are we losing?' there are people who don't want to know what the answer is. And I understand that. Water science is fairly simple, but water policy management is complicated. If you know you're doing something wrong, there's the temptation to keep doing it wrong, because at least that's familiar."

The solutions, Blanken points out, will never completely halt evaporative loss, but it could be controlled. "We could reduce evaporative water demand," says Blanken. "It might mean building new reservoirs, where there's less evaporation. You could change the timing of water delivery. You could also store water in underground aquifers, where there's no evaporation."

Policy managers are correctly concerned with costs. Some of them may have cast at least a furtive glance at one estimate of the price of evaporation, furnished by the Glen Canyon Institute. As the Imperial Irrigation District was getting set to sell its share of Colorado River water to the city of San Diego, some opportunistic number cruncher multiplied the price that fair city was paying per acre-foot by the number of acre-feet lost to evaporation, as estimated by BuRec, at Reservoir Powell alone. Annually, the clouds produced by Powell come to $225 million. Since 1963, the year the Glen Canyon Dam was completed, those Reservoir Powell–derived billowy ephemeral container ships of Colorado River water come to $9 billion. If BuRec's evaporation pans are underestimating losses, which Grossman and Blanken contend they are, that cost would be even higher. A paper that Grossman co-authored estimated that volume of evaporated water is worth up to $370 million annually.

When not studying clouds out the window, Grossman has taken the trouble to study the history of western water. "There's lots of clues there as to how this situation came about," he says. "Early boosters of water control, they knew there was no way a farmer was going to make a living on [an allotted] 160 acres. They also knew if you were going to make the desert bloom, you'd have to move water out of desert river canyons. Ergo, reservoirs." But Grossman remains fundamentally a scientist at heart. "We need a whole new kind of research," he says. "There's so much we don't know. Air flow through canyons, various kinds of air conditions, coupled atmospheric plus reservoir models. That would give you a better picture of what's required in terms of risk analysis."

This subject gets technical, and like the veteran science teacher he is, Grossman returns to a simple analogy. "A couple of years ago I was asked to be a judge at a school science fair," he recalls. "And I spent a lot of time with a girl whose experiment measured evaporation rates from different kinds of vessels. It turns out," Grossman sums up, "that a shallow bowl has more evaporation potential than a tall cylinder. As the upstream end of a reservoir gets shallower, the water is more easily warmed, and you clear the way for more evaporation. You've created, in effect, the 'shallow bowl' that's more conducive to losing more water. It's another of those positive feedback loops with climate change that could really wreak some havoc." He describes "runaway evaporation" that occurs when vaporizing water meets with other physical reservoir phenomena, like increased sedimentation. Why risk more dire consequence than necessary? "Why the heck," asks Grossman, "would you send precious Colorado River water into the desert to evaporate?"

Reservoirs as Sediment Traps

To appropriate Grossman's analogy, the transformation from tall glass to shallow bowl in any given reservoir depends on a host of variables. Engineered to last centuries, some reservoirs have proven they won't last even a couple decades. One that has become nothing more than a giant evaporation pan with a quicksand bottom can be observed in the hills outside Ventura, California. Thousands of people know it as the dam where activists painted giant scissors on its surface, which was featured in the 2014 film about dam removal called *DamNation*. Situated within the Los Padres National Forest, fifteen miles from the ocean, the Matilija Dam was completed in 1948. Cost overruns and safety concerns plagued the project from the start. Originally, it was opposed by the California Department of Fish and Game, and even by the US Army Corps of Engineers. In 1964, a study completed by the Bechtel Corporation, not exactly an antidam organization, recommended lowering the dam as a viable option to deal with the reality that the dam would be condemned in 1965. Instead of demolition, a reasonable fate for any condemned public works project, a notch was cut in the top of the dam to allow flows during high-water events to spill down the face. By the mid-1970s, its reservoir was rendered useless. Sediment build-up had reduced the storage capacity of the reservoir from thirty-eight hundred acre-feet to less than five hundred. It cost $4 million to build Matilija, and it will cost somewhere between $13 and $30 million to tear it down.

As early as the 1980s, worldwide reservoir sedimentation has been estimated to have filled in one-fifth of the planet's dam-created water storage capacity. Some river systems do this work more quickly than others.

The muddy Colorado River—too thick to drink, too thin to plow, as that time-worn adage goes—is busy supplying ample evidence that original estimates of the life span of Glen Canyon Dam and Reservoir Powell have been greatly exaggerated. In *Dead Pool: Lake Powell, Global Warming, and the Future of Water in the West*, distinguished scientist and author James Powell painstakingly describes the forces at work that are revising downward the remaining years of the impoundment with which he shares a surname. Powell writes that climate chaos has hit the arid American West harder than much of the rest of the planet. The West's average temperature increase of two degrees Fahrenheit from 1950 to 2000 is greater than the worldwide average temperature increase over the whole of the twentieth century. In the Colorado Basin, two degrees hotter, with its attendant increase in evaporation rates, correlates to a 14 percent reduction in the river's annual flow volume. A 1 percent decline in average rain and snowfall translates to a 22 percent flow decrease. In the first twenty years of the twenty-first century, average flows in the Colorado River have decreased 20 percent. All forecasts predict further reduction as the warmer years roll by.

This insidious process is a problem made more acute by increasing water demand. The American Southwest remains one of the fastest-growing regions in the United States. Phoenix, Arizona, added more people—two hundred sixty-two thousand of them—from 2010 to 2020 than any other American city. The Las Vegas area, which housed half a million people in 1980, is home to 2.8 million thirsty souls in 2022, and is the second-fastest growing city in the United States. Both metropolises depend on Colorado River water.

Agriculture in the basin still gets the lion's share of water for now—some 70 percent of Colorado's water budget. And though total farm acreage has shrunk, demand for water has actually risen with farmers planting water-intensive crops like alfalfa. The growth proceeds as if the Colorado River will never run out of water, even though, since the year 2000, withdrawals from the Colorado's flow have exceeded deposits in every year.

And yet the real killer of Reservoir Powell, contends author Powell, may well be the river's prodigious sediment load. Each day, the Colorado delivers enough sediment to the reservoir to fill fourteen hundred cargo ship containers. As the reservoir shrinks, sediment deposits that were laid down when the water level was higher are resuspended. Powell cites a study that calculated that in five years of sediment deposition, the reservoir received twenty-two years' worth of sediment, due to these "recycled" reservoir deposits. Decreasing flows and increasing siltation are shortening the life of Powell. At full pool, boaters once enjoyed access to the water from eleven different boat ramps. In the summer of 2021, there were three, and only one of those, Bullfrog, was fully functional.

It was once estimated by BuRec that it would take seven hundred years for Reservoir Powell to fully silt in. That estimate assumes that in most years, the reservoir would refill each spring to near capacity. But at less than a third of capacity, it will silt in and dry up much faster. Sedimentation and evaporation have a synergistic relationship. The less water in a given reservoir, the faster the remaining water will evaporate, given shallower depths and warmer water temperatures. Sediment left high and dry by shrinking reservoirs is remobilized during less frequent high-water events, and is moved downstream, settling out in the reservoir's slack water, making deep water shallower. Then that shallower water will evaporate faster.

Given the climate chaos–induced dynamics now at play, author Powell estimates the impoundment has but fifty-five years—and even that may be cut short. He also outlines some nightmare scenarios that will unfold as Powell approaches "dead pool"—the level at which everything the dam and reservoir was designed and built to do can no longer be done.

Currently, Reservoir Powell has accumulated two major sediment plumes—one at the north, upstream end of the impoundment, and another at the foot of the dam. While the northern, upriver side is doing the work of creating the "shallow bowl"—effectively shaping its own river delta where the river flow slows and drops suspended sediment—the pile at the foot of the dam has the potential to reduce the entire flow of the Colorado below Glen Canyon Dam to an anemic trickle. The sediment pile at the upstream side of the dam's base could eventually grow to plug the river outlet works, 237 feet above the original bed of the river. Even if that submerged egress remains unplugged by sediment, serious questions remain about whether the pipes that would conduct water through the dam down there would hold up. They were not designed to handle the volume and pressure that would occur.

The openings for the turbine bays—at low water, the only other path the river has to flow out of the reservoir—lie another ninety-six feet above the outlet works. As the reservoir level recedes below these turbine bay openings, the river would effectively have no outlet. Everything downstream of Glen Canyon Dam, including the Grand Canyon, Reservoir Mead, and the forty million people dependent on Colorado River water, would be quickly dehydrating under a merciless sun in a more or less waterless desert.

Of course, BuRec assures the public it has options. Bypass tunnels below the elevation of the current outlet works could be drilled, likely at great expense; how much, no one seems to know. In the meantime, BuRec can continue to call water from upstream impoundments. Farmers can be paid to let upper basin water rights remain in stream, letting Rocky Mountain snowmelt fill the reservoir. And praying might yield results: You never know when the good Lord will bestow the Great American Desert with a few wet years. But be careful of what you pray for.

Because of siltation, even if the Southwest's climate were to reverse to a series of wet years, Reservoir Powell will never be able to hold the twenty-four million acre-feet of water as originally designed. Reduced reservoir capacity has already led to a commensurate reduction in hydropower capacity. Once capable of producing 1,320 megawatts of electricity, with less water to spin the eight giant dynamos in the bowels of Glen Canyon Dam, generation is down by a third.

It isn't clear at all anymore that an extended forecast of rain would fix Reservoir Powell. With wet weather, upriver tributaries produce higher runoff, which carries more sediment. Exposed stretches of temporarily stranded river sediments will continue to be remobilized. The more water, the more sediments will continue to pile up at Glen Canyon Dam. The less water, the faster the upper end of the reservoir will continue to dry out.

So, the better bet, science indicates, is that the Lord will forsake, for the foreseeable future anyway, his insatiably thirsty desert people of the metastasizing American Southwest. When scientist and author James Powell published *Dead Pool* in 2008, the hydrological dystopia he described seemed to many to be far-fetched. It is now within reach. "It did not take a genius to make those predictions," Powell says via a Zoom call in early 2022. "Just a scientist who accepts the science on climate change. At the time, the Bureau of Reclamation did not, and probably still does not." Powell, who retired in California after a long career that included stints as a museum director and college president, and appointments by Presidents Bush and Clinton, is worried about his grandchildren's future. "I didn't want to give up on science, so I write books. I like to start with a really big question."

One of those questions for Powell has been what the future holds for the American Southwest. "I wish these predictions were not coming true," he says. "But all is not lost for the future—if we choose to act." Correcting the mistakes of the past will be difficult, he concedes, without widespread recognition of those blunders. "Glen Canyon Dam, at least, never should have been built," says Powell. Without a major course correction, the future looks silted in. "In seventy-five to a hundred years, these dams will be big traps full of wet sediment."

Having dropped 140 feet in twenty years, given the consensus prognostication of the long, climate chaos–driven drought to continue, by the year 2042, it seems reasonable to at least begin preliminary planning for the day that Reservoir Powell will have dropped another 140 feet. As I write this, its elevation sits at 3,537.33 feet. Another 140 leaves it at 3,397.33 feet, 92 feet below the formerly submerged openings that feed water into the dam's prodigious hydroelectric turbines.

Then what?

All Dams Are Dirty: The Methane Problem

In the meantime, dams on the Colorado River, and everywhere else, have another problem. It turns out they're all significant emitters of a greenhouse gas that, in the short term, is much more potent than carbon dioxide. Methane made headlines in late 2021 at COP26, the United Nations gathering of world powers held in Glasgow, Scotland, to discuss climate change. Methane is a colorless, odorless gas that's produced both in natural processes (cow flatulence and underwater plant decomposition) and in industrial activity. Fossil fuel production and consumption produces a lot of methane. Unlike carbon dioxide,

the world's reservoirs are annually producing ... as much greenhouse gas as ... Germany, the world's sixth-largest contributor to climate change.

which will persist in the atmosphere for centuries, methane dissipates relatively quickly but does a lot more damage while it's there. According to the EPA, over a century's time, methane is twenty-five times more effective at trapping atmospheric heat than carbon dioxide. Over a twenty-year period, methane is eighty times more effective at heat retention than carbon dioxide. Commitments to cutting methane emissions worldwide became one of the most heralded accomplishments of COP26. Sticking to these commitments will require some fresh scrutiny over existing and planned dams, and at least a passing familiarity with a

Next spread: The Klamath River's Iron Gate Dam and Reservoir—an emitter of the potent greenhouse gas methane. Note the bright green hue of the water, the sign of a dangerous algal bloom. Klamath River Shasta Indian Nation ancestral lands, California. ECOFLIGHT

rapidly growing branch of limnology, the study of biological, chemical, and physical properties of water.

In the early 1990s, a small team of scientists in Brazil started measuring greenhouse gas emissions produced at dams and reservoirs. Led by Philip Fearnside, these scientists found surprising results, indicating that large hydropower projects in tropical countries emit high levels of greenhouse gases, especially methane.

In 2000, Vincent St. Louis, Carol Kelly, Éric Duchemin, John W. M. Rudd, and David M. Rosenberg published a paper in the journal *BioScience* that described how reservoirs contribute to greenhouse gases. The five scientists furnished data from reservoirs in Brazil, Canada, Finland, Panama, French Guiana, and the northern United States, and called for reservoir emissions to be included in inventories of anthropogenic greenhouse gases.

In 2008, Fearnside published an article in an academic journal, *Oecologia Australis*, titled, "Hydroelectric Dams as 'Methane Factories': The Role of Reservoirs in Tropical Forest Areas as Sources of Greenhouse Gases." In the article, Fearnside put forth credible evidence that some large hydroelectric projects in tropical locations spew greenhouse gas emissions equivalent to that of large, coal-fired power plants. Around the same time, other scientists around the world launched new studies that supported the conclusions of Fearnside and his colleagues.

Over the past twenty years, international studies of dams and their reservoirs confirmed in dozens of peer-reviewed research papers that dams and reservoirs are net contributors to climate change.

In 2016, the climate cost of large dams was further affirmed when an international team of scientists synthesized dozens of studies from around the planet indicating that methane emissions from dams and reservoirs have been widely ignored and dramatically underestimated. Published in *BioScience*, the article, titled, "Greenhouse Gas Emissions from Reservoir Water Surfaces: A New Global Synthesis," was funded by the US Army Corps of Engineers, the Environmental Protection Agency, and the National Science Foundation. The study made international news and recommended that the United Nations' Intergovernmental Panel on Climate Change (IPCC) revise its calculations and include dams, and reservoirs' significant emissions in climate change scenarios.

Part of the "global synthesis" service, this seminal paper provides an inventory of almost 270 dams worldwide and their estimated methane emissions. Included were Glen Canyon Dam and Reservoir Powell, and Hoover Dam and Reservoir Mead. Per megawatt hour of electricity produced, Powell emits an estimated 228.8 kilograms of carbon dioxide equivalent. Mead spews 1,079 kilograms per megawatt hour. For comparison's sake, per megawatt hour, an average-sized, gas-fired electricity generating plant emits 407 kilograms of greenhouse gases. According to a report commissioned by the Glen Canyon Institute, from 2010 to 2014, Glen Canyon Dam averaged 4.08 million megawatt hours of power production annually. Do the math: multiplied by the estimate of emissions of methane in the Global Synthesis study, the clean, green hydropower coming out of Reservoir Powell produces 933 million kilograms of carbon dioxide equivalent greenhouse gas in the form of methane each year, equal to the climate cost of 205,000 cars on the road over the same time span.

How Dams and Reservoirs Produce Methane Emissions

Rivers move more than water. Vegetation, sediment, algae, phytoplankton, wood—all are carried downstream, settle out where river currents slow, and are trapped at the bottoms of reservoirs behind dams. In reservoirs, organic matter becomes a fuel stream for methane production. Subsurface anaerobic decomposition—organic flotsam and jetsam that sinks, then rots without oxygen—is dramatically intensified in dam and reservoir systems. This organic matter produces methane. If reservoir conditions remain stable, the methane diffuses—kind of oozes—slowly back to the reservoir surface and, eventually, to the atmosphere. Constant pressure from the water keeps methane from being quickly released into the atmosphere. But when reservoir levels fluctuate, as reservoirs were designed to do, pressure on the bottom sediment is decreased. Under these conditions, methane-laden bubbles rise to the surface and release directly into the atmosphere. Methane can also escape directly to the air via downstream degassing, which occurs when methane-rich water passes through a dam, either via a spillway or through a powerhouse to spin a turbine.

Reservoir greenhouse gas emissions are often more intense where:

- the dam is bigger and the reservoir is larger, and especially where the surface area of the reservoir is larger;
- the weather is warmer and wetter, and the water temperature of the reservoir is warmer;
- the initial flooding of the landscape submerges large areas of vegetation;
- more vegetation and sediment runoff into the reservoir occurs;
- the reservoir's water level fluctuates up and down, either seasonally or during hydropower-ramping cycles, causing vegetation to grow on the dry banks of the reservoir, and then become submerged when the reservoir level rises causing that vegetation to drown and decompose;
- the reservoir is newer or made larger, and the vegetated landscape more recently flooded;
- the reservoir receives runoff from agriculture, forestry, and disturbed areas where erosion and fertilizer-heavy water feed into a reservoir, amplifying the biological cycle that grows and decomposes algae and other submerged vegetation; and
- where any other type of heavy nutrient load is pouring into a reservoir, including human wastes, stormwater runoff, or wastewater treatment plants.

How serious is the reservoir methane problem? More so than the already significant trouble described in the 2016 Global Synthesis study. In 2021, some of the same authors of the Global Synthesis paper updated their research in another paper published in *Global Biogeochemical Cycles*. A new model improved the accuracy of methane measurements in reservoirs. Emissions were 29 percent higher than previously predicted. All told, the world's reservoirs are annually producing 1.07 gigatons of carbon dioxide equivalents as methane.

This is as much greenhouse gas as is emitted annually by Germany, the world's sixth-largest contributor to climate change.

John Harrison is a professor at Washington State University and a leader in the field of studying reservoir methane emissions. He was part of a working group that presented the results of their research to the IPCC. "We were responsible for developing guidance for national [greenhouse gas] inventories," recalls Harrison. "That's basically where each country calculates and reports greenhouse gas emissions from different landscape types." In 2006, there was an effort to provide similar guidance for reservoir emissions, but the science was new enough that it was relegated to an appendix. By 2019, the data gathered by Harrison and many others was convincing enough that the IPCC now includes a category for reservoir emissions in their inventory procedure. The IPCC protocols have been adopted by policymakers at the US Environmental Protection Agency, which is recommending a reservoir emissions calculation in its manual for adding up greenhouse gas emissions from individual states.

The acceptance of methane emission science by respected international bodies and influential federal agencies hasn't come a moment too soon. Climate change has the potential to intensify the phenomenon. "Laboratory studies show there's a metabolic relationship between temperature and methane production," says Harrison. He points out that, in addition to stimulating more rapid methane production, warmer water holds less oxygen, potentially expanding the anaerobic environment required for methane production. Reservoir water levels, and related greenhouse gas emissions, could also change as climate changes, but the net result of these changes is not well-understood. "There's a possibility that decreasing the surface area of a reservoir might allow for the oxygenation of some of those shoreline sediments, which would then be released as carbon dioxide rather than methane," Harrison says.

Of more immediate concern is the downstream degassing that can occur when water is released from the bottom of a dam's outlet works, as occurs at Reservoir Powell. This fact complicates a favored fisheries management tool, releasing "bottom draw" as a means of keeping cold-water dependent fish species out of hot water in the increasingly longer, hotter summers.

A tangle of complex factors also provides possible opportunity. Harrison points out that agricultural pollution, especially in the form of phosphorous and nitrogen, leads to increased algal production, which leads to increased methane. "So there's a double incentive to clean up that kind of nonpoint source pollution," says Harrison. "You get cleaner water, which is better for aquatic life, but you also have the potential to reduce greenhouse gas emissions."

In any case, difficult decisions, including the removal of offending methane-producing dams, will have to proceed with the knowledge that hydropower and the sprawling water storage and delivery systems of the twentieth century are nowhere near as clean and green as hydropower advocates have claimed. "We are confident that these systems are net producers of methane," says Harrison. "In every system where we've measured methane emissions, reservoirs are producing methane and releasing it to the atmosphere."

Climate chaos has turbo-charged sedimentation, evaporation, and methane production at all reservoirs. Reservoir Powell offers a glimpse of what could happen to any dam and reservoir complex blocking a sediment heavy river system and situated in an arid location. Measured in terms of its greenhouse gas contribution, two hundred and five thousand cars worth of pollution may seem like an acceptable risk compared to a similar amount of fossil-fuel generated electricity. But it's worth remembering that greenhouse gases are not the only form of ecological havoc that dams have wreaked.

Because it threatens not only the health but the flowing existence of everything downstream of it, because it loses through evaporation five times more water every year than Denver uses, because it drowned Glen Canyon, because its bathtub ring rivals the height of the Statue of Liberty, because its marinas are silting in—Reservoir Powell is a growing mess. Like all man-made messes, the longer it takes to reckon with the disaster, the harder it will be to clean up.

A buoy sits high and dry on cracked earth that was previously under the waters of Reservoir Mead. June 2022. In October, federal officials announced a plan to pay farmers to not take water. Southern Paiute ancestral lands, Arizona. AP IMAGES / JOHN LOCHER

SAFETY FIRST

In February of 2017, on the Feather River in Northern California, under the strain of a torrential rain, the main spillway spectacularly failed at Oroville Dam. The tallest dam in the United States at 770 feet, completed in 1968, its namesake reservoir is the second biggest freshwater body in the state. It's a crowning achievement of the California State Water Project, one of the largest water storage and delivery systems in the United States, serving more than twenty million people, irrigating hundreds of thousands of acres of farmland, and lighting up a significant portion of the state's utility customers by generating hydropower. How close Oroville Dam came in 2017 to complete failure—and how much risk remains for such a catastrophe—isn't fully known. The disaster in 2017 exposed some painfully obvious weaknesses.

As the disaster unfolded, and damage to the main spillway mounted, flows to the spillway were shut off while officials tried to figure out what to do about the damage. Meanwhile, the emergency spillway—little more than a concrete weir and an earthen embankment off to the side of the dam—was pressed into service for the first time since the dam

A survivor of the destruction of Longarone, caused by the failure of Vaiont Dam, prays on her knees on the flattened ruins where the parish church stood. 1963. Italy. MARIO DE BIASI / SERGIO DEL GRANDE / GIORGIO LOTTI / MONDADORI / GETTY IMAGES was built. It was completely inadequate to the task. The soil quickly eroded, compromising its structure, precipitating a disaster water managers described with bureaucratic understatement: "loss of crest control." Nearly two hundred thousand people downstream were evacuated. The emergency spillway was quickly shut off, and the damaged main spillway was reopened, risking further damage to that structure. The dam held, sparing downstream communities from the destruction of a Feather River rampage. But the spillway was a wreck, the massive concrete slide splintered, the earthen fill beneath eroded to bedrock. Initial estimates for repairs came to $500 million—which proved to be a gross underestimate. In September 2018, the bill for repairs to the spillway topped $1.1 billion dollars, with more to come. Damage to the dam structure itself will cost another billion. Meanwhile downstream businesses, residents, and municipalities are pursuing litigation against the California Department of Water Resources (DWR), the owners of Oroville Dam. The plaintiffs have a compelling case.

Even as the disaster at Oroville was unfolding, news that dam managers had been warned of the inadequacy of the emergency spillway made headlines. The failure of this secondary spillway occurred at less than 4 percent of the three hundred fifty thousand cubic-foot-per-second capacity the Federal Energy Regulatory Commission (FERC) had deemed its maximum. The potential for loss of crest control was predicted with precision only a dozen years earlier. In 2005, as California officials applied to have Oroville Dam's fifty-year operating license renewed, three conservation groups, Friends of the River, the local Sierra Club chapter, and the South Yuba River Citizens League, wrote comments that were filed in the application to FERC that warned that piled up dirt would not make even a temporarily adequate spillway.

Patrons of the services Oroville provides, among them the Metropolitan Water District of Southern California, providers of water for twenty million citizens of Southern California, and the State Water Contractors, an affiliation of some of the state's largest water utilities, including the Metropolitan Water District, Kern County Water Agency, the Santa Clara Valley Water District, and the Alameda County Water

The damaged Oroville Dam spillway on February 27, 2017. Downstream, one hundred eighty thousand people were evacuated. Konkow and Enterprise Rancheria Estom Yumeka Maidu ancestral lands, California.
DALE KOLKE / CALIFORNIA DEPARTMENT OF WATER RESOURCES

District, deemed the dirt adjacent to the dam's only other spillway to be adequate, and stated their opinion in a 2006 letter to FERC. Their customers would be the ones on the hook for the cost of the safety upgrades. Attorneys for the State Water Contractors urged FERC to reject improvements to the emergency spillway, citing costs in the "tens to hundreds of millions of dollars," and FERC engineers obliged. One of that federal agency's civil engineers, John Onderdonk, estimated that the erosion that would accompany any overflow volume of water on the dirt embankment "emergency spillway" would not threaten the integrity of the dam's concrete. At a small fraction of its rated capacity, the weather made fiction out of Onderdonk's estimation.

The main spillway, as it turns out, has also been suspect from the beginning. A post-spillway failure report by Robert Bea, co-founder of the University of California, Berkeley's Center for Catastrophic Risk Management, cited dam managers and engineers for poor design, low-quality concrete, and continued use of out-of-date standards, guidelines, and processes as major contributors to the disaster. One of the most shocking findings of Bea's report: the main spillway was engineered to be built on bedrock or concrete, but was instead built on "graded fill," rocks and soil dumped during the construction of the dam. Such material, as the failure of the spillway demonstrated, simply won't withstand the forces brought to bear against it. Other findings in Bea's report, titled "Root Causes Analyses of the Oroville Dam Gated Spillway Failures and Other Developments," should be cause for serious alarm.

As far back as 1998, inspection reports, photographs, and other documents had identified problems with the section of spillway that failed. The DWR tried patching cracks, even filling up voids beneath the concrete spillway. Some of these repairs trapped water, further degrading structural integrity.

Headgates—the structures that control water releases from the dam—are a serious liability. Corrosion, large cracks in two gate control tendons, and some gates that don't open and close completely increase risks for everyone and everything downstream.

In a telephone interview, Bea pointed out what might be the most worrisome of all the observations he compiled in his report: green grass growing on the abutments. "The grass shouldn't be green in that part of California during the summer and fall. It should be brown, so when you see lush green grass, it indicates there's seepage through the dam face. What's particularly worrisome is evidence we found indicating this seepage has been going on for about fifty years. DWR says that it's just some natural springs, and that it's no cause for worry. But a natural spring in that area would have to flow uphill, which runs counter to the laws of physics," Bea said in an interview with the Cal Alumni Association of UC Berkeley. In a telephone interview, Bea added that, "When you see seepage on the downstream face of a dam, run. Get out of the way. These early warning signs are really important."

Bea, who began his career as a civil engineer at Shell Oil, later pioneered the field of forensic engineering. He's compiled a database of more than six hundred engineering disasters and has been on-site post-calamity at failures ranging from the explosion of the space shuttle *Columbia*, to the wreck of the *Exxon Valdez*, and the *Deepwater Horizon* oil spill. The engineering department at the University of California, Berkeley, where he taught, affectionately refers to him on their website as "Dr. Disaster." It was his expert testimony that was key in British Petroleum admitting criminal liability and paying out a $4.5 billion settlement in the *Deepwater Horizon* disaster, a service for which he was recognized by the United States Senate.

In a 2016 paper, Bea, whose pioneering work in forensic engineering seems to have fallen on deaf ears in the world of dam operations and maintenance, published a paper in the *Journal of Modern Civil Engineering*, titled "What Is Safe?" Here, Bea recounts his long experience as an engineer, and how, with few exceptions, standards of safety always seem to fall short. Bea begins with the dictionary definition of *safe*: freedom from undue exposure to injury or harm. Use of the word among engineers, writes Bea, "makes me wince." Not only do systems age physically, he writes, but also in the daily increasing distance from the knowledge of design standards that existed at the time of construction. Risk will always increase as long as humans can look to the past with varying degrees of regret and remark, "If I'd known then what I know now."

The surrounding environment in which a thing is built is also subject to change, due to forces both natural and human engineered. We like to build a dam, then build a city downstream. Bea writes, "Additional challenges develop when the potential consequences of failures have increased as a result of changes in the natural or 'social' environments in which the systems exist. What was deemed safe for the original environments can no longer be deemed for the changed environments."

High-risk systems, writes Bea, require low probability of failure. Dams are a high-risk enterprise—the bigger the dam, the bigger the risk. Due to the passage of time, an increase in knowledge, and changes in landscapes around dams, all dam risks are on the rise. A commensurate boost in scrutiny over what comprises a safe dam has not been made. The results of this ongoing lack of care will be costly, and quite possibly, deadly.

A failure at Oroville, Bea points out, would set California's water delivery system back so far it might never recover. "A breach at Oroville would send a wall of water down the Feather River, through the Sacramento Valley, and ultimately into the Sacramento/San Joaquin Delta," says Bea. "It would destroy towns along the Feather and Sacramento Rivers, flood major portions of Sacramento, and blow out levees throughout the Delta, permanently flooding much of the region. The huge government pumps near Tracy, that send water to Southern California cities and farms, would be incapacitated. There would be tremendous loss of life and property, and it would be years before a permanent water delivery system to the south state could be reestablished. Furthermore, it wouldn't necessarily take a tremendous amount of rain and uncontrolled releases as we saw in February to trigger such a failure. It could happen on a bright, sunny summer's day. The situation is that serious," Bea told the UC Berkeley Alumni Association.

Bea recounts his experience working with Boeing back in the 1990s when a persistent pilot with an enduring concern about the safety of the planes he flew took up correspondence with him, eventually visiting the professor in his office at Berkeley. "His name was, and still is, Captain Chesley Sullenberger," recalls Bea, of the pilot who famously emergency-landed a passenger jet on the Hudson River. "What the safety culture around dams could really use is someone like him. There're some obvious signals that the risk factor is almost to the point where a major disaster will be hard to avoid."

... as of 2019 there were fifteen thousand six hundred high-hazard dams in the United States ...

There's no emergency landing for a dam once it fails. And until the hydro-equivalent of a Captain Sullenberger materializes, there's reason for grave concern over a looming crisis facing the country's dams. Well into the twenty-first century, dams fail. And it isn't just old dams that give way. All dams fail at a predictable rate, about one in ten thousand each year. The Association of State Dam Safety Officials (ASDSO) keeps a database of dam failures; more than three hundred fifty are on that list. According to an annual report issued by the American Society of Civil Engineers (ASCE), as of 2019 there were fifteen thousand six hundred high-hazard dams in the United States, more than double the amount from two decades prior. High-hazard dams are those which would likely result in significant loss of life should any one of them fail. Another 11,343 dams are classified as "significant hazard," meaning should they crumble, maybe no one gets killed, but the man-made flood would cause catastrophic damage.

Dams in the United States are well into middle age, fifty-seven years old on average. By 2030, 70 percent of the US inventory of dams will be fifty years old or more. It isn't just the inexorable aging under pressure of cement that risks failure for these dams. As ASCE notes in their 2017 report, "Fifty years ago, dams were built with the best engineering and construction standards of the time. However, as the scientific and engineering data have improved, many dams are not expected to safely withstand current predictions regarding large floods and earth-quakes. In addition, many of these dams were initially constructed using less-stringent design criteria for low-hazard dams due to the lack of development below the dam." A review of dam failures over the past century reveals several kinds of dam-generated disasters that have already happened. Given the national inventory of more than ninety-one thousand dams, a failure rate of five to ten dams per year would seem to be expected. But the failure rate far exceeds that number.

The ASDSO report also noted that "from January 2005 through June 2013, state dam safety programs reported 173 dam failures and 587 'incidents'—episodes that, without intervention, would likely have resulted in dam failure." In addition to the risks of aging, it's become clear that the nation's water infrastructure, dams included, wasn't built to withstand the extreme precipitation events that accompany twenty-first-century climate chaos. Research from Dartmouth University found that the frequency of high- or low-water events, measured at more than five hundred gaging stations across the United States and Canada, has doubled over the past fifty years.

Another climate change–research query by Stanford University found that, from 1988 to 2017, 36 percent of the more than $200 billion in flood damage was attributable to weather extremes driven by climate change. That percentage is expected to increase.

The past is prologue, the saying goes. No one eagerly awaits the next dam disaster, but the record of catastrophe hints at what the future might bring.

In February of 2014, a worker at Wanapum Dam in central Washington noticed something unusual. The deck atop one of the gargantuan spillway bays, an area of sufficient square footage to park two semitrucks side by side, was listing downstream. Divers were sent into the chilly river to inspect. They found a sixty-five-foot tall, two-inch-wide crack.

A mile long and 185 feet high, Wanapum features twelve spillway bays, with gates that are fifty feet high and sixty-eight feet wide. It came online in 1963 by the local public utility district, Grant County

PUD, at a cost of $93.3 million, according to the *Capital Press*. At peak-generating capacity, its powerhouse can crank out 1,203 megawatts of power. Together with Grant PUD's other Columbia River facility downstream, Priest Rapids Dam, the utility district produces far more power than the forty thousand utility customers in Grant County can use. The surplus is sold onto the grid.

The swift and decisive reaction of PUD personnel protected life and property from a potentially catastrophic failure of the dam. Nonetheless, the fix was anything but cheap, quick, or easy. Right away, the reservoir behind Wanapum was lowered thirty feet to relieve pressure on the crack. To accommodate this drop, water behind the next dam upstream, Rock Island, was also lowered. The fissure closed, but with the start of irrigation season a month away, the fruit orchards adjacent the river that rely on the reservoir for water were left high and dry. Just as pressing were soon-arriving adult salmon, estimated at some seven hundred thousand strong, who would need a way through Wanapum Dam. Normally, fish ladders provided this service, but with the reservoir level lowered, the ladders wouldn't work.

Then there were the complexities of the solution to the crack itself; the dam needed some new tendons. Crews drilled thirty-seven shafts, each sixteen inches in diameter, into the support columns that frame the spillway bays, down through the concrete, and into the river-bottom bedrock at the base of the dam. Then, tendons—sixty-one steel cables aggregated to make a twelve-inch-diameter bundle—were fed through the shafts, anchored into bedrock, and grouted at intervals into the dam's concrete. Finally, from the top, each tendon was pulled taught with 2.5 million pounds of pressure, fitted with a waterproof sleeve, and capped at the crest. Little more than a year after that crack was discovered on a gray February morning, the reservoir began to refill. In the interim, an emergency adult salmon transportation program had gotten adults past the out-of-service fish ladders. Temporary extensions of irrigation pipes kept the bloom on apple and cherry trees in orchards. Crisis averted. Yet what happened here may be only one instance of a systemic problem plaguing aging dams.

The Dow offices and a large industrial complex stand surrounded by flood waters after two dams failed in Midland, Michigan, in May 2020. Mississauga ancestral lands. EMILY ELCONIN / BLOOMBERG / GETTY IMAGES

The crack at the Wanapum Dam spillway bears some striking similarities to ongoing problems at Oroville Dam. In 2017, California's Department of Water Resources, owners of Oroville, came clean on the nature of a large crack in the headworks of the dam to a state legislature subcommittee. (The damaged spillway, in the process of being repaired at the time, is an adjacent structure.) At fourteen feet long, and four inches wide, the crack at Oroville is plainly visible to the naked eye. In testimony at this hearing, Robert Bea pointed out that the US Army Corps of Engineers issued a report in 2013 over concerns of increased failure risk at dams due to old and aging steel anchor tendons. Oroville Dam test data, gathered by the California Department of Water Resources in a report issued in 2000, shows that every single gate of the spillway has defect "flaws" in steel anchor tendons with noted crack dimensions "considered significant." Bea confirmed in an email to me that the problems at Wanapum and Oroville appear to be similar.

The official culprit at Wanapum was a fifty-year-old math flub. The original planners for the gravity dam—claims dam owner Grant County Public Utility District—did not correctly calculate the enormous pressure of water on the structure's concrete. Some of the largest dams must be able to withstand science-fiction worthy loads. Oroville, the tallest dam in the United States, has to withstand pressures at its base of ten thousand pounds per linear foot. (Imagine the weight of three midsize import cars condensed to push on a brick.) At the Wanapum incident, calls for the engineer's head could not be answered, because that man is now pushing up daisies instead of designing dams. Scapegoating long-gone engineers may be convenient, but it doesn't address the added risk climate change poses to dams.

On May 18, 2020, heavy rainfall in Michigan topped out Wixom Reservoir, impounded by Edenville Dam. The next day the dam failed. The runaway freight train of water raced down the Tittabawassee River, destroying Sanford Dam downstream. The toppling of the two dams damaged or destroyed more than twenty-five hundred structures and handed Michigan a $200 million tab for its rampage. Ten thousand people were evacuated; downtown Midland, a city of just over forty thousand, was under nine feet of water. Residents watched in horror as the flood inundated a chemical plant and hazardous waste sites adjacent the river. The cost of rebuilding the dams, which began in late 2021, will run into the hundreds of millions.

Spencer Dam on the Niobrara River in Nebraska failed in March of 2019, killing one person. The ninety-two-year-old structure will not be rebuilt by its owner, Nebraska Public Power District. Fifty million dollars was earmarked by Congress in 2021 to remove what's left of the dam and shore up riverbanks downstream that were leveled by the eleven-foot-tall wave that carved a new path for part of the Niobrara.

The deadliest small-dam failure in the United States in the last fifty years was the Black Hills Flood in Rapid City, South Dakota. Huge thunderstorm cells parked themselves over the eastern escarpments of the

Black Hills, dumping prodigious amounts of rain. Flooding was bad and getting worse, when, at 10:45 p.m. on June 9, 1972, the Canyon Lake Dam failed. A deluge of water was unleashed on the downtown Rapid City area. Several other tributaries added to the raging waters that killed 238 people, injured 3,057, and destroyed 1,335 homes and 5,000 cars.

Unlike the Black Hills flood, the failure of Kelly Barnes Dam some ninety miles outside of Atlanta, Georgia, on November 6, 1977, was the sole cause of a flash flood that killed thirty-nine people, mostly students at a religious college. Killing budding young bible scholars in the south gets on the news quickly, and the Toccoa Falls disaster, which came on the heels of a much larger but less lethal dam break in Idaho a year before, made national headlines. Lack of adequate maintenance to the structure was cited as the cause.

In March of 2006, a small earthen dam failed on the north side of the Hawaiian Island of Kaua'i, draining Ka Loko Reservoir, and sending a wall of water rushing downstream. Seven people were killed, including a toddler and a pregnant mother. The structure had never undergone inspection by state officials.

In September of 2013, another record rain event caused widespread flooding in Colorado. Nine low-hazard dams failed. The event called attention to safety concerns at much larger projects. Colorado has 431 dams on the high-hazard list, including Vallecito, Lemon, Ridges Basin, McPhee and Jackson Gulch, Narraguinnep, Totten, Summit, Stagecoach, Terminal Dam at Electra Lake, and Durango Terminal Dam. All have the potential to kill if the potential for failure goes kinetic.

Some little, privately owned dams suddenly don't seem so small when disaster strikes. In Iowa, in July of 2010, the nearly sixty-foot-tall, seven-hundred-foot-wide Lake Delhi Dam, which had plugged the Maquoketa River to create a nine-mile-long lake, overtopped, then collapsed. The dam was completed in 1929, and was owned by the Lake Delhi Recreation Association, comprised primarily of property owners along the artificial shore. An inspection of the dam a year prior to the disaster advised the recreation association to fix a spillway gate that

The floodwaters from the failed Teton Dam left denuded topsoil
and death in their wake. Shoshone–Bannock ancestral lands, Idaho.
US BUREAU OF RECLAMATION

had fallen into disrepair. A summer rainstorm dumped ten inches of rain
in twelve hours and made the repair of the spillway a moot point.

In October of 2015, South Carolina was hit with record rainfall. More
than twenty-four inches of rain fell in seventy-two hours in locations
around Charleston County. At least thirty-six dams in the state were either overtopped or failed completely. Eighty-four others were closely
monitored for signs of failure.

Each of these dam cataclysms illustrates the paradox of dam-based
water control. Dams do allow for storage of water for irrigation and
power production. And they can control the potential for flooding—but
only to the point at which the dam is overtopped or fails. Then dams
only make floods worse.

The problem with larger dam catastrophes: the bigger the dam, the
more destructive the flood. The collapse of Teton Dam near Rexburg,

Idaho, was a peculiar mix of federal government agency hubris and a major miscalculation about the porous nature of soil in this part of the country. Welded ash is a type of soil that occurs when volcanoes spew their nonliquid innards over the landscape. In these eruptions, superheated gases heavier than air rush downslope. Particles of ash ride the wave, then cool when they hit the ground, and fracture upon cooling, forming a soft rock called ignimbrite or welded ash. This is exactly what happened 2.1 million years ago in what is now Yellowstone National Park, when an early Pleistocene supervolcano blew its top and buried the Tetons and a portion of the Snake River Valley in welded ash.

In the 1930s, the Bureau of Reclamation had their sights set on a dam in these parts. They knew from the moment they scrutinized their first soil sample that welded ash didn't hold water very well. The soil type was identified as "unsuitable for dam construction." The site was also found to be sitting atop an active earthquake zone. Nonetheless, construction for Teton Dam began in 1972. Disturbingly, while excavating footings on the side of the dam, another fractured layer of ignimbrite was discovered. Still, BuRec engineers were confident that they could seal the leaks. Two hundred thousand cubic yards of grout were originally included in the construction estimate for sealing such fissures. Nearly five hundred thousand were poured into the sieve-like ignimbrite. But it was all for naught.

On the morning of Saturday, June 3, 1976, clear water springs were discovered on the downstream face of the dam. By the morning of June 5, seeps were recorded staining the face on the north end of the dam. BuRec engineer Robert Robison later recalled that a leak developed at about 10:30 a.m. and let loose with a loud roar. At 11:00 a.m., a whirlpool developed on the upstream side of the dam. Two bulldozers were deployed to try and plug the hole. Word went downstream that evacuations should commence. Half an hour later, both bulldozers, after being abandoned by their drivers, were swallowed as embankments atop the dam on which the heavy equipment was riding gave way. At 11:57 a.m., the north half of Teton Dam collapsed. Nearly three hundred thousand acre-feet of water raced at a million cubic feet per second along an eighty-mile path. Floodwaters inundated nearly three hundred square miles of the Snake River plain. The deluge found its way to the south fork of the Snake, and on Sunday morning, twenty-four hours after the breach, Idaho Falls residents living anywhere near the river were treated to a marathon session of sandbagging and quick evacuation. Most of Idaho Falls was spared, but upstream, the man-made flood killed eleven people. It did at least $400 million worth of damage in a weekend. Thirteen thousand cows drowned. The towns of Wilford, Sugar City, Salem, Hibbard, and Rexburg—a college town of ten thousand souls—were devastated.

In the United States, massive losses of human life wreaked by the failure of large dams has so far been avoided. But the rest of the world has not been so lucky. In northern Italy in 1963, what some considered to be the crowning achievement of the country's post-war recovery, 860-foot-tall Vaiont Dam, a gleaming white concrete plug at the foot of a narrow tributary of the Piave River, loomed just east of the town of Longarone. Photojournalists admired Vaiont for the way it lit up around sunset, Longarone and its satellite villages in the foreground, just a mile from the dam. But experts ignored local warnings that the high walls of the river valley in the foothills of the Alps were prone to slides. Ominous rumblings around the valley, in fact, had brought a group of forty-five scientists and engineers who were quartered in a dorm adjacent the crest of the dam. Movements of slopes across from their dorm were alarming and had been monitored for three years by then. They wouldn't get a chance to investigate further.

A little before 11:00 p.m. on the night of October 9, 1963, a slab of mountain above the south bank of the reservoir, approximately a mile square, sloughed off and slid toward the impounded waters behind Vaiont Dam. Less than a minute later, that entire hulking landmass hit the man-made lake at approximately fifty-six miles per hour. The result-ing impact sent a wall of water estimated between two hundred and five hundred feet high into the valley below. At least two thousand peo-ple were killed, among them the scientists gathered to assess the risks presented by Vaiont Dam. The massive wall of water pushed a pocket

Rescuers search the rubble in Longarone below the Vaiont Dam. Italy.
GETTY IMAGES

of air in front of it more powerful than the winds created by the nuclear bomb dropped on Hiroshima; it stripped the clothes off nearly all the victim's bodies. Many victims were never found, much less identified. Longarone was wiped off the face of the planet. (It has since been rebuilt.) Photos taken the day after the devastation look similar to grainy images of dry riverbeds on Mars.

The ravages of the Vaiont failure hinted that large dam disasters of the future would rival modern warfare in their potential to destroy life and property. Twelve years later, Banqiao Dam in the Henan Province of China became quite likely the worst dam disaster in human history.

In the 1950s, China rushed headlong into the industrial age, in part by embarking on a mad frenzy of dam construction that continues to this day. Over one hundred dams were built in the Zhumadian prefecture of Henan Province alone. Despite the warning of at least one state hydrologist, the dams were celebrated as part of an ambitious package of modernization. But the first week of August in 1975 brought to the region the worst storm in China's long-recorded history. More than three feet of rain fell in one day. Panicked citizens described dead and disoriented birds that had crashed in the maelstrom. When it became apparent that Banqiao Dam would overtop, a sandbag brigade worked feverishly to keep the water below the crest of the dam. After midnight, a few stars became visible. The rain abated. A tentative sense of relief came over the scene. Then there was a sound, according to one survivor, "[as if] the sky was collapsing, and the earth was cracking." Seven million cubic meters of water burst forth from behind Banqiao. Accurate accounts of fatalities are much disputed. Western knowledge of the carnage came forth slowly, due to the hardline *what-happens-in-China-stays-in-China* policy of the day. But as relations with the West warmed, records, as well as eyewitness accounts of the flood, have emerged. Credible estimates are that as many as 171,000 people were killed.

While three feet of rain in a day seems like a storm invented for mythology, increasingly, what was once considered meteorologically impossible is becoming a frightening new reality. Climate change will tend to make things more unpredictable, with each passing season becoming more prone to extremes. But even without climate change as a factor, previous dam disasters are making clear that the records upon which reasonable tolerances in design and construction were made were based on too little data.

The size and strength of modern dams are guided by a principle known in the industry as "probable maximum flood." To arrive at this number, a hypothetical engineer would delve into local meteorological archives, locate the wettest storm on record, and assume a similar-sized storm will fall again, but this time on already fully saturated soil atop a full winter's snowpack (if the dam was designed at a latitude where snow falls.) They would then calculate the runoff from this storm and instruct the lead excavator to begin digging footings for an appropriately sized concrete monster to catch this prodigious flow.

The problems with this approach are manifold.

The annals of weather records are too short to make any definitive conclusions about the maximum probable flood in a given basin, especially in North America. The United States has existed as a nation for less than a quarter-millennium. Most stream flow and weather data goes back less than a century, the rest goes back no more than half a century. To build a dam based on observations from this brief window of time should only reinforce the reality that, in geologic time scales, humankind has been on the planet for an instant, building giant cement things for only a sliver of that moment. At Oroville Dam, during the decade it took to build that structure (1968–1978), the Feather River saw two thousand-year floods and one ten-thousand-year flood.

Still, you have to give credit to the busy-beaver mindset of engineers: A 2018 manual from the US Army Corps of Engineers, titled "Hydrological Engineering Requirements for Reservoirs," recommends that probable maximum flood be calculated not on the largest recorded flood in history, but rather on a guesstimate of the largest flood physically possible in the chosen valley. "The probable maximum precipitation [...] is based on the maximum conceivable combination of unfavorable meteorological events." Put aside for the moment the phrase "maximum conceivable combination," which begins to stray a good distance into the realm of imagination rather than engineering, and belies the reality that, year after year, the weather conjures up events that seem to disprove the conceit that humans can imagine every possible scenario or outcome. More to the point, this manual reflects the manner and methodology by which some rather unimaginative engineers come to improve their ideas: If nature foils the best laid plans, pour more concrete. But this damn-the-torpedoes approach has at least one fatal flaw.

Until recently, the order of engineers that build modern dams didn't like to admit that there's even a statistical probability that any structure they design and build has a chance of failure. There is some truth to the notion that with an endless supply of time and money, a dam could be proofed against every vagary of weather and geology. But all built things have a construction budget and timeline. Engineers strive to create a bomb-proof design; economists, politicians, and project managers want a design that balances safety concerns with cost. The latter group also wants the public perception that a project is proceeding at a reasonable pace. When problems arise—say, a tuft of welded ash large enough to bury a small town inside it at the foot of a dam site, as was the case at Teton—the strictures of budget and timeline tend to temporarily supersede the laws of physics the engineer is obliged to obey. Errors are made, uncertainties glossed over. The latter tendency helps to explain why the most dangerous time in the life span of a modern dam is not at the end but the beginning: About two-thirds of all dam failures happen when the reservoir behind it is filled for the first time. An engineer's math error or some unforeseen geological detail will present itself when the pressure of millions of pounds of water comes to rest on a giant, man-made drain plug for the first time.

The weight of all that water presses down as well as out. As such, there's good data that show a compelling correlation between dam construction and earthquakes. Not a decade after Hoover Dam was completed, scientists found it had triggered quakes there. According to the International Rivers Network, at least a hundred cases worldwide of "reservoir induced seismicity" have been documented, and there are likely more. In a paper prepared for the UN's World Commission on Dams (WCD), V. P. Jauhari wrote: "The most widely accepted explanation of how dams cause earthquakes is related to the extra water pressure created in the micro-cracks and fissures in the ground under and near a reservoir. When the pressure of the water in the rocks increases, it acts to lubricate faults which are already under tectonic strain but are prevented from slipping by the friction of the rock surfaces."

This proverbial greasing the wheels for large earthquakes may have caused a quake in Sichuan Province in China in 2008, a 7.9 on the Richter scale that killed eighty thousand people and has been the subject of much scrutiny by Chinese and American scientists, who are examining the very real possibility that Zipingpu Dam was the cause of the quake. The weight of the water behind Zipingpu tipped the scales at 320 million tons. The dam was built five hundred meters from the earthquake's fault line; the epicenter of the quake was 5.5 kilometers (3.3 miles) away from the dam.

In spite of the case study China provides, the risks posed by dams, whether they cause a quake or just make a randomly occurring one worse, goes largely unexamined. Dams inevitably are built along fault lines, since rivers often follow valleys formed by the fracture lines that occur where faults lie. The probability of large dams adding immense doses of risk to areas where millions of people have settled, in the now-predictable intervals between catastrophic quakes, hasn't been taken into account much.

In July of 2015, the New Yorker featured a story by journalist Kathryn Schulz that described in gory detail what will happen to the wet, steep, and, in geological time scales, very recently urbanized corridor between Portland and Seattle when the next major earthquake comes—which it inevitably will. This stretch of verdant coast has the misfortune to lie along the Cascadia subduction zone, which delivers a shaking that has come, on average, about every 250 to 300 years. These are no mere Bay Bridge-collapsing California shudderings. The Pacific Northwest goes longer between quakes, but when they come, they make up for lost frequency by an exponential increase in intensity and duration. The upper registers of the Richter scale, on the other side of 9.0, isn't out of the question. Old masonry buildings from Bellingham to Bandon will crumble, soil will liquify, perhaps toppling office towers in violent sequences. What will happen to dams in this mossy, mildewed upper-left corner of the country? Bonneville Dam, less than an hour east of Portland on the Columbia River, is often celebrated as a beacon of American dam ingenuity. But one of the most dramatic scars of the last big quake is massively visible above the north abutment of Bonneville Dam, dwarfing one of the flagship engineering projects of twentieth century America.

When Lewis and Clark came floating down the Columbia in the fall of 1805, at Cascade Locks they miraculously survived the largest series of rapids on their journey—whitewater likely created by one of those giant quakes. After their wild and improbably successful ride, the explorers

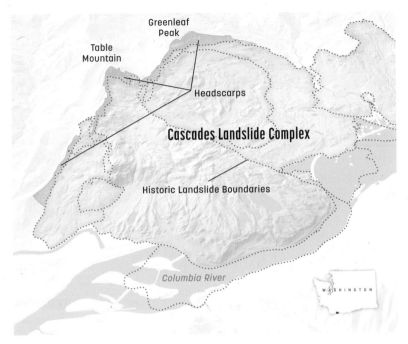

At the current day site of the Bonneville Dam is the remains of historic earthquake-caused landslides. The region is due for another quake anytime now.

were regaled by stories of a massive slide that had blocked the entirety of the Columbia River for at least a few months. Local Chinook Indians recalled to the intrepid explorers that the slide allowed them to cross the mile-and-a-half-wide Columbia before the river finally washed the temporary land bridge away on its south end, creating the rapids Lewis and Clark successfully ran. The size of this slide— what geologists now call the Cascades Landslide Complex—dwarfs what happened at Vaiont Dam in Italy a half century ago.

The westernmost headscarp, the top of this massive slide zone, is Table Mountain, a thirty-four-hundred-foot-high, pyramid-shaped cross section of Cretaceous basalt that sits atop an older clay layer; the eastern headscarp, a few miles upriver, is Greenleaf Mountain, similarly shaped and two hundred feet lower than its downstream counterpart. The slide "complex" begins on a ridge between the two peaks and extends for several miles all the way to the riverbank twenty-eight hundred feet below. Overlapping debris paths indicate that the area has experienced several landslide events rather than a single one. The physical signs of multiple episodes of subsidence are obvious. Slides pushed the Columbia's riverbed a mile to the south, toward the Oregon shore. In the episode recounted by the locals for Lewis and Clark, a temporary lake seventy miles long extended upriver. The height of the natural dam that blocked the river was twice the height of today's Bonneville Dam—situated precariously just downstream of the path of these slides.

Rivers don't make mistakes. People do. "Nature," says Bea, "is very unforgiving of ignorance."

In their journals, Lewis and Clark describe conifer trees buried in debris. The slide that buried these trees was likely caused by a big Pacific Northwest earthquake.

The last big slip of the Cascadia subduction zone occurred on the evening of January 26, 1700. Anthropologists and geologists have corroborated their knowledge base to arrive at this precise date. A tsunami hit the Japanese coast that day. Radiocarbon dating and dendrochronology (dating derived from studying the growth of tree rings) affirm that buried trees along flood zones experienced their last season of growth in 1699. Stories told by First Nations and Native American coastal people offer further confirmation. More geologic investigation reveals a major rattling, on par with what happened in January of 1700, hitting the region almost like clockwork every 243 years. Ominously, the region is now more than three-quarters of a century overdue. A study by scientists at Oregon State University determined that over the past ten thousand years, there have been nineteen 8.7 to 9.2 magnitude earthquakes between southern Vancouver Island to around the Oregon-California border. By the year 2060, if the region has not experienced another quake, citizens of the Pacific Northwest will be the luckiest inhabitants of the late Pleistocene: 85 percent of all the known intervals of earthquake recurrence will have been surpassed.

So, what happens to Bonneville Dam, or any of the other major dams in the Columbia River Basin when the big one hits? The majority of US dams, after all, were designed before anyone had much of a clue about the intricacies of seismology.

Years before Wanapum Dam cracked due to a deceased engineer's math error, Grant County Public Utility District set out to answer that question. Along with two other utility districts, a study was commissioned to see whether dams they owned would remain standing after a major quake. The verdict, based in part on what happened to dams in Japan in the 2011 quake there: damage would occur, but no catastrophic failures would result. The utilities agreed, nonetheless, that it would be good to invest in some seismic retrofits of their dams.

That assessment seems cursory to "Dr. Disaster," Robert Bea, whose investigation of the disaster at Oroville Dam, and his subsequent warnings about its future, have thus far gone largely unheeded. "It's a patch and pray approach," says Bea. The most dangerous risk factor, says Bea, is the human tendency to look the other way as disaster approaches. Rivers don't make mistakes. People do. "Nature," says Bea, "is very unforgiving of ignorance."

PATIENCE AND PERSEVERANCE

Those who say "it cannot be done," should stay out of the way of those who are doing it. – Unknown

Commercial fishers are known as a durable bunch, a quality shared by at least one of their attorneys. "Fishermen are always at the end of the line in negotiations over water," Glen Spain tells me over lunch one gray autumn day. "But we're not the quietest. People forget that my clients are used to shouting at sea over diesel engines."

Spain, bespectacled, bearded, smiling as often as not, and always dressed in a manner somehow at once appropriate for office work or standing on a boat deck, is general legal counsel and Northwest Regional Director for the Pacific Coast Federation of Fishermen's Associations. The Eugene, Oregon-based attorney is a veteran of western river wars. Since 1982, a major portion of Spain's job has been trying to fix the mess that is the Klamath Basin; its fish-killing dams and its hotly contested water rights. "I was a young environmental attorney in the Bay Area, and I kept running into this feisty commercial fishing

Klamath tribal members are trying to restore critical habitat along Upper Klamath Lake for endangered species like the C'waam and Koptu, historically a staple of their diet. Klamath and Modoc ancestral lands, Oregon. PAUL ROBERT WOLF WILSON

147

group, at that time led by a charismatic Northern California fisherman named Nat Bingham, who was already talking about taking out dams. I admired how they were kicking the shit out of the agencies, and kicking the shit out of their opponents in the public relations arena, too. So, I went to work for them," Spain recalls.

Squaring off with opponents of fishermen in the Klamath has meant squaring off with an entrenched irrigated-agriculture lobby. Historically, the Klamath was one of the country's top salmon-producing rivers, third only behind the Columbia and the Sacramento. Draining a massive swath of sparsely populated Southern Oregon and Northern California, it was also one of the richest wetland ecosystems on Earth, harboring some three hundred and fifty thousand acres of marsh, swamp, and savannah. Home to the Klamath, Hoopa Valley, Yurok, and Karuk Tribes,

Water rights here have been as contentious as any place on Earth.... If a deal can be struck to take out dams here, it can be done anywhere.

the river nurtured cultures rich in fish, game, and timber, and in the upper basin, bird life as riotously rich as any place on Earth. The Upper Klamath Valley was a vital stopover on the Pacific Flyway, the migration route for millions of migratory waterfowl. Little more than a century ago, up to ten million birds could be found in and around Upper Klamath Lake.

But in 1905, the Bureau of Reclamation made the Klamath one of its pioneering projects. A network of dams and canals was built to deliver water, mostly to upper-basin farmers. The marshes were drained, replaced by the standard BuRec formula: farmers growing subsidized crops with subsidized water and subsidized electricity, an arrangement the farmers came to view as their birthright. The birds were reduced to a mere fragment of their former glory. One of Oregon's early fish and game commissioners, William L. Finley, wrote of the loss of

Before it was drained a century ago, the Klamath Basin was a seasonal stopover for millions of migratory birds. Lower Klamath National Wildlife Refuge, Klamath and Modoc ancestral lands, California. DAVID HOFFMAN

avian plenitude: "Today, Lower Klamath Lake is but a memory. It is a great desert waste of dry peat and alkali. Over large stretches, fire has burned the peat to a depth of one to three feet, leaving a layer of white loose ashes onto which one sinks above his knees. One of the most unique features in North America is gone. It is a crime against our children."

Reparations for ecological crimes have proven difficult to settle. But the Klamath River is tantalizingly close to setting a major precedent in efforts to set things right again. Four dams—one in Oregon and three in California—are slated for removal. Water rights here have been as contentious as any place on Earth and have been that way for more than a century. If a deal can be struck to take out dams here, it can be done anywhere.

This was Glen Spain's operating principle in his long years of trial on the Klamath. It all begins with an unwavering commitment to patience and persistence. That faith has come to fruition. The Klamath dams are coming out. Oregon and California have set aside more than adequate funding for the task, and the owner of the four dams, PacifiCorp, has turned over the title to these dams to a recently formed nonprofit entity whose sole purpose is to liquidate those assets. The two states have issued water quality reports and permits. When Spain began representing commercial fishermen's interests on the Klamath, all indications were that it would be a cold day in a waterless hell before any farmer gave up a drop of water for any fish. Spain and his allies insisted that both sides take into full account a litany of facts based in law, policy, and science. They had to overcome the mythology of water in the West that had become almost as stubborn a reality as the law.

A River Upside Down

At a time when the population of white settlers was sparse, justice for Native American tribes a secondary concern, and environmental values nonexistent, the Bureau of Reclamation had no trouble establishing a water right that gave farmers the lion's share of Klamath water. "Under the Bureau's historic water right, their demand has no cap," Spain says. "It is unlimited demand. If there's water available, and they can use it for irrigation, then there is no upper limit. The original water right was literally all the water that's left in the system." The troubles with this arrangement were until very recently considered to be intractable, mostly because it was widely assumed that irrigators owned the river. But they don't. Some farmers and politicians still deny this fact. But the law of the land dictates there should be water for farm and field, fish and fowl. This doctrine has been upheld in court, as will be detailed later in this chapter, but it owes something as well to the unique shape of the Klamath Basin.

The National Geographic Society once described the Klamath as "a river upside down." Most of the agricultural work for which the river's water is diverted is in the upper portion of the drainage. This portion

Drought leaves its fractal-patterned punishment on once-wet ground.
Upper Klamath River, Klamath and Modoc ancestral lands, Oregon.
MASON TRINCA

of the Klamath Basin seems more suited to what the "delta" of a river system should look like: a network of marshes, ponds, lakes, creeks, and tule flats situated in a broad, flat valley. The fecund waterfowl stopover that William Finley eulogized. The lower 120 miles runs through a steep narrow canyon, and drains some of the most remote country left in the Lower 48 states. It's also in this lower portion of the river that the Yurok, Karuk, and Hoopa Valley Tribes have lived and fished since time immemorial.

In the middle of the river's run sit four outdated, fish-killing, water-polluting dams whose owner, PacifiCorp, had indicated they would prefer to decommission. "These dams produce almost no power," says Spain, "and it would actually cost the company more to fix them up to modern standards than it does to tear them out." Due to the

Next spread: The Williamson River, a major tributary of the Klamath, augments short-lived seasonal flooding on the north end of Klamath Lake, where over-allocation and drought are shrinking a once vast store of freshwater. Klamath and Modoc ancestral lands, Oregon. AL SEIB

upside-down nature of the Klamath, farms and fields were watered far upstream of the dams. Removing them would not affect a single farm irrigated by the Klamath Project. But advocates of dam removal were about to learn that some watersheds have ties more political than ecological.

Since the Bureau of Reclamation drained most of the marshes in the upper basin, then over-allocated limited water to farmers, geopolitical factors have complicated efforts to amend BuRec's short-sightedness. It's hard to get people outside the region, politicians in particular, to care about the Klamath, in part because it is relatively unpeopled, encompassing the least populated parts of both Oregon and California. No major cities lie within its sixteen-thousand-square-mile territory. Median income lags far behind the national average. On the Yurok Reservation along the Northern California coast, some households still do without electricity. The rough-and-tumble landscape has cultivated analogous attitudes among some of its citizens.

Where water politics are concerned, upside down really does serve as an apt description of Klamath Basin water wars. Violence is an all-too-common undercurrent in discussing water-related matters here—death threats and armed confrontation are part of its past. Glen Spain maintains an ability to see the better angels of his opponents' nature. Several former adversaries have become friends. "Fishermen and farmers are both basically blue-collar food providers," Spain observes. "We have as much in common as not. What I've found is there are really a bunch of essentially good people trapped in a very bad system."

"The biggest problem you have in the Klamath Basin isn't the dams," says Oregon Wild's Conservation Director Steve Pedery, who began working on the Klamath's water shortage problems in 1999. "It's that the basin's water is over-allocated. And the part no one wants to talk about is that even if Congress somehow had approved dam removal, the basin's water will still be over-allocated." Over-allocation is a problem that plagues many western watersheds. It has a century-and-a-half-long history. Those like Pedery and Spain who were in on the early rounds of discussion about removing four dams far downstream of upper-basin farmers could not fully anticipate how profoundly this history would affect their early negotiations. "These farmers basically crashed the talks on dam removal," recalls Pedery. "And they made it clear that if the dams were to come out, they were going to try to extract water guarantees out of the process. Now keep in mind these dams are more than a hundred miles from the federal irrigation project upstream. The dam removals weren't going to affect their operations one way or the other. But there they were. It was brash, and it was divisive when some parties decided to hear [the farmers] out." Pedery and Oregon Wild didn't like that. "There was too much water being given away in exchange for dam removal, really, for us to stomach," he says. According to Pedery, Oregon Wild was shut out of the negotiations due to that opposition.

Spain, whose constituency is commercial fishermen, not conservationists, sees it slightly differently. "It might be the case that we find that after the dams come out, we still don't have enough water for fish," says Spain. "But one problem at a time, please. If that scenario arises, and we have four fewer dams to contend with, then the water negotiation and solution will be that much simpler."

The needs of Spain's clients dictated that more fish as soon as possible was a higher priority than calling bullshit on farmers' eleventh-hour party crashing. Solutions are not always perfect, Spain observes, because law and policy are not perfect, nor are people. "The Klamath is not only a perfect example of everything wrong with western water law, but it also presents a model of some ways that that can be cured. It's a good model. We've created a scenario where it's now quite certain that the dams will come out—the money is there, and the majority of stakeholders agree it's something that should be done." The slow recognition of the reality that water, especially in semi-arid climates, is of limited supply, has been a major catalyst for this change.

Yet this reckoning with reality has not yet arrived at the offices of certain western congressmen. Perhaps the most significant testament to the will of those who want the lower Klamath to run free is that a deal was struck in spite of a congressional attempt to sabotage the process.

Spain is one of the primary architects of a deal twenty-five years in the making that was forged to go a long way toward balancing water and healing old wounds in the Klamath Basin. The prize for farmers, a stable supply of water—gained via their insistence on becoming part of the negotiations over Klamath dam removals—has been axed from the Klamath settlement. In explaining how this happened, Spain warns of the dizzying array of abbreviated terms. "We like to joke that whoever shows up with the most acronyms buys lunch," he says.

This original agreement, the Klamath Basin Restoration Agreement (KBRA), which would have guaranteed minimum flows for farmers and fish, and its sister bill authorizing dam removal, the Klamath Hydroelectric Settlement Agreement (KHSA), would have become one of the largest conservation wins in American history. Signed by the governors of Oregon and California in 2010, congressional approval of KBRA-KHSA would have meant tearing down four dams on the Klamath, thereby reconnecting the upper and lower basin and salmon to habitat they haven't seen for a century. PacifiCorp would have capped the cost of dam removal and been immune from liability in the removal process. BuRec project farmers, and even some off-project upper-basin farmers, would be guaranteed water delivery amounts for the next fifty years. *Would* is the verb of choice in the previous sentence, because the KBRA died. Congress, or rather one congressman, killed it. "The KBRA had written into its language what was deemed a 'terminable event,'" says Spain. "Which basically says, that if Congress did not approve the KBRA by February 1, 2015, that the agreement would be dissolved, that all parties would be free to walk away from it." To make short another long, sordid tale of congressional ineptitude, now-retired Oregon Republican Congressman Greg Walden delayed crafting, for five years, a bill authorizing removal of the Klamath dams. When he finally did, within weeks of the 2015 deadline, Walden floated a bill that contained no language green-lighting dam removal but had plenty to offer about turning over timber-rich federal lands within the Klamath Basin. His bill quickly died.

It wouldn't be altogether wrong to blame the snuffing out of the hard-won agreement on Walden. But in a twist of fate for irrigators, it now appears that the minimum flow guarantees extracted by farmers in the KBRA will simply not be revisited. Dam removal, on the other hand, could be. "The language of the KHSA [the portion of the agreement pertaining to dam removal] contains some provision for parties to pick up the pieces if they indicated a willingness to do so," says Spain. "And so, after the Walden bill killed the KBRA, the parties—the tribes, PacifiCorp, the states of Oregon and California—went back to see if they could devise a way to pursue dam removal in a way that didn't require Congress to act. And it turns out that procedure exists, and that it's simply the one that all utilities have to go through to get their dams licensed or decommissioned. FERC grants or denies these licenses. So as is the case with any other privately owned dam, those commissioners will vote to approve or deny the new application to remove the Klamath dams."

Ironically, Spain points out, Walden and his fellow conservative representatives in Congress had a chance to do something for their constituents back home. By crafting a bill that would have approved the KBRA, the historic perception on the part of farmers that they controlled the Klamath's water would have continued. "Now it's irrigators are angry, and they should be," says Spain. "Republican congressmen who refused to endorse this deal also screwed their own farmers. Because of their inaction, the next time there's a shortage of water in the Klamath, project irrigators are going to be cut off." The courts, Spain observes, have upheld tribal water rights as superseding all others, and the KBRA, unratified by Congress, cannot supersede the court's decision.

Courts intervening in Klamath water matters were a long time coming, a factor again owing to the politics and culture of the region. The Klamath Basin is a place that has cultivated a powerful aversion to federal oversight. For almost a century, with an iron grip on the controls of the Klamath Project, the federally owned irrigation project, farmers had come to view themselves as sole proprietors of Klamath water. They succeeded in implementing a kind of virtual reality based on this illusion of ownership, a misconception of which they were slowly, but thoroughly disabused.

The beginning of the end of single-party water rule in the Klamath came with the resurgence of Indigenous Nations' rights in the 1960s and '70s. Upstream, the Klamath Nation had emerged from the nightmare of the Cold War–era Policy of Termination and Relocation, wherein the federal government absolved themselves of responsibilities to tribes, a matter of policy and law that had existed since the early nineteenth century. The plan was simple: pay off individual tribal members for the dissolution of tribal lands and transfer them into private ownership. This was meant to hasten the "progress" of Indigenous Nations in the effort to remake them into ordinary white Americans. Thanks in large part to Douglas "Giveaway" McKay, a car dealer and Eisenhower booster whom the latter appointed to be his Interior Secretary, the Klamath people were among the first to be volunteered as guinea pigs in this experiment, which began in 1953.

The theft of Klamath land and water was swift and immediate. The largest remaining contiguous ponderosa pine forest in the United States stood almost wholly within lands on the Klamath reservation. Turned over to federal ownership, and christened the Fremont-Winema National Forest, Weyerhaeuser and other corporations treated themselves to a nearly six-hundred-thousand-acre frenzy, clear-cutting, high-grading, and hauling logs on Klamath reserved lands so fast that by the time Klamath people regained their federal status in 1986, their forest had been greatly diminished.

Meanwhile, more dams were constructed on Oregon's upper basin portion of the Klamath during the Termination years, further eroding Indigenous Nations' rights to fish, hunt, and gather. Nonetheless, in the early '80s, Klamath tribal citizens immediately set about re-establishing hunting and fishing rights. A significant opportunity to further this cause was the adjudication of water rights within the state of Oregon. This meant sorting out whose water right came first.

The western doctrine of prior appropriation—"first in time, first in right"—was, like a host of other nineteenth-century natural-resource giveaway laws, meant to facilitate white settlement of western lands. In theory, the first party to settle in any western US river basin was entitled to all the water they could use from that basin. But a 1908 Supreme Court decision, *Winters v. United States*, established that Indigenous Nations' claims to water supersedes all others, not only on reserved Indigenous lands, but off-reservation as well, in what is dubbed an "implied water right," places where tribes traditionally hunted, gathered, and fished. Largely ignored for better than a half century, the Winters decision holds enormous implications for the future of federal irrigation projects, especially in places like the Klamath, where water is scarce. "The Klamath and other tribes had their water rights reestablished," notes Spain. "It took irrigators forty years to come to grips with the fact that they lost their perceived right to use all the water. They appealed every step of the way. And they lost every step of the way."

One of those steps was indirectly related to water rights via fishing rights and came in 1969. A Yurok fisherman named Raymond Mattz was arrested for deploying fishing nets near Brooks Riffle, twenty miles from the mouth of the Klamath. Fishing with gillnets in the state of California is illegal. But as Mattz patiently pointed out, Brooks Riffle is not in California. The Yurok Reservation was granted in 1855 by Executive Order by President Franklin Pierce. From its terminus at the Pacific Ocean, a mile on either side of the river, upriver to mile forty-four was Yurok land, carved out of territory that was quickly being overrun by gold seekers and other mostly white settlers.

Of the more than three hundred treaties negotiated by the United States concerning Indigenous First Nation territories and reserved fishing, hunting, and gathering rights, none have been upheld in their original form. All have been amended to the overwhelming disadvantage of Indigenous people. The Yurok experience was no exception. In 1892, Congress passed "an act to provide for the disposition and sale of lands known as the Klamath River Indian Reservation." The law stated that "... all of the lands embraced in what was Klamath River Reservation in the State of California, as set apart and reserved under authority of law by an Executive Order ... are hereby declared to be subject to settlement, entry, and purchase under the laws of the United States granting homestead rights and authorizing the sale of mineral, stone, and

timber lands." An appellate court ruled that the Yurok's Klamath River Reservation ceased to exist and with it the Yurok fishing rights. Almost eighty years later, Raymond Mattz decided that was wrong, and found a legal team that took his case all the way to the US Supreme Court. In 1973, in the matter of *Mattz v. Arnett*, the plaintiff prevailed. A majority of the court held that the Yurok should have retained reserved fishing rights even if their land had been sold out from under them.

As was the case to the north in Puget Sound, with Billy Frank Jr. and the Nisqually Tribe in Washington State, during this tumultuous period of the late 1960s and early '70s, the right to fish, once granted, was hotly and sometimes violently contested by white commercial and sport fishermen. Bullets chambered in rifles accompanied nets in boats on the water. State fish and game commissions, including California's, were slow to recognize the significance of what federal courts had decided on behalf of the Yurok and others.

In 1978, a fishing ban off the mouth of the Klamath was proposed. California state biologists cited logging and excessive take by commercial fishing as the reasons. The Yurok were being punished for a deteriorating watershed, a crime they didn't commit. Eschewing conflict, the Yurok turned to science and the law.

Amy Cordalis is an attorney for the Yurok, as well as an enrolled tribal member. Raymond Mattz was her uncle. She loves everything about the ancient Yurok tradition of netting salmon each season, the sights, smells, sounds, and communal camaraderie of the whole affair. She didn't grow up on the Yurok Reservation, but the experience of frequent trips to fish with family on the Klamath made an indelible impression on her. It was on these trips that she began to hear of the conflicts that had arisen around reinstated Yurok fishing rights. "It was in the process of re-establishing fishing rights that we realized if we wanted to continue fishing, we would have to start looking at what was happening in the whole watershed. So, we established our own biology department, and I would say the science program we have is as rigorous as any the state of California or Oregon has," she says. "But our reasons, or motivation, is not just science based. It's cultural and even religious. Our

The Yurok Tribe depends on healthy, wild salmon runs for their way of life. Decreased river flows combined with agricultural runoff have made Klamath River susceptible to deadly disease. Klamath River mouth, Yurok ancestral lands, California. MARTIN DO NASCIMENTO creation myth directs us to take care of the salmon, to take only what we need from them, and that in turn, we will be taken care of. If salmon on the Klamath go extinct then the Yurok people will go extinct, that's because we simply wouldn't be able to live as Yurok people. That's why we started looking upstream, at fish passage problems at the dams, at water problems because of irrigated agriculture above the dams."

Like Spain, Cordalis is now an attorney whose clients are fishers—the Yurok Nation. Their livelihood depends on the health of the Klamath, from its headwaters 250 miles from the coast in the Cascade Range to the estuary encompassed by the Yurok Reservation. Making sure the Klamath is producing fish, whether the motivation is commercial, re-

> ...the Yurok Nation's livelihood depends on the health of the Klamath, from its headwaters 250 miles from the coast in the Cascade Range to the estuary encompassed by the Yurok Reservation. Making sure the Klamath is producing fish, whether the motivation is commercial, religious, or cultural, is common cause.

ligious, or cultural, is common cause. "After we won the Mattz case, President Nixon signed a law that made federal money available for tribal governments," Cordalis says. "This contributed to the establishment of our fisheries program, and we're really proud of the science we've produced." The Yurok fisheries department employs fifty to sixty-five people depending on the season, and monitors everything from catch levels to water quality. "We started speaking up—and quickly figured out we needed data to back up what we were contending. We came to water meetings, to fish meetings and started saying 'we have rights. And we're going to assert them,'" she says.

As Klamath tribes from the mountains to the coast asserted their treaty-guaranteed rights to water and fish, Northern California commercial fishers were beginning to put pressure on Oregon and California officials to do something about the destruction of upriver habitats that had occurred as the result of dam construction. Meanwhile, the US Congress passed a suite of the most progressive environmental laws in history. The Endangered Species Act (ESA), along with the Clean Water Act, provided fishers, tribes, and conservation groups with traction in the push to manage water for fish. For thirty years, upstream irrigators, especially those with generous allocations from the upper-basin Bureau of Reclamation project, steadfastly stuck to a strategy of opposing these laws. "What happened is that the irrigators lost," says Spain. "First they were going to prevail over tribal rights in court. They lost. Then they challenged the initial decisions made under the ESA. And they lost. Then they endeavored to have the ESA overturned. This turned out to be a more popular law than they thought. So, they lost. They tried the same thing with the Clean Water Act, and that law proved to be even more popular than the ESA. So, they lost again."

Upper-basin irrigators were going to be stuck obeying the law of the land, a reality they tried to undo in 2001. "Real breakthrough came in 2001 because of ESA restrictions," says Spain. "For the first time ever, users of a federal irrigation system were cut off." The shock caused a wave of deeply conservative activists to take to the streets. They marched ten thousand–strong on downtown Klamath Falls. They sawed and blow-torched locks on headgate valves that would have put Klamath River water back in empty canals. All to no avail. The dawn of the twenty-first century era of sharing water had arrived—at least for a year.

Monitoring the Klamath from a distance was Dick Cheney. In early spring of 2001, not long after being sworn in as Vice President, Cheney placed a call to the office of Sue Ellen Wooldridge, a low-ranking official at the Department of the Interior whose job description included oversight of the Klamath. According to a 2004 article in the *Washington Post*, Cheney requested weekly briefings on the Klamath crisis. According to the Post, that phone call was the first in a series of events—including a

Cheney-instigated challenge to the science that protects salmon—that led to a one-year, White House–orchestrated return to the good old days of farmers' unfettered access to water.

In February 2002, Interior Secretary Gale Norton presided over a ceremonial twisting of a spigot valve that marked the return of what farmers saw as "their" water. Republican operatives had energized the base. Fishers wept, not just for that year but for several years after. In addition to the adult fish mortalities, millions of out-migrating juvenile salmon died. As Spain tells it, the Cheney-orchestrated backroom deals gave irrigators all the water they wanted in 2002. "The result was the fish kill," recalls Spain. "At least seventy thousand dead adult Chinook salmon on the Klamath. But because of the juvenile fish kill, which meant no returning adult fish to the Klamath a few years after, we had a [fishing] closure. . ." The colossal fish kill struck Cordalis hard back in 2002. Before she had decided on law school, she was working as a seasonal fisheries biologist on her home river. "You'd see a fish come down a riffle, gasping, on the surface like a person suffocating or choking," she recalls. "These fish would float by, and then we'd find them not far downstream, belly-up. Dead. Pretty soon the dead were two and three fish thick along the banks of the river. We stopped all our fishing. It's hard for me to describe how devastated we were. Remember: these are the creatures we're given the task of caring for, and we had to sit on the bank and watch them die. More than any other experience, this is what drove me to go back to school and get a law degree."

Cheney's meddling in Klamath affairs, all for political gain, cost US taxpayers $60.4 million dollars in federal disaster relief funds granted to coastal communities in Southern Oregon and Northern California, whose boats were idled due to poor fish counts in 2006. "The effect of this was felt all the way from just south of the Columbia River to Monterey," says Spain. "You might have only 2 percent of the catch in Monterey Bay coming from the Klamath. But if weak-stock management rules dictate that the take on an at-risk population has to be zero, everyone is shut down." Disaster aid didn't begin to cover the consequences of the economic downturn.

The irony of all Cheney's interference was that it led directly to settlement talks in 2004. For more than thirty years, tribes, fishers, and conservationists had argued that fish were entitled to their fair share of the water. Irrigators had ignored them, a ploy that would no longer work. Dam removal and an equitable share of river water were on the negotiating table. Emboldened by the cover provided by the Bush administration, Steve Kanda, an upper-basin irrigator, had challenged the 2001 water cutoff in federal court. He was trying to get an injunction, but a federal magistrate in Eugene, Oregon, Thomas Coffin, instead offered court-facilitated settlement negotiations. Coffin ordered a bailiff to be stationed at the door of the hotel conference room where hearings were held. During work hours, no one could leave, except to use the bathroom. "No one had ever held that broad a stakeholder meeting before," recalls Spain. "Off-project irrigators came in. Downriver tribes came in. At first there wasn't very much to talk about. But then some of the state agencies furnished us with some numbers. It was too soon to say if settlement was possible—but the numbers were very intriguing. No one had ever seen them all on one table before. We started talking about possibilities. It turned out to be very threatening for a lot of the project irrigators. It started to look like a settlement negotiation rather than a slam dunk win for the irrigation districts. So, they pulled the plug on it. They felt like they were losing control over it—and they were. The reality is you can't control a negotiation. You negotiate."

The Klamath détente was tenuous at first. "That was the point of all those potato and salmon bakes that we went to," recalls Spain. "Potatoes and salmon. Neither can exist without water. A very wise person once said, 'If you want to make peace, you must talk to your enemies, not your friends.' That was, and still is, true. When the timing and the chemistry is right, you have to sit down with the opposing side and negotiate. And this is where you have to give the farmers and ranchers who came to the table some credit," continues Spain. "They didn't exactly come with their hats in their hands. But they came. I said before, you can't control a negotiation. You have to negotiate. And they, to their credit, did just that. It took a long time. But we hammered out the KBRA, and the

KHSA. And even though those agreements are dead, the relationships that came out of that remain. And that's what got us the KRRC."

The latest incarnation of the alphabet soup of Klamath dams removal effort acronyms (KRRC, or Klamath River Restoration Corporation) was hatched out of the abandoned shell of the KBRA agreements. "After Congress refused to act [in 2015]," recalls Spain, "parties to the dam removal portion of those agreements got together. It was established that we all still wanted to pursue dam removal. Turns out there was not only a lot of momentum toward continuing to angle toward removal, but that there were still a lot of factors on our side." The state of California had passed its own omnibus water bill in 2012. It included setting aside some $250 million toward the removal of the Klamath dams. PacifiCorp

Prior to the restoration of the Penobscot, the count of alewife in a good year might clear ten thousand fish. In 2021, there were 1,953,153.

also received approval for a rate increase around this same time, the proceeds of which have been set aside for the express purpose of decommissioning the Klamath dams. The two revenue streams combined mean there's $450 million already set aside for freeing the Klamath. "Best cost estimate we have for removal of these dams is $446 million," says Spain. "So, we're looking at a dam removal project that is already more than adequately funded. We [the board of directors of the KRRC] got busy assembling a team. Hiring staff. Interviewing engineering firms. Over the past few decades there's quite a body of knowledge that's been amassed on dam removal ... and we intend to take full advantage of that body of knowledge."

The impetus for forming the KRRC had much to do with the needs of the current owners of the dams, PacifiCorp, which has been unwavering in its support for Klamath dam removal, with one condition. "They needed a way to be free of the liability that comes with taking out dams,

Alewife returning to the Penobscot River. Penobscot ancestral lands, Maine. BRENT DOSCHER

which would give them what they want, a means to exit the Klamath Basin gracefully and legally unencumbered. So, the title of each of the four dams was transferred by PacifiCorp. The KRRC will own the dams, and the liability that goes along with them, and then we'll go ahead and begin the removal process," Spain says.

If buying up dams only to secure the privilege of destroying them seems a vaguely familiar scenario, the name of one of the KRRC's board of directors might also ring a bell. Laura Rose Day is the former Executive Director of the Penobscot River Restoration Trust (PRRT). She was tapped for a leadership role in the KRRC based on the wildly successful plan she hatched years ago, while in a meeting with recalcitrant utility executives over the fate of the Penobscot's beleaguered fish. Someone in that meeting cracked a joke that the only way dams on the Penobscot could come down would be if the rag-tag bunch of fishers and conservationists came up with the coin to buy them. Rose Day's response: "How much?"

Sixty-three million dollars and the better part of two decades later, Veazie and Great Works Dams on the Penobscot River are gone. A fish bypass around Howland Dam was constructed as well. The fish have undeniably appreciated the investment the PRRT made. River herring, or alewife, are making a comeback to rival the one their cousins made post–dam removal in the Kennebec River, just to the south, where in 2021, more than three million herring returned. Prior to the restoration of the Penobscot, the count of alewife in a good year might clear ten thousand fish. In 2021, there were 1,953,153.

The fish that eat alewife, most notably shad, are also on the mend. The Penobscot has been touted as the last best chance for Atlantic salmon to thrive in the Lower 48. It's too soon to tell if this endangered salmonid will take advantage of the opportunity afforded on the Penobscot. In the meantime, Laura Rose Day finds herself in a position all too rare for professional conservationists. She's worked herself out of a job. "A project may be over, but I don't think any river's work is ever done," says Rose Day. "It's crucial that the restoration work, along with monitoring and evaluation, goes forward. But I am certain that the Penobscot River's prospects for the future is in far better shape now than when we began negotiating in 1999." In addition to sitting in high-stakes negotiations with utility executives, Rose Day spent countless hours knocking on doors, getting to know people along the river. "It's not just about creating a movement of supporters," she says of her grassroots efforts. "It's also about getting people to understand what you're asking for, so that you're also creating a lack of opposition. Congresspeople will stand down in their opposition to something if they don't readily see their constituents as adamantly opposed. I can't tell you in how many people's kitchens I sat drinking coffee and eating brownies, hearing out their concerns. You have to do this not as a representative of an organization, but person-to-person. The majority of folks are not pro- or anti-dam removal out of the gate. They just want questions answered, assurances made."

With the major component of a historic river mission completed on one coast, Rose Day is looking forward to working on an equally significant set of dam removals on the other coast. "The fact that the utility

[PacifiCorp] is on board, and the money is set aside, is a big head start," says Rose Day.

Though prospects for dam removal on the Klamath look positive, there are factions within the watershed who are vehemently opposed to dam removal, and politicians willing to exploit the vocal opposition. Yet Spain points out that any argument for keeping the dams in place is a very difficult one to make for conservatives. "Property rights are the cornerstone of Republican values," he says. "And the Klamath dams are property that owners should be free to improve or dispose of as they see fit. That's the ideological hurdle. The practical one is that the economics of keeping the dams just doesn't pan out. The estimate we had to bring these dams up to modern standards came in at around $500 million. No entity in the basin has that kind of money. And even if that money were spent, the company that owns the dams would still be on the hook for all the liability, to tribes, for fish, for water quality."

While the KRRC maintains a low profile, it's a busy place these days. Contractors are bidding on different phases of the work, from improving roads and bridges, to native seed propagation, to dam removal itself. A detailed timeline for completion of the project shows that by 2024, one of the West Coast's major salmon-producing rivers will have undergone a dramatic and globally unprecedented restoration.

THE RETURN OF THE ELWHA

Dam removals reveal buried treasures. Fish move quickly to reclaim habitat that was walled off from them, sometimes for centuries. Dissolved oxygen in free-flowing water breathes new life into the whole aquatic food chain, from benthic macroinvertebrates to beavers, otters, even wolves. The river's banks, once recolonized by vegetation, become a habitat for birds and bugs. These have become standard forecast outcomes for a river renewed by dam removal. On the recently dam-free Elwha River in Washington, draining the Olympic Mountains in the damp northwest corner of the state, hope is a thing with fins.

Historically, the Elwha was among the region's most prolific rivers, bearing ten varieties of anadromous salmon and steelhead. But in the early twentieth century, the river was dammed for hydropower. Though an 1890 state law required dams to have a passage for fish, the Elwha River dam had none, and blocked off some 90 percent of upstream spawning ground for hundreds of thousands of fish and decimated the Chinook salmon population. The Lower Elwha Klallam Tribe, who have fished the Elwha since time immemorial, were severely affected as

Rewilding the Elwha; four miles from the former Elwha Dam site, nature is taking back the river. Lower Elwha Klallam ancestral lands, Washington. JOHN MCMILLAN

Concrete isn't forever: the Elwha was freed of its dams in 2014. Lower Elwha Klallam ancestral lands, Washington. JOHN GUSSMAN

the fish they depended on all but disappeared. But a decade after two dams were removed on the Elwha, the recovery is well underway. The river is already in some ways defying expectations, and in the process, buoying the hopes of those who've come to love and depend on it. The first step in bringing salmon home to a place like the Elwha is re-establishing the habitat to which they have become accustomed over thousands of years of evolution.

Over a century, enough sediment had been trapped by the two dams on the Elwha River—located about a hundred miles west of Seattle—to fill the Seattle Seahawks' football stadium to capacity eight times over with sand. Skeptics fretted that the load of muck would spoil restoration efforts. Casual observers rightly wondered what would happen when it all got uncorked. The work of deconstructing the dams took place from 2011 to 2014. By the time the river was running unimpeded, the Elwha had built itself a whole new estuary.

Where the Elwha runs into the saltwater, in the Strait of Juan de Fuca, a beachcomber's delight of roughly a hundred acres of sand, gravel, driftwood, and river channel was laid down by the newly unfettered river. Out beneath the sea, beyond the hundred acres of new earth, a sub-sea-surface delta—formed from additional sediment—raised the seafloor bed six to fifteen feet in height. All told, the estuary is about three times larger than it was before the dams came out. To the east of the Elwha's mouth, the positive effects of sediment returning to an ecosystem deprived of its river-born soil for a century are visible as far as the discerning eye can see.

A host of nearshore fishes, not seen in such diversity and abundance off the mouth of the Elwha since the Model T was a novelty, quickly colonized the estuary habitat. Surfers relish riding a now-regular break that used to be seen only once in a blue moon. Beavers appear to be making a comeback. Pools and channels sculpted by the push and pull of tide, wave, and river action are a haven for juvenile fish.

Elwha's newly expanded beach is accessed down a steep, winding two-lane road that dead-ends inside a neighborhood at the east end of Freshwater Bay. A sign says, "No overnight parking," and there's a porta-potty and a couple of trash cans, attesting to the spot's growing popularity. As happens with any desirable location, the brand-new estuary is in some ways burdened from the fresh love it's receiving. Dog shit has become a problem, and bonfires set amongst the prodigious supply of driftwood don't help much either. The Lower Elwha Klallam Tribe, in whose reserved lands the new delta lies, have closed part of the area so that recovery can proceed without compromise by too many visitors. Yet it's hard to blame anyone for enthusiastic curiosity here.

On a bright weekday February morning, after a rare sea-level snow storm the night before, I expect to see no one, but immediately get welcomed by a family and their rambunctious, slobbering chocolate lab. They depart in one of about a half-dozen cars parked in the neighborhood dead-end. "This is nothing," one of a trio of twenty-something men tells me as we pass on the path atop a low dike that accesses the beach. "When the surf is up, you won't find a place to park anywhere near." Without the crowd on a calm winter morning, the placid scene nonetheless makes a wild impression. Scads of trees, branches, and sticks in various states of decomposition litter the vast beach and tempt even the most dull-witted beachcomber to try a hand at building some daringly creative structure out of the ample supply. The beach is full of such ad hoc sculptures, some tending toward teepee shape, others more wickiup, still more that look like cast-offs from some post-modern sculpture exhibit. Bisecting the beach is the sinuous flow of the Elwha, curving gracefully to meet saltwater in a braided channel that enters the Strait of Juan de Fuca at an oblique angle.

Anne Shaffer is the executive director and lead scientist of the Coastal Watershed Institute. Founded in 1996, the CWI came on the scene a few years before a law passed in Congress that would eventually lead to the two Elwha dams being demolished. Her office is on the waterfront in Port Angeles. Step outside and on a clear day, you can see a hundred miles to the hulking mass of Mount Baker. It's a fabulous view, but Shaffer doesn't spend all her time in the office, preferring wetsuits and seine nets to proximity to the coffee maker. Balancing desk and field time is juggling act enough for most scientists. Add politics to the mix and things get downright nutty. The 1992 legislation that OK'd the dam removals didn't specify where the funding would come from. Washington Senator Slade Gorton and a number of other legislators blocked funding for years. Even after he was voted out of office, it took several years for the funding to come through. "Then when it came," recalls Shaffer "everything happened so fast, there was almost no time to establish pre–dam removal conditions." It wasn't ideal from a science perspective. If the lead-up to dam removal left her small research nonprofit in something of a lurch, the results since then, which the CWI has tracked, have been nothing short of astonishing. "Lots of people were hoping something like this would happen," says Shaffer. "And it's not only the extent of new habitat creation for the nearshore, but how fast it happened. Where else are you going to get a hundred acres of new land and a totally redesigned, better functioning estuary, essentially for free?" Restoration is still underway.

With the dams out, the freed sediment has restored the estuary of the Elwha River. Lower Elwha Klallam ancestral lands, Washington. AP IMAGES / ELAINE THOMPSON

The revitalized Elwha mouth is a positive development in otherwise dire times for similar spots around the globe. The fifty-eight thousand five hundred largest dams in the world have blocked 3,155 gigatons of sediment since the middle of the twentieth century, according to Jai Syvitski, a professor emeritus at the University of Colorado, Boulder. That's enough muck to bury all of California fifteen feet deep.

Nearshore environments have fared poorly with the onslaught of dam building and shoreline development over the past century. Worldwide, shorelines have faced more rapid urbanization than any other ecosystem type. About half of the world's population lives within 125 miles of a coastline. Half of the world's major city centers lie within fifty miles from a given seashore. As of the year 2000, 11 percent of the world's total population was coastal. By 2060, as many as 1.4 billion people will live near the beach. Unbeknownst to many of them, along too many beaches around the world, the ground is literally disappearing beneath their feet.

The transport of sediments from mountains, hills, and valleys via rivers to the coast and its subsequent distribution through the action of tides, waves, and storms is a phenomenon easily comprehensible by middle school science students. Yet these processes have been altered and interrupted by dam construction and other forms of shoreline development. Dams, and associated shoreline armoring, prevent river-born sediment and other key portions of shoreline ecosystems from reaching the sea. Meanwhile, the sea is always eating away at sediment-starved coastlines when storms, large waves, and big tides hit. The modern human response to these inexorable facts has been shortsighted. Cities and towns build bulkheads, jetties, riprap, revetments, seawalls, and other structures known as shoreline armoring. In many of the world's largest ports, half of adjacent shorelines have been armored. In the United States, 14 percent of all the coastline miles in the Lower 48 states have been armored, with 64 percent of that portion of shoreline adjacent to estuaries and coastal rivers.

The absence of sediment makes for poor marine habitat. Intact nearshore environments are among the richest marine ecosystems on the planet. But as researchers from the University of Washington and East Carolina University found, "armored shorelines overall are associated with lower biodiversity, vegetation cover, and [lower] abundances of invertebrates and fish." Without nourishment in the form of sediment, the nearshore habitat, along with the sand that creates it, gets scraped away by the inexorable wave action of the sea.

Shoreline armoring actually performs the opposite of its intended purpose. "Armored" shorelines can accelerate erosion as waves are deflected off protective structures, pulling sediment with them on their bounce back oceanward. The vitality of coastal ecosystems is greatly diminished as shallow intertidal habitats give way to dramatically steepened shorelines. Steep drop-offs translate to narrower zones where sand and large woody debris can settle out. The transition between nearshore and deep-sea environs becomes abrupt, to the detriment of a startling variety of sea-going critters that depend on this transition zone.

One cure for this disappearing-beach syndrome has been discovered at the Elwha Delta. The recovery here has been nothing short of astonishing. Before dam removal, Shaffer had figured it would be. But back in the days before dam removal, she was treated as something of a discount prophet. "Getting the nearshore on the agenda prior to dam removal, it was like pulling teeth," she recalls. "In the fish management meetings leading to dam removal the nearshore would always be last on the agenda. Discussions would run long, and then, as people were piling papers and packing their bags it would be me rushing through all the nearshore information as people were heading out the door. Now? The nearshore is the poster child of the project. Because this isn't just dam removal. It's an ecosystem restoration reconnecting of the hydrodynamic processes between river and shoreline."

Now that the sediment is readily available, the wisdom of disarmoring the stretches of beach that were starved of sand can be realized. The CWI sponsored one local effort on this front. They have paid crews to come in with heavy equipment and rip out old riprap. "We had noticed there was a piece of property with maybe a half mile of heavily armored shoreline along the east Elwha Delta beachfront that had come up for sale," says Shaffer. "So we wrote some grants to purchase the land, with the idea of getting rid of the armor and restoring the beach. Well, we did it. And in one twenty-four-hour tide cycle—in one day—the beach came back." She takes the time to scroll through some photos pointing out landmarks—an old snag of a tree that was on the edge of a rocky shore, then the same tree twenty-four hours later with a healthy beach in front of its base. These conditions have persisted for years after the shoreline armoring was removed. Surf smelt, an indicator species for nearshore ecosystem health, responded immediately too.

She shows me an aerial view of the whole new estuary and points out the dike that for now is the causeway serving as public access to the new beach. "But we know that if we could somehow reconnect the ponds on the west side of the dike here," she points out in the photo, "we think this would be the richest habitat for rearing fish."

Alas, the landowners don't seem up to the task of remodeling the dike, even if the financing were to come from somewhere other than their own pockets. The old way of thinking, that the dike equals protection from the vagaries of waves and weather, hasn't completely died out. It's a source of mild frustration for Shaffer, who doesn't blame the landowners. "When we started [the Coastal Watershed Institute] literally a career ago," she says, "scientists didn't know what they know now about dam removal, about fisheries science, including hatcheries, and habitat disruptions, including shoreline armoring and diking. We're in a completely different universe. A lot of management has not kept up. We now know what we need to do regarding hatcheries and shoreline management to protect and restore coastal ecosystems. We need to take these steps."

Outdated policies were not the only problem hobbling the restoration of the Elwha. It took years of lawsuits by parties necessary and ancillary to the dam removal process to finally sign off on the proposition of a free river. The final bill for everything associated with dam removal came to $325 million. The actual work of removing the dams ($35 million) and restoring the exposed, denuded land around the former reservoirs ($27 million) was cheap. By contrast, $163 million went to fish hatcheries and water treatment facilities, an astronomical sum that threatens to climb even higher given the dubious benefits.

Port Angeles rightfully insisted on a guarantee from the National Park Service, the federal agency ultimately on the hook for liabilities associated with dam removal, that their water supply remain in dependably good condition. For reasons that remain unclear, the city and the Park Service appear to have chosen the most expensive route to clean water rather than the most effective. The Park Service spent $79 million on a water treatment facility in 2010, the keys to which were slated to be turned over to city officials after the dam removals were completed. But city officials claim that after weathering the sediment load from two dam removals, the new facility needs repair. They also noticed, somewhat belatedly, that the complexities of the modern treatment plant required more resources. Operation and maintenance budgets for the new plant will rise ten-fold, from $60,000 to $600,000 a year.

Still, it looked like a sweet deal for Port Angeles even just a couple years ago. A free, modernized water treatment facility would pay huge dividends. At the time, Nippon, a Japanese corporation, owned and operated a paper mill that was a profligate water user, one of the area's largest employers, and a primary reason for the push for a Cadillac water treatment infrastructure. But the mill produced phone book and newsprint paper, commodities heading the way of whale-oil powered lanterns. Nippon sold the operation to a Mexican-owned conglomerate, McKinley, and it retooled the facility to recycle corrugated cardboard.

That bureaucratic sideshow takes a back seat to the news on salmon recovery on the Elwha. Bad news first: the year after Elwha dams were taken out was one of the worst years of the last fifty for Pacific salmon. "The Blob," a marine heatwave, arrived in the northern Pacific Ocean in 2013 and spread south over the next few years, meaning no snow in western American mountains. If a juvenile salmonid was lucky enough in the spring of 2015 to find its way to the ocean on the warm, meager river flows, this same fish was greeted with an ocean producing a fraction of the salmon food that it normally produces, mostly copepods. The result, both during the Blob and in the years after it dissipated, has been a population crash affecting every salmon species in the eastern Pacific. The Elwha salmon are no exception. While salmon numbers have increased, the pace of recovery has been tempered by the Blob.

The two fish hatcheries don't seem to be helping much, and could well be impeding long-term fish recovery.

The hatchery controversy continues to shadow the demolition of Elwha dams and the recovery of the river. While Chinook and coho numbers returning to the river continue to climb, no analysis has been done to determine what proportion of these increases are a result of the increase in hatchery production. Shaffer and colleagues in 2017 concluded that these jaw-dropping hatchery releases were overwhelming the Elwha estuary, and likely suppressing every species of wild salmon using the shoreline and their recovery. "Chum salmon historically were the backbone of the Elwha system," says Shaffer, "and are almost extirpated today, a reflection of this suppression."

The Elwha, the Klallam People, and the Fight for Indigenous Treaty Fishing Rights

Meanwhile, the Lower Elwha Klallam Tribe has lived and fished their river since time immemorial. In 2012, as the removal of the dams progressed and the river ran free, it was the culmination, in some ways, of a half a century of fighting for tribal recognition as well as the right to fish and operate fish hatcheries.

The Lower Elwha Klallam were front and center during the Puget Sound fish wars of the late 1960s and early '70s. Billy Frank Jr., from the Nisqually Tribe on the eastern shore of the Salish Sea near Tacoma, was arrested more than fifty times during that tumultuous period, insisting that fishing rights be honored as they'd been spelled out in treaties made with the US government more than a century before. Frank was as tireless and fearless a civil-rights activist as any in those days, and his inspiration spread like wildfire to tribes around the Pacific Northwest. The Lower Elwha Klallam were no exception.

A federal investigation into state enforcement of wildlife laws, and then a court ruling in 1974 mandated respect for the tribe's nineteenth-century treaty rights. *United States v. Washington*, known as the "Boldt decision" after the presiding judge, held that local tribes are entitled to a fair share of the total catch. A subsequent court case clarified the definition of "fair share": half the annual commercial harvest. As sovereign nations, the court's ruling found, they should co-manage fisheries on equal footing with the state.

Yet in the nearly two decades that passed ... the science on hatcheries became clear-cut: Hatchery salmonids are a detriment to the existence of wild ones.

Not long after the Boldt decision, the federal government granted the Lower Elwha Klallam Tribe 372 acres of reservation land along the river. Encouraged by the winning streak, the tribe established its own fish hatchery. "We did it because no one else was going to help us," recalls Robert Elofson, who fishes commercially and is the tribe's harvest manager. "Even back then there were a handful of people who made a living fishing on the lower river. We wanted to make sure that kept happening."

By the mid-1980s, the Lower Elwha people had teamed up with some visionary environmentalists to make what was then a radical proposal. The dams on the Elwha should come down. "Honestly, we joined up with the idea in those early days, but we—or at least I—didn't think it would actually happen," recalls Elofson. "It seemed like a good way to draw attention to our issues. But then there was a delegation that went back to [Washington] D.C. and all of a sudden, the idea was going somewhere." That the dams were illegally built within the confines of a national park was an argument that Elofson hadn't taken into consideration. Others were hell-bent on leveraging that, and other pertinent legal points, into an earnest effort to get the dams torn down.

It took another nineteen years, but in 2011, what started for the Lower Elwha people as a long shot has ended with a free river. Yet in the nearly two decades that passed between authorization and funding of the Elwha dams removal, the science on hatcheries became clear-cut: Hatchery salmonids are a detriment to the existence of wild ones. But the position of the Lower Elwha people was just as clear: We are fishing beings for as long as we have been, they proclaimed, and we're not going to stop fishing just because some dams are coming down. Thus far, $20 million of the Elwha restoration budget has gone to building hatcheries. An ichthyological and cultural divide was quickly formed, a new conflict borne out of the old adage that conservationists who love salmon want to count them, whereas Native American people who love salmon want to eat them. As part of the settlement agreements around removing the Elwha dams, the National Park Service agreed to build the Lower Elwha Klallam people a hatchery. Conservation groups, the Wild Fish Conservancy, the Federation of Fly Fishers' Steelhead Committee, Wild Salmon Rivers, and the Wild Steelhead Coalition filed suit against the Park Service and other federal agencies over their approval of the hatchery.

The science on what this hatchery will do to the recovery of wild fish in the Elwha is quite clear. Jack Stanford, a retired PhD ecologist from the University of Montana, testified in federal court that the tribe's hatchery "will most likely cause severe and long-lasting harm" to native Elwha steelhead. He had more than a hundred peer-reviewed scientific papers to choose from that have drawn that same conclusion. Federal courts, however, found that while the science of salmon certainly influences policy and legal matters pertaining to fish management, it isn't the only factor. The conservation groups lost in district court. That decision was upheld on appeal.

The tribe, for their part, felt vindicated in their half-century-long fight to keep on fishing. The Lower Elwha's sacred place, the site where their creation myth takes place, was drowned in 1913, when the Elwha Dam closed its floodgates. In the summer of 2012, with both dams removed and the river resuming its natural course, the creation site re-emerged. Members of the Lower Elwha Tribe hiked up the river and scooped water from the rock's holes into little bottles. They fashioned the vials into necklaces for elders unable to make the trip.

For the Lower Elwha people, dam removal has afforded glimpses of a better time. Before white settlement, nearly a half-million anadromous fish swam up the Elwha Basin every year, spawning and dying in their native streams. Today, the salmon are returning, already in the low thousands—not bad by current standards. "Even if we have good runs coming back, we're going to let them go back to the river for spawning," says Elofson. Long term, he hopes for something more significant: a harvest big enough to lift the economic fortune of the Tribe. The hatchery, he says, is a necessary, if imperfect, step toward restoration. "We look at the long haul," Elofson says. "We're not going anywhere. We know we have things to protect."

The Hatchery Impeding Chinook Salmon Recovery

For all the controversy the lawsuit generated over federal funding of a tribal hatchery, the state of Washington's Chinook operation on the Elwha looks like the bigger problem. "There are two hatcheries operating on the Elwha," says Shaffer. "Between the two hatcheries, they release now well over three million juvenile Chinook, coho, and steelhead here every year." Of the two, claims Shaffer, the Washington Department of Fish and Wildlife (WDFW) hatchery is the most problematic. She points out that the tribal hatchery releases coho and steelhead in relatively low numbers, and volitionally (meaning when the fish are ready to swim on their own from the hatchery). Until recently, the WDFW facility released the Chinook salmon in a much more abrupt manner. "This hatchery," says Shaffer, "flushed the fish within twenty-four hours of their delivery from the hatchery in very large numbers, on occasion, over one million fish at a time. We take every precaution to avoid these fish in our sampling, but we have intercepted them in large numbers. In one sample, ten thousand hatchery fry in one set [of the net], eight thousand in another. The scientific literature of the last twenty years clearly indicates that interactions with other recovering wild fish is a valid concern. The results of our decade-long study indicate that, even after dam removals, the estuarine salmon community composition continues to simply reflect hatchery releases."

Despite mounting evidence of hatcheries' biological failure, salmon-centric tribes see them as the only solution to their treaty-guaranteed fishing rights and sustaining their way of life. No fish, no fishing rights. Yet there's increasing evidence the hatchery cure is unsustainable. Washington state has the largest hatchery program in the country, 140 hatcheries producing over two hundred million juvenile salmon a

Washington state has the largest hatchery program in the country. ... Yet ten of fourteen salmon and steelhead populations are listed as threatened here.

year. Yet ten of fourteen salmon and steelhead populations are listed as threatened here. And despite $2.2 billion of federal investment in hatcheries over the past twenty years—at a cost of $250 to $650 per returning adult fish—annual salmon numbers continue to plummet.

That controversy as well as some disappointment has arisen from a project as large and unprecedented as the Elwha dams removals, the largest in US history, isn't really a shock. Lawsuits make the front page. Snorkel surveys and other evidence of ecosystem recovery, proceeding more or less as planned, are relegated to the occasional human-interest story.

John McMillan shares with fellow scientist Anne Shaffer an allergy to too much time indoors. He is the former science director of Trout Unlimited's Wild Steelhead Initiative. He recently jumped ship and went to work as the Science Director for The Conservation Angler. "I can't work in an office; I've got to be with the fish," says McMillan. "All I want to do other than love my wife and dog is snorkel and fish."

In some ways, McMillan seems like the true-life avatar of Gus Orviston, the protagonist of David Duncan's fly-fishing novel *The River Why*. His home outside Port Angeles feels coastal and cabinesque. His office is festooned with photos, books, flies, rods, and reels. McMillan's father is renowned angler and author Bill McMillan. Like Gus, John has

Chinook carcasses reintegrate into the web of life, upstream of erstwhile dams on the Elwha. Lower Elwha Klallam ancestral lands, Washington. JOHN MCMILLAN proven to be afflicted by as powerful a case of fish-on-the-brain as his old man. "For years, I fished 350 days a year. I caught thousands of steelhead until I realized I didn't want to do that anymore. I wanted to do something to help wild steelhead, because I could see just from personal observation that they're in decline," says McMillan. With a graduate degree in fisheries biology from Oregon State, he became a professional snorkeler, contracting with NOAA to complete in-stream (and underwater) survey work of salmonid populations in the Elwha prior to dam removal. "What I found there in the lower five miles of river [before

The most destruction occurs when hatchery fish mate with wild fish and reproduce. The resulting offspring have a lower survival rate and that gets passed along to future generations.

the dams were removed] was this: Alaska-league level of habitat and species diversity and abundance," he recalls. "That told me all I needed to know about the potential for recovery."

McMillan was also cautious toward a hatchery-dependent approach to Elwha recovery, though he understands why they were ultimately used. "You know my background," says McMillan. "I was definitely raised in the skeptical philosophy [with respect to hatcheries]. Back when people thought hatcheries were the answer, my father was an early skeptic—and for good reason. Hatcheries for fisheries basically follow an agricultural model. Unfortunately, the returns are far less predictable, however, so input doesn't always equate to output. But in some cases, that is all fishers have. Some rivers can no longer support wild fish. From my perspective, we have to admit that the Chinook and coho hatcheries preserved some of the original native Elwha genes and it would have been too risky to not save some of each species in hatcheries during dam removal. I don't have an issue using those fish to jumpstart recolonization. Beyond that, I'll let the fish tell us what works."

The hatchery programs so far have provided a mixed bag of results. McMillan was a co-researcher and author on a recent study that looked at the success of coho salmon in the Elwha during and after dam removal. "We basically had two tributaries that enter the Elwha across from one another a few miles above the former Elwha Dam," he says. "They were the first tributaries that adults would find on their way upstream, so the Tribe and others moved adult hatchery coho into each of the creeks beginning one year prior to dam removal. They produced quite a few juveniles, and adults from those juveniles have returned to spawn, without ever being in a hatchery. The returns last fall were the best to date, so the hatchery helped jumpstart the recolonization process." That is the good news, McMillan says.

The most destruction occurs when hatchery fish mate with wild fish and reproduce. The resulting offspring have a lower survival rate and that gets passed along to future generations. Washington's hatchery-based Chinook recovery program on the Elwha demonstrates this fact, suggests McMillan. "The program helped provide a fishery when the dams were in place, but it also had some of the lowest survival rates of any hatchery on the West Coast. Essentially the program had to plant a few million fish to get a solid return. And, so far, it doesn't look like those fish are as successful at spawning in the wild as the coho were. Chinook are different from coho, and hatcheries affect species in different ways."

McMillan pointed out that one of the most serious consequences of hatchery-dependent salmon production is the loss of diversity and size. "With pink salmon, for example, because they have the least diverse life history of any Pacific salmon species, the life history you produce in the hatchery is fairly close to what you get with natural reproduction. Steelhead are at the other extreme, being really diverse, and not surprisingly, hatcheries seem to have stronger effects on them than other species. For Chinook the concern is size. Hatchery Chinook tend to be younger and smaller as adults than wild Chinook and can have smaller eggs. Reducing the size of something that relies so heavily on being big, that seems important to me."

Over the long haul, McMillan sees a longer road to recovery for Chinook than any other salmon species in the Elwha. The problem, as he sees it, goes beyond hatchery production in the Elwha. "The biggest obstacle to Chinook recovery in my opinion is recovering their age and size, which means thinking about how we harvest them," says McMillan. Research indicates the size of Chinook is declining in several parts of the North Pacific, he says, and this is likely because we have caught and killed too many large kings. "Some fisheries have taken steps to reduce impacts on larger fish, but there is still a long legacy of taking big fish that doesn't disappear overnight. And, consider this, to get a fifty- or sixty-pound king, that fish will need four to five trips around the Alaskan gyre [the system of currents rotating in the Gulf of Alaska] or wherever the local stock goes to sea. If it survives fisheries in those areas, it will likely face additional fisheries in freshwater. I hope that one day we will see eighty-pound kings in the Elwha, and in reality, there will be the occasional big one. But I don't think they will be more than an anomaly unless there are larger-scale changes in ocean fisheries."

What keeps McMillan hopeful and inspired is the rapid recovery of Elwha habitat, and the growing number of signs that fish and the whole array of creatures who depend on them are making a comeback. Steelhead, still his favorite salmonid, have become a leading indicator that recovery continues apace. "The densities of rainbow trout are the highest I've seen on any river," he says. This is important because a resident male rainbow trout and an anadromous female steelhead may pair up and spawn in the absence of a suitable anadromous mate. The offspring they produce can be ocean-going steelhead. This phenomenon helps explain the presence of a significant number of summer steelhead up some twenty miles above the site of former "Lake" Mills, the impoundment created by the Glines Canyon Dam. The Elwha Basin is not noted for its abundance of summer steelhead, but as McMillan notes, that is likely because of the dams. Seeing them meant believing—if the habitat becomes available, salmon will return—and steelhead will probably be the first to get there. "All we need now is better marine [ocean] survival," says McMillan. "Assuming ocean conditions rebound, I think that we'll see the salmon and steelhead do the same. That could take ten years, it could take forty. The ultimate goal is to have all-natural reproduction, but each species is different. For steelhead, they appear to be doing relatively well amongst the species."

McMillan cautions against expectations for a miraculously fast recovery. "All the timelines for full recovery of the ecosystem were in decades, not years," he says. "And from what I'm seeing I'd say we're off to a pretty good start." Shaffer concurs. "If you're talking about long-term recovery, of a complex species like salmon, it's going to be generations," she says. The political side of Elwha Dam removal was less likely, in some ways, and less predictable, than the recovery after the removal of the dams. "When we started planning this, we were in a different reality than we are now," says Shaffer, of the growing acceptance of destroying dams as a means of recovering rivers. "There are a lot of frustrations with the way things have happened with these dams removals. But from my perspective, it happened, and we can only take the perspective that we got them out just in time."

Time is an increasingly precious commodity to Robert Elofson, the Lower Elwha Tribe's natural resource manager. Last time we talked, he was prepping a new boat for another season of fishing. The giddy expectations of a fresh season were discernible in his voice, even over the phone, and it seemed to me that he was as excited for this year's fishing as he was for his first season more than half a century ago. I ask him what his long-term expectations are for the recovery of the Elwha. His answer is surprisingly personal, a testament to the notion that hope can grow with age: "When I was a young man in the early 1970s," he begins, "I have this vivid memory of hiking a long way into the Elwha, with a backpack on, setting up camp, fishing early in the morning, catching a trout and having it for breakfast. What I'd like to do—and boy would I have to take some time to get in shape to do it—I'd like to hike back to that same spot, catch a salmon and eat it."

With the dams gone, the fish can now do their part to make Elofson's wish come true.

DAM REMOVAL 101

The urge can strike anytime, anywhere. Whether nostalgically flipping through tattered paperback pages of an old copy of *The Monkey Wrench Gang*, or by watching the fishing turn from bad to worse on a favorite local stream, or by fretting over the safety of children swimming in a plugged-up local creek: you want to become a dam buster. Welcome to the fray.

What follows is an introduction to terms and concepts, a compendium of good advice, and an amalgamation of recommended steps that have resulted in dam removals around the country. First, a few words to the wise: While considerable time and care has been taken to synthesize many hours of interviews, emails, and notes, it would be wrong-headed to call it a manual or blueprint for dam removal. What's offered here are broad guidelines, with some specific examples of successes and challenges. There are several reasons for this disclaimer.

In nearly every conversation with veterans of dam removal campaigns from around the country arose the caveat that there was no substitute for practice. Most states still don't have guidelines, much

An official from the Division of Safety of Dams inspects Bowman Dam in the Tahoe National Forest in Nevada County, California, where earthquake risk is high. Nisenan ancestral lands. KELLY M. GROW / CALIFORNIA DEPARTMENT OF WATER RESOURCES

less rules for dam removal, and only a handful of states provide any pa-
rameters for what constitutes a small dam. Beyond the lax regulatory
environment, no two dam removals are alike, certainly because no two
rivers are the same—but also because the people that live in that watershed are unique to that place. Relationships with people, it was unanimously emphasized, is the key. Get to know the specific concerns of
residents of a creek or river where dam removal is proposed. Listening
to concerns and taking those concerns seriously—as vexing a challenge
as that can be—are essential, foundational steps to getting concrete
ripped out of a riverbed. Or even getting some people to think about
that step as a positive one.

The work of getting a dam removed is unlike the work of most other
environmental campaigns, for reasons well-articulated by Sam Mace,
the former inland director for Save Our Wild Salmon, a group that for
nearly a third of a century has been doggedly pursuing the removal of
four dams on the lower Snake River in eastern Washington: "Dam removal is about building consensus. It's about saying 'yes' to an alternative view of the future of a river. Consensus building around a 'yes'
is more complex than building a critical mass of people to say 'no' to
something—no to development, no to clear-cutting, no to drilling.
Both kinds of activism are important. There are no silver bullets to make
a dam go away. The only way to do it is to keep forging relationships,
keep the conversation going, especially with people who you don't
see eye-to-eye with right away."

Laura Rose Day, former director of the Penobscot River Restoration
Trust, and a key player in freeing a large section of the Penobscot River
in Maine, echoed this concept: "I got to the point where I stopped
being intimidated by all the faces that would show up at public meetings. And I realized it was because even the people there that didn't
agree with me, I knew them. I had taken the time to get to know them; I
spent hundreds of hours in their kitchens and living rooms chatting with
them, sipping their coffee, and trying to understand where each of us
was coming from. You have to remember that you're not often going to
make converts out of people. Just as important as advocates are people

who move from being opposed to being neutral, to being willing to hear you out because you were willing to listen to their worries."

Dam removal, in other words, is not purely an engineering game, nor strictly an exercise in ecological improvement. It's a grassroots organizing project, an endeavor in door-to-door diplomacy, a revival of the practice of community-level democracy to which politicians are always vaguely alluding, and which the vast majority can't quite seem to remember how to perform.

Your dam removal effort will not be free of conflict. Dams are owned by irrigation districts, influential landowners, public and private utilities, corporations, municipal and state governments, and the federal government. Dam owners, with a few notable exceptions, own dams because they are convinced that doing so is a net economic benefit rather than a liability. The logic they see in balance sheets is often difficult to get past. Some proprietors of dams are convinced that plugging a river is also a net social and even ecological benefit. It will require, among other virtues, a Zen-like detachment from outcomes to do the work of convincing these respective parties that they may be wrong.

Finally, where dam removal is concerned, size does matter. According to the US Army Corps of Engineers, there are over ninety thousand dams fifteen feet tall or higher in the United States. Estimates of the number of small dams nationwide that have not been placed on any kind of official list run into seven figures. Of course, anything saddled with the descriptor "nationwide" runs the risk of immediate generalization. A million of anything spread over the breadth of a continent can be too easily rendered meaningless.

Denise Hoffert, who began her career as a small dam removal specialist for American Rivers fifteen years ago, and has since started her own consulting firm, offers some context for the scourge of small dams plaguing the waterways of the United States. Some twenty small dams have come out in Oregon because of Hoffert's work. She's also the author of an eighty-page primer commissioned by the state of Oregon, simply titled *Small Dam Removal in Oregon: A Guide for Project Managers*, that remains, more than a decade after its publication, one

**US Dams over Six Feet in Height
Removed Since 1981**

- 2011–2021
- 2001–2010
- 1991–2000
- 1981–1990

of the most comprehensive manuals available on the subject. Just as importantly, getting to know dams at a watershed scale has earned her a kind of awe-struck appreciation for how much work remains to be done. "West coasters love to point to the Rogue River as an example of a successful, basin-wide large dam removal campaign," Hoffert says of the nine dams that have been removed on that river system. "And they are right in one respect. Savage Rapids, Gold Ray, and Gold Hill dams are gone. But no one knew how many small dams on tributary creeks existed, until we started to count them up."

The fifty-one-hundred-square-mile Rogue River basin, in southwestern Oregon, drains steep mountain country from roughly the western boundary of Crater Lake National Park 215 miles farther west to the coast, a significant watershed, but merely midsized as far as major watersheds go. "You can free the mainstream, which gets all the press coverage, which then leads to this tendency to think the problem is solved," observes Hoffert. "And so, everyone who has a small impoundment on even the littlest stream thinks the problem can't possibly be here, with this dam, which might only be three feet high. But three feet high for a juvenile salmonid is a mountain range. And you have to remind people that these little feeder creeks are where the majority of spawning and rearing goes on." And the number of impassible mountain ranges remaining in the Rogue Basin? "We're up to five hundred eighty," says Hoffert matter-of-factly. Put another way, there is roughly one low-head dam for every ten square miles in the Rogue watershed. Conceptually, if you zoom out from this single watershed to a continent-wide scale, two million small dams, a rough estimate for how many might exist around the United States, looks plausible. A satellite-height image emerges of just how clogged the country's aquatic arteries really are.

Far from being daunted by the scale of work remaining to be done, Hoffert is optimistic. "Concrete has a life span of around sixty years. These small dams were built at a time when they were needed to serve the economy of their time," says Hoffert. "Most dams were built to divert or store water for irrigation, or to power a mill, or to water livestock. But that economy has changed. We don't need the majority of these dams anymore, and a lot of them are crumbling. I think what we'll see is the pace of dam removal increasing significantly in the years to come."

DAM REMOVAL NUTS AND BOLTS

Small dams, then, are the proverbial low-hanging fruit of the movement to restore rivers. Much of the good advice that follows is tailored to the task of small dam removal. The vast majority of the nearly eighteen hundred dams that have been removed over the past century are smaller, low-head projects. If you've got your heart set on taking out a big dam, recognize that there will be more of everything required to get the job done: more regulation, more resistance, more stakeholders, more permits, more meetings, more time, more money, and more determination. Regardless of the size, keep your eyes on the prize. Hoffert describes a favorite project that took nearly a decade to complete. "And then the jackhammers showed up, and the whole thing was gone within two weeks. I felt the edge of this kind of emotional cliff, you know? Like what do I do next?"

For prospective dam busters, feeling crestfallen as the concrete disintegrates looks like a nice problem to have. Hopefully what follows will help get you there.

IS THE DAM YOU LOATHE A VIABLE CANDIDATE FOR REMOVAL?

While the pathos of dam removal still very much evokes romantic notions of idealistic activists engaged in the guerrilla graffitiing of some monolithic, multi-story, blank concrete face, the reality of dam removal is much more pedestrian. The main reason dams come out is simple: The cost of upgrading and maintaining the structure outweighs the benefits. This fact is often overlooked, perhaps for the simple reason that most dam removals have been prompted by small citizen groups whose sense of injustice at the presence of a dam finally precipitated action. In other words, the river and offending dam often "pick" advocates rather than advocates seeking out a dam to remove.

Although most small dams aren't held accountable through the federal licensing process overseen by the Federal Energy Regulatory Commission (FERC), they are still subject to federal and state safety and environmental laws. The leverage points for removing an outdated dam often can be found in projects that are out of compliance with these laws.

State laws vary by location, but applicable federal laws include the Endangered Species Act and the Clean Water Act. In addition, the Federal Emergency Management Agency (FEMA) issued a set of guide-lines in 2013 that encourages dam operators to have an emergency plan on file in case of dam failure.

Safety standards have moved many dams from the asset to liability side of the ledger. Even small dam failures on private land can cost downstream residents life and property. Dam owners face legal li-ability, not only in the event of catastrophic failure, but for hazards created by the presence of the dam, dangers that could cost the lives of recreational boaters, swimmers, and property owners upstream and down.

Insurance costs, public safety risks, and adherence to environmental law may outweigh an aging dam's benefits. The aim of removal, then, is to relieve the dam's owners of liability while providing benefits that can be enjoyed by a larger segment of a given watershed's population.

Benefits of dam removal include, but are not limited to:
- restoring habitat for anadromous and resident aquatic species;
- restoring natural flow regimes;
- improving water quality;
- eliminating a maintenance liability; and
- removing a public safety hazard.

QUESTIONS TO ASK WHEN
CONSIDERING A DAM FOR REMOVAL

What kind of river is it plugging? The more established theories of river processes have been developed for the eastern United States, where a hundred-year flood can be as much as fifty times the average annual flood. Flooding in the more arid West is less common—but when it happens, can have a much more dramatic effect. Climate change will increase the frequency and severity of these floods.

Is the river (and dam that occupies it) large or small? Small streams have simpler hydrology and sediment regimes. Management tools used for small streams are better understood, and where questions arise, more easily researched. The larger the river, the more complex the system and—as mentioned in the introduction—the more complex the dam removal proposition.

Is the dam on public or private land? Land ownership, not only where the dam in question is sited, but around access points (roads and bridges that get to the dam) have to be sorted out at the outset of any removal campaign. Questions surrounding easements, multiple generations of family ownership, inter- or intra-family ownership, should be sorted out before any formal removal proposal or campaign begins.

Is the dam safe? Many states have an office of dam safety, and some even publish annual lists of high-hazard dams. The Association of State Dam Safety Officials (ASDSO), while not advocates of dam removal, are nonetheless strong advocates of dam safety. Their website features a resource page that includes advice for determining whether a dam is safe. Don't underestimate the role of safety in pitching the notion of dam removal to any community where the future of a dam is in question. Lots of people don't know or care about the difference between a benthic macroinvertebrate and a bull trout, but would happily dynamite a dangerous dam where their dog nearly drowned.

Who are the stakeholders?

- Who holds the keys to dam removal in your watershed? Find out:
- Who owns the dam?

The Gold Ray Dam, removed in fall of 2010. With its removal, the lower
157 miles of the Rogue River in southern Oregon flowed freely for the
first time in 106 years. Shasta Indian Nation and Cow Creek Band of
Umpqua Tribe ancestral lands. MATT STOECKER

- Who benefits from the dam being maintained and operated as it
  has been in the past?
- Who benefits from the dam's removal?

ORGANIZING A CAMPAIGN

Outreach strategies

Dam removal can be a dizzyingly complex and intensely emotional decision for a community, a situation where rational knowledge is not always well recieved. Nonetheless rational knowledge will be your most reliable ally. Glen Spain, who's worked for thirty years to have dams removed on the Klamath River, has this to say about his approach to meeting with stakeholders: The trick, he says, is to talk in a way that passes a test invented by none other than Albert Einstein and has become one of Spain's favorite platitudes. "For an idea to really mean anything, you have to be able to explain it to your grandmother."

Count on stakeholders in the community having little or no knowledge of watershed processes and functions, native fish populations, or applicable state and federal law. Expect a negative public reaction and be ready to respond to the expected concerns. Be prepared for a timeline of years, not months. But have faith in the process.

There is one key component for a successful dam decision-making process: Involve all key community stakeholders early and often. Open and frequent communication is essential to success. Share the information you gather widely. Build relationships with key partners. Invite key agencies and funding organizations to participate in your organization's discussions about the dam's impacts to your watershed. Let people see your process. Be open about what your ultimate goals are.

- Involve key community leaders early in the process. Gain their support for the project. Enlist their help in spreading information on the project.
- Plan plenty of time for discussion at public meetings. If you anticipate a "tough" crowd, plan ahead and enlist support from key community members to attend and speak in support of the project. Those who like to hear themselves talk attend and speak at public meetings. Supportive people either do not attend or do not want to stand up to vocal opposition. Those who want to maintain the status quo are generally more eager to be loud and negative at a public meeting.
- Be patient. The decision to remove a dam takes time to percolate through the community's consciousness. People who are initially opposed may not maintain that view once they understand all of the reasons removal is being considered and what is involved in keeping the dam.
- Ask questions. Why are some folks unhappy with the proposed removal? Make an effort to fully understand the opposition's concerns.

Establish Goals and Objectives

Goals are general; objectives are precise and should be measurable.

Goals for your dam removal might include:

- restoring natural ecosystem functions and processes including improved water quality, functioning stream channel morphology, natural hydrological processes, etc.;
- restoring passage for aquatic species;
- protecting and enhancing existing cultural resources; and
- removing a potential hazard and liability affecting dam owners.

Objectives might include:

- increasing the number of stream miles that will be accessible to aquatic species following the removal;
- increasing the number of adult fish spawning upstream of the former dam site;
- quantifying improvement in water quality indicators (stream temperature, pH, dissolved oxygen);
- increasing the recruitment of gravel to downstream gravel bars for a specific distance downstream of the former dam or increasing the formation of gravel bars; and
- increasing the amount of public open space or park area created (in the formerly impounded area that is recovered after the reservoir drawdown).

Event Planning

Frequent meetings—both small and informal and large and widely publicized—throughout the decision-making process offer stakeholders the opportunity to receive information and exchange ideas. Where the opposition seems utterly recalcitrant, meetings can be used to attract further public support. It's also important to meet informally with pretty much everyone you can think of that might have some influence or expertise in the dam removal process. Some possible groups with whom to meet include key stakeholders, affected land owners, the dam's owner, local government officials, concerned citizens of the local community, and natural resource professionals who work in the watershed in question. You may want to avoid meeting with all these groups at once at first. Smaller, more informal meetings can serve as stepping stones to a well-publicized, wide-ranging public meeting later on.

Possible items for discussion in these smaller meetings:

- Watershed background: Community education prior to exploring dam removal to describe river processes, watershed functions, how the dam is impacting the river, condition of the dam, and management options. Offer to host site tours, provided access is open to the public.
- Remediation alternatives: Provide the science and social costs of various alternatives designed to remediate stream function and fish passage issues at your soon-to-be-gone dam.
- Questionnaires, focus groups, and surveys can help collect information on community opinions in a way that does not require people to speak up in a public meeting.
- Outline the dam removal decision-making process with the dam's owners and any other interested parties.

Spread the Word

Give presentations to community groups and members. Attend city council meetings, chamber of commerce meetings, and Kiwanis, Rotary, and other civic and social service group meetings. A webpage, a presence on social media, and other digital forms of outreach can't hurt.

- Submit articles to the local paper to provide information on each step of the process and announcements for upcoming public meetings.
- Conduct door-to-door outreach to affected landowners. Let them know in advance when you will be in their neighborhood, and otherwise avoid surprising them by showing up on their front porch unannounced.

When to Seek Technical Assistance

Land and water management agencies, environmental NGOs, and natural resource–dependent companies and corporations all rely on third-party technical assistance whenever complex decision-making is required. Sometimes local, state, or federal agencies themselves are the technical experts; sometimes that role falls to a private consulting or engineering firm. Do not hesitate to seek formal, third-party technical assistance. Several states even have a path to gain technical assistance funding for dam removal projects.

The most obvious circumstance in which an expert is required occurs when pressing issues or questions arise for which no stakeholder has a solid answer. Uncertainties about sediments stored behind a dam, fish passage, engineering issues related to dam deconstruction, channel reconstruction, or post-removal revegetation are all technical issues you likely won't have a good answer for. Find the experts and forge relationships with them. A good answer is always worth paying for. There are also good political reasons for seeking technical expertise. Those technical experts can act as facilitators, and in some cases, as mediators.

As a grassroots activist, you may run into trouble knocking on the door of a dam owner and telling them you think their dam is a hazard and needs to come down. Delineating a path toward a third-party inspection of the project is a better bet, especially if there are resources to share the cost. Ergo the expert.

Dams on public land draw a larger cross section into the debate. If there's a perceived recreation benefit, or as is more common, a perceived flood control benefit, you'll immediately have a more hostile opposition. Here again, third-party expertise is worth the investment. Small, low-head, run-of-the-river dams by definition don't have any flood control capability. In most cases, removing dams like these results in a net flood control benefit. High water and small dams are a good recipe for intensifying floods. Yet several dam-busting veterans noted the myth of flood control capability of these types of dams has been the hardest misconception to overcome.

Pushing for regime change: free-river advocates making their opinions known in 2015. Free the Snake Flotilla, Confederated Tribes of the Colville Reservation ancestral lands, Washington. BEN MOON

As your dam removal campaign grows, it's probably a good idea to recruit some technical experts to serve either as informal advisors or as part of a formal technical team. Utilize this expertise in different phases of the project, including forming the project goals and objectives, contracting with a project, engineer, and providing design review.

Whether by experts in engineering or fisheries biology, or just an ad hoc group of concerned citizens, prior to winning approval of your dam removal plan, formal reports addressing two key areas—a project engineer and funding the removal—should be written and distributed as widely as possible.

Does my dam removal require a project engineer?

The short answer: hopefully, yes, assuming your eventual success. Even small dam removal requires engineering expertise; and engineering firms are licensed and bonded for their construction and deconstruction projects. Your nascent dam-busting nonprofit or even the Sierra Club won't have the wherewithal to take on the liability of a dam removal.

Unless you have experience in the commercial construction business, it's quite likely that you're not familiar with the cumbersome process of Requests for Proposals and Requests for Qualifications and scads of drafts of scope of work documents that accompany hiring for a major project like a dam removal. Seek advice from those with experience in this arena.

If you can cobble together the funding to hire a project engineer before you get the green light to tear out your dam, as the campaign gains momentum toward final approval of your plan, all the better. Project engineers should be capable and experienced in many areas that will help get you closer to the day the concrete is toppled. A competent project engineer should be able to:

- conduct engineering design and map creation;
- conduct site assessment and any necessary data collection;
- create a hydraulic model, as necessary, for design and permitting;
- prepare dam removal designs;
- be well-versed on state and federal permit requirements and options;
- handle all technical aspects of permit applications;
- coordinate communication on permit applications between the various permit agencies;
- handle the bidding process with construction firms;
- act as the construction administrator for on-the-ground work;
- implement the dam removal design;
- conduct any turbidity monitoring required under permit conditions;
- provide oversight of post–dam removal site restoration;
- possess good working relationships with permit agency staff; and
- possess good landowner presentation skills.

How will I pay for my dam removal?

Financing the freeing of a segment of a creek is not without its difficulties. Twenty years ago, federal agencies like NOAA and the US Fish and

Wildlife Service had seen the light on the benefits of dam removal and began making grant-based funding available for small dam removal nationwide. In relatively recent times, such grants were still available.

Some states have stepped up their fiscal support for low-head dam removals. A dizzying variety of state agencies offer grants, matching grants, and other forms of financial aid for dam removal. Offices of dam management in several states have personnel, expertise, and even funding available for some types of dam removal projects.

Private foundations are stepping up as well. In late 2016, the William and Flora Hewlett Foundation announced a $50 million fund earmarked for dam removal. Hewlett Foundation officers announced the fund by saying they hoped the money would be "catalytic," which was a thinly veiled invitation for other foundations to join in Hewlett's commitment to restoring rivers.

Some private dam owners, utility companies in particular, may be willing to seed a dam removal fund, or pay outright for removal. Fort Halifax Dam, on the Sebasticook River in Maine, was torn out in 2008 after the utility that owned it, Florida Power and Light, figured out that the meager power output of the dam's hydroelectric operation wouldn't adequately finance the expensive fish lift required. So they paid for removing the dam instead.

Regardless of the source, in making a pitch for funding, emphasize economics that show dam removal is a net positive for the dam's owners. James G. Workman, who was a top assistant to former Secretary of the Interior Bruce Babbitt, has spent a significant portion of his career in subsequent years making the case for a market-based approach to dam removal. He points out there is, as estimated by the US Association of State Dam Safety Officials, a $75 billion backlog of dam upgrades and maintenance in the United States, a number that will only increase as dams age. Leveraging mitigation needs against removal costs might one day yield a market for dam removal. Until that day comes, grant-seeking from private foundations alongside state and local agencies will be your best bet.

Network with as many like-minded people as you can find to identify grant opportunities and other forms of funding. Read the fine print

Dam removal on the Musconetcong River. Lenni Lenape ancestral lands, New Jersey. SAED HINDASH

in applying to grant-makers. Many foundations with an environmental focus are willing to fund the actual dam removal, but less eager to fund the steps to get there. This can quickly get complicated, especially if you're trying to cobble together several grants to get your dam to come down.

Going after funding means you've at least identified a constituency that believes your project should move forward. Ballpark estimates for the total cost of your dam removal will look daunting. Of course, you can't know the entire cost of the project at the beginning. For this reason, and because it's often easier to raise big chunks of change in smaller increments, it makes sense to draw up a fairly detailed timeline. Divide the project into phases and submit applications for each phase over the course of the project. The number and scope of your project phases will depend on your project's complexity. Here's four suggested phases that you might add to or subtract from to suit your needs.

PHASE 1
PUBLIC OUTREACH AND TECHNICAL
ASSISTANCE

Here you'll seek funds to work with the community in developing and evaluating options for the future of the dam in question. Need a dam removal alternatives analysis, sediment analysis, sediment and flow modeling, or an archaeological survey? Any of these pre-project permitting investigations should be funded and implemented in this initial phase.

PHASE 2
TECHNICAL ASSISTANCE FOR DESIGN
AND PERMITTING

This phase will need to take your project from design of the dam removal through its permitting costs. This is a phase where costs are frequently underestimated. The design of the removal will likely have to be created by an engineering firm, which will also be responsible for procuring the necessary permits. Plan on several weeks worth of billable hours from the firm of your choice. A ballpark hourly rate for such expertise is $150 to $300 per hour.

PHASE 3
PROJECT IMPLEMENTATION

The actual work of removing the dam, the cost of which you'll know to the penny after completing phases 1 and 2.

PHASE 4
MONITORING AND SITE RESTORATION

Frequently overlooked, but vital for building the body of data on the restorative power of dam removal.

When creating timelines and budgets, keep in mind that costs will grow over the life of the project. Historically, inflation has run at roughly 3 percent. If you want to be precise, there are construction inflation indices available online that you can easily plug into cost calculations.

HOW MANY PERMITS DO I NEED TO
TAKE OUT A DAM?

It depends on the state, county, and municipality where your dam will be torn down. In addition to state and local permitting requirements, there are federal permits. You will need to identify, understand, and acquire all necessary permits before proceeding with dam removal. One way to learn a whole lot in one day about your particular permit scene is to host a pre-application permit party. This is where you provide coffee and snacks to representatives of every pertinent permitting agency you identify. The variability of local government shape and size makes it impossible to list whom you might want to invite. But at the state level, you'll want a name tag for representatives from the departments of environmental quality, fish and wildlife, state lands, state water, and the state historic preservation office. Federal permit party invitees might include personnel from NOAA Fisheries, the US Army Corps of Engineers, US Fish and Wildlife Service, the Natural Resource Conservation Service, and the Environmental Protection Agency.

The goal of getting everyone involved in permitting in one room is to create a list of applicable permits and a timeline for acquiring each one.

You should be ready with following party favors:
- site map (including labels for dam site, proposed staging area, site access, proposed work bench, proposed erosion control measures);
- ownership map;
- site photos;
- dam dimensions;
- year the dam was built;
- type of construction;
- condition of dam;
- amount, size classes, and quality of stored sediment;
- presence (historical or current, native or introduced) of all fish species;
- presence of ESA species or state species of concern and critical habitat in the basin;

- potential for presence of historic artifacts;
- existing watershed water quality issues directly up- and down-stream of the dam site;
- proposed removal method;
- proposed site dewatering plan; and
- anticipated condition of the river following the dam's removal.

The second goal of your permit party is to establish warm, friendly relationships with the faces behind the bureaucracy at each of these agencies. If this is not possible, for the love of all that is sacred, do not piss these people off. You need all the required permits to proceed, and bad relationships are not conducive to getting them into your hands. Be transparent as glass in your intentions with permit-granting agency personnel. They don't like surprises. It's their job to read permit applications every day, and for that reason alone, you should be nice to them. And since permits are of vital importance to your endeavor, keep track of your communications with them, including emails and a phone log. You should have a single point of contact within each agency, and by turns, there should be one person in your by-now budding organization that handles the interface with permit agencies.

If you've hired an engineering firm to design and implement the dam removal plan, you're in luck. It's customary for the firm to take over the acquisition of all necessary permits. Even so, you should be familiar with the list of permits that you need and be in touch with your project engineer on permit matters.

LET'S TALK ABOUT FEDERAL PERMITS

The US Army Corps of Engineers will be the agency you'll become most familiar with in the effort to bring your dam down. You'll need a 404 permit. The number refers to section 404 of the federal Clean Water Act, which lays out the rules for discharging dredged or fill material into rivers, lakes, streams, and wetlands. If you jump through all the hoops, you'll either be issued a Nationwide Permit (good for sixty days) or an Individual Permit (good for 120 days). The former is generally considered by dam removal specialists to be more desirable than the latter, based on the level of detailed information required during the application process.

The corps will review the application, and launch any number of reviews and assessments they deem necessary, based on the information found therein. The good news is that you don't need to pay for any of these reviews. The bad news is they will often proceed at a seemingly glacial pace. Here's the short list of possible assessments to which your dam removal may be subject:

Biological Assessment: Will your dam removal activities jeopardize the existence of threatened or endangered species or adversely modify their habitat? The Biological Assessment will determine whether a more extensive process to answer this question is necessary.

Biological Opinion: The Biological Opinion is issued by NOAA or the US Fish and Wildlife Service, based on either respective agency's reading of the aforementioned Biological Assessment. As the name suggests, the agency will opine on whether the proposed action (in this case, your dam removal) will jeopardize the existence of threatened or endangered species, or adversely modify critical habitat. If NOAA or the USFWS decides you need a BiOp, you may be asked to give more information than you issued in the 404 permit application. You should be ready, willing, and able to do this.

A programmatic consultation is a kind of streamlined biological opinion; it offers a blanket assessment and opinion for a particular activity in a given region. For instance, NOAA and the USFWS have offered joint programmatic consultations on a suite of ecosystem restoration activities. Some small dam removals may be covered by this kind of agency action.

ESA/EFH Consultations: If your dam is on a salmon-bearing stream, be prepared for the Endangered Species Act (ESA) and/or Essential Fish Habitat (EFH) consultations. The ESA mandates that if your dam removal affects species of fish listed under that law, a comprehensive consultation with pertinent federal agencies must be undertaken. Another law specific to fish, the Magnuson–Stevens Fishery Conservation and Management Act, calls for a very similar type of assessment of EFH to be performed for many of the same reasons outlined in the ESA. In fact, pertinent federal agencies cover both of these legal mandates, when required to do so, with a single document. ESA/EFH consultations have the most potential to significantly delay your acquisition of a 404 permit. If deemed necessary, the agencies may call on you for more information, which you should be prepared to give.

HOORAY!

The permits are all in place, a date has been set to actually begin tearing out concrete at your dam. It's time for the actual, long-anticipated work of getting rid of your dam. It's also time to answer the question you've long been waiting to ask:

Will explosives be used in demolishing my dam? It's possible. The method of deconstruction depends on the configuration of the structure in question. The most common method of dam deconstruction involves heavy equipment, but no dynamite. If you're new to the process, you might be surprised to learn that in some cases you'll be temporarily adding a dam to your river. A short-lived cofferdam will divert the flow of the river into a bypass channel, creating a dry work area during deconstruction. Some complicating factors: if your dam provided fish passage up- and downstream, the design of the cofferdam and bypass channel must preserve this same opportunity. And if boaters frequent the stretch of stream you'd like to free, you'll have to shuttle them around your deconstruction zone. These two provisions can add time, effort, and money to the final bill for freeing another river.

Some dams require no cofferdam for removal, and many have been removed with a jackhammer and excavator to extract the larger pieces of rubble.

The most dependable hassle, as the 404 permitting process doubt-lessly made clear to you, will be sediment management as the dam you love to hate slowly disappears. Gravels will settle out quickly, becom-ing habitat for all manner of aquatic life, generally not far downstream of where the structure once stood. Smaller chunks of soil and rock known as "fines" will merit closer scrutiny. Where such material has been con-taminated with pollutants, some dredging or transport will have to be undertaken. Other unpleasantries: wherever possible, try to reduce the amount of old concrete hauled away to some recycling facility near or far. Placing as much material as possible in situ can reduce expense. This works with smaller dams; the bigger ones, not so much.

THE FINAL STEP:
SITE RESTORATION AND MONITORING

The good news for small dam removals in this last phase is that there isn't often any restoration actions that will be required of you. In many instances, you can plant a few willows if you like, and call it good. If more planting or bank stabilization is required, you'll need to budget for plants, and the cost of personnel to make sure that some of the plants survive. Brace yourself: riparian plant costs can add up in a hurry, and the headache of locating a regiment of willing caretakers of flora vulnerable to the predation of birds, beaver, mice, deer, wind, weather, vandals, and thieves will give you fits.

Post-removal monitoring is too often overlooked: Post-removal monitoring is a chance for the growing army of dam busters to add an-other success story to the body of evidence that dam removal is one of the most powerful tools of restoration biology. It's been a challenge to find funding for small, post-project removal monitoring. But evaluating how closely the recovery of your stream bears out the predictions you made prior to removal will be a worthy endeavor. In many instances, small dams have far exceeded predicted benefits in ecologic, eco-nomic, and recreational benchmarks. Monitoring is another kind of megaphone you can use to add to the momentum for clearing up the

The dam upstream of Saint-Étienne-du-Vigan was removed in 1998, reviving the stream ecology on the Allier River. Haute-Loire, France.
LUC OLIVER

concrete still plugging the planet's waterways. Take pictures, write a glowing report, and share the tale of bringing water back to life, and life back to water, to as many folks as you can find who'll listen.

SMALL DAM REMOVAL SUCCESS STORIES

Freeing rivers from dams is complex work, but all the hassle has, with one notable exception, been totally worth the effort. Results of dam removals have been stunningly positive. According to American Rivers, nearly eighteen hundred dams have been relegated to history over the past century, with the vast majority of these coming out since the year 2000. With one notable exception, dam removals have met or exceeded the expectations of those who plan them, and those who live with them afterward. The exception was Fort Edward Dam on the Hudson River, where in 1973, dam removal allowed contaminated sediment stored in the reservoir to be released downstream, caus-ing fish kills and a host of other troubles. Based on ecological and economic indicators—aside from Fort Edward Dam—you can't find a dam removal where facts would elicit a legitimate response of regret. In other words, there is no constituency represented by the slogan "Rebuild our demolished dams."

Instead, the body of evidence grows in favor of freeing rivers. It's not possible in a single book to tell every good tale of undamming, even in brief narrative form. After all, there are nearly eighteen hundred of them, which would be an encyclopedic volume of hydrologic happi-ness. Here's the next best thing: American Rivers, in cahoots with the US Geological Survey and a few other partners, have joined forces to create DRIP, the Dam Removal Information Portal, which is, as the USGS describes it, "a living database of information on dying dams."

Two locales featured on DRIP are profiled here. Projects on the Scioto River, in downtown Columbus, Ohio, and dam removals in New Jersey, most of them less than an hour by car from New York City. The opportunities for small dam removals east of the Mississippi are legion, for reasons having to do with hydrology, topography, population den-sity, and the historical timing of the wave of the industrial revolution. As the outcome of each of these recent projects suggests, if you give a river an inch of a chance, it will it take a mile toward a better place.

COLUMBUS

Cities require parks and open spaces to make them civil. In the twenty-first century, the consensus seems to be that the more green amidst the concrete and asphalt, the more civilized a town looks and feels. It's a challenge, however, to carve significant greenspace out of urban areas that grew up in the heyday of rust-belt industrial development. But vi-sionary planners in Columbus, Ohio, added thirty-three acres of trails, grass, gardens, and river access in late 2015. Key to creating this new bit of earth was removing an old dam.

The Main Street in Columbus was built in 1920. Before that, there was a wooden dam built from the west bank of the Scioto River, which bisects downtown Columbus. This diversion dam, which jutted about three-quarters of the way across the river, directed water into the Ohio and Erie Canal, a critical trade gateway for nineteenth-century Columbus.

The wooden dam was destroyed in a 1913 flood, and in 1920, a concrete dam spanning the entire river channel replaced it, widening the structure to twice its original three hundred feet. That dam turned the Scioto into a giant muck collector. It backed up the river, creating a sediment pond that stretched for two miles upriver from the dam. It wasn't more than a couple of inches deep, save for a narrow semblance of the original river channel out in the middle.

Columbus is the fifteenth-largest American city, home to Ohio State University, and its current identity as a center of research and technology didn't match up with the appearance of its downtown area at the dawn of the twenty-first century. The Columbus Downtown Development Corporation (CDDC) aimed to fix that.

An automobile-centric shopping mall met the wrecking ball and was replaced with a park, outdoor concert area, and the conversion of an old department store into an office/retail complex. A five-lane riverside highway got squeezed into two lanes, leaving room for a greenspace along the abandoned banks of the Scioto. Still, the heart of Columbus had no detectable pulse by five o'clock on weekdays and was seldom visited on weekends. The CDDC launched phase two of its ambitious urban renewal project in 2010. The notion of tearing out the Main Street Dam was floated at a series of public meetings.

A year and a half later, Scioto Greenways, as the dam removal plan came to be known, began working its way through the eighteen different regulatory agencies that had to sign off on the dam's removal and the river's reclamation. Demolition began in November 2013 and was done before year's end. Almost a century's worth of sediment parked behind the dam was recycled, furnishing half of the five hundred thousand cubic yards of fill the CDDC used to reconstruct the riverbanks and recreate the river channel. A trail system now stretches from Scioto Audubon Metro Park to the campus of Ohio State University.

The grand reopening of the river took place in November of 2015 and immediately began reaping design awards. The awards were followed by visitors—lots of them. Kayakers drift through downtown, past a fifteen-thousand-square foot, kid-friendly fountain. America's largest outdoor climbing wall keeps vertically minded midwesterners in shape for their next visit to the mountains. People get married here. Bird watchers perch along the 175 green acres of the Mile, intently glassing avian life where, for the previous half a century, five lanes of Columbus commuters would rush to get the hell out of a lifeless downtown. Now some Columbus homebuyers are wanting to park here permanently.

According to the CDDC's Amy Taylor, downtown Columbus's population peaked immediately following World War II, at nearly thirty thousand. Then, a mass exodus: the 2000 census counted slightly more than three thousand. But by 2021, the downtown population had rebounded to eleven thousand two hundred residents.

Economically, removing a useless, silted in, concrete clog in the Scioto has paid huge dividends for Columbus. The resculpted riverbank and surrounding environs has generated nearly $300 million in private residential, office, and retail construction around it.

The turnaround has spurred interest in freeing a stretch of the Olentangy, the lower few miles of which run through Columbus before joining the Scioto. A suite of lowhead dams plague the Olentangy, one of which, the Fifth Avenue Dam, was removed in 2014.

RARITAN AND MUSCONETCONG RIVER RESTORATION, NEW JERSEY

Conventional wisdom dictates that most people residing in or visiting New Jersey these days aren't there because of the fishing. The overblown stereotypes of Garden State waterways existing as a toxic industrial swampland or as a repository for those who saw too much of some nefarious mob activity still supersedes an emerging reality: Jersey has been busy healing some of its rivers, after a few centuries of abusing them. The fish are back, with one species in particular demonstrating a resilience bordering on the miraculous.

When American shad last ran up the Musconetcong River, Abenaki, Massachusett, Mohegan, and Wampanoag Native Americans were organizing to make what would become the last Indigenous push to get the British out of New England. The Musconetcong was already known as a key tributary of the Delaware, and it was around this time that the first dams were being built on local rivers and streams. In the days before electricity, the power of falling water was harnessed by gears, wheels, pulleys, buckets, and belts, mostly to power mills that ground wheat into flour. These gristmill dams were the precursors of larger wooden dams, built to aid navigation, and later, concrete dams that produced hydropower.

As far back as the late eighteenth century, local citizens expressed regret at having traded a little technological convenience for the wealth of marine-derived plenitude. Jim Waltman is the executive director of the Watershed Institute. A few years ago, a staffer ran across the journals of a German traveler who quartered with some local settlers. "This was in the 1780s," recalls Waltman, "before the United States even was a country. And even then, this German wrote that the locals were still complaining about the loss of fish runs, which, according to this account, had all but disappeared by the 1740s."

Dam removal is an exercise in patience. In this case, 280 years' worth. At least a dozen dams, all within an hour's drive of New York City, have come down in the past decade. On the Musconetcong River, Gruendyke Mill and Seber Dams in Hackettstown are gone. In 2011, Riegelsville and Finesville Dams were removed. The deconstruction of Hughesville Dam was completed several years ago, clearing the way for removal of the Warren Glen Dam, located in the Musconetcong Gorge. Scads of American shad have come back to the Musconetcong.

Brian Cowden is one of New Jersey's full-time dam busters. Trout Scapes River Restoration LLC is a design-and-build river restoration company, and dam removals in Cowden's home state of New Jersey are keeping him plenty busy. "I always tell people you can learn from what we've done [on rivers] in the East—both what we've done wrong and what we're doing right," says Cowden. "On the 'Musky' we were getting not just a few shad, but large pods of them moving upriver to the next dam. This made it easier of course to make the pitch that that next dam should come out."

Cowden notes that financing dam removals, while still a tall order, is made somewhat easier in the Garden State because of a good law and a bad industrial past. "As far as I know, New Jersey and Michigan are the only two states where water quality standards exceed the federal standard. So, there's a higher bar for polluters, including dam owners," he explains. "And then the settlements with polluters—when there's a judgment against them, they're responsible for returning not only the good water quality, but all the wildlife, including species of fish, that went missing because of the company's abuse. And it turns out the most cost-effective way to restore species is to tear out dams." In spite of recent success, there's more work to be done in Cowden's part of the country than almost any place else. "Count them all up, and in the past ten years I've worked on over twenty dam removals," he says, counting dams that are already gone and projects still underway. Cowden says his company isn't the only one in New Jersey taking out dams. "But there are literally tens of thousands of these size projects that need to come out," he notes.

Three more dams have come down on the Raritan River, a watershed neighbor of the Musconetcong, and more are planned. In late 2021, federal and state agencies announced a $25 million settlement over the polluted Superfund site of a former electronics manufacturer. The fund will go a long way toward financing more dam removals. Two more dams, the Headgates and the Blackwells Mills Dams are soon to be gone. A comprehensive restoration effort aims to recreate a functioning, whole, intact ecosystem out of the Raritan River.

Jim Waltman got to witness the removal of the Weston Mill Dam on the Raritan's largest tributary, the Millstone River, and can attest to the recovery of native fish that ensued. "We get back shad, alewife, striped bass, and blueback herring," says Waltman of the immediate return on investment in dam removal. "But true recovery is a long-term prospect, something I probably won't see come to fruition in my lifetime."

He describes the challenges ahead—creating natural flood control by restoring wetlands and loosening the grip of development in flood-prone areas. But the short-term rewards—the ones Waltman will be able to witness in the near term—have been astonishing. "When again in this life are you going to have the chance to put a species back in its natural habitat that's been missing for three hundred years?"

ANATOMY OF A DAM, FROM A TO Z

Like any form of technology new or old, dams have their own peculiar vernacular describing their types, parts, and pieces and how they work. A basic knowledge of dam anatomy and a few related terms from hydrology will at least furnish an initial working vocabulary, establishing credibility with agency professionals as well as those opposed to your cause. The following definitions are from www.ussdams.org.

Abutment: The point of contact between objects or parts that are adjacent or next to each other. That part of the valley side against which the dam is constructed. The left and right abutments of dams are defined with the observer viewing the dam looking downstream.

Acre-foot: The amount of water that would cover one acre of land one foot deep. One acre-foot equals 325,900 gallons, 43,560 cubic feet, or 1,233 cubic meters.

Alluvial: Sediment deposited by flowing water, such as in a riverbed.

Aquifer: An underground layer of rock, sediment, or soil that is filled or saturated with water.

Arch dam: A concrete, masonry, or timber dam with the alignment curved upstream so as to transmit the major part of the water load to the abutments. *See page 224.*

Baffle block: A block, usually of concrete, constructed in a channel or stilling basin to dissipate the energy of water flowing at high velocity.

Base flow: The sustained portion of stream discharge that is drawn from natural storage sources, and not effected by human activity or regulation.

Beneficial use: The use of water for any beneficial purpose, often defined by statute or court decisions. Such uses include domestic use, irrigation, fish and wildlife, fire protection, navigation, power, industrial use, etc.

Berm: A nearly horizontal step in the sloping profile of an embankment dam. Also a step in a rock or earth cut.

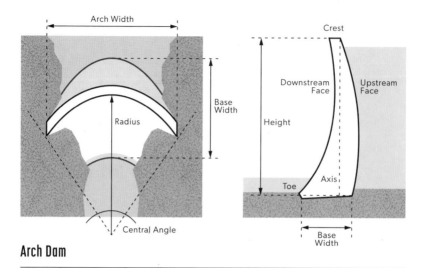

Arch Dam

Breach: An opening through a dam that allows the uncontrolled draining of a reservoir. A controlled breach is a constructed opening. An uncontrolled breach is an unintentional opening caused by discharge from the reservoir.

Buttress dam: A dam consisting of a watertight part supported at intervals on the downstream side by a series of buttresses. Buttress dams can take many forms, such as a flat slab or massive head buttress.

Bypass system: A channel or conduit in a dam that provides a route for fish to move through or around the dam without going through the turbine units.

Cofferdam: A temporary structure enclosing all or part of the construction area so that construction can proceed in a dry environment. A diversion cofferdam diverts a stream into a pipe, channel, tunnel, or other watercourse.

Consumptive use: Quantity of water lost to evaporation, agriculture, manufacturing, and industrial process loss.

Crest of dam: Top of a dam.

Crib dam: A gravity dam built up of boxes, crossed timbers, or gabions, filled with earth or rock.

Cubic feet per second (cfs): A unit of measurement describing the flow of water. A cubic foot is the amount of water needed to fill a cube that is one foot on all six sides, about 7.5 gallons.

Dead storage: The water behind a dam that lies below the lowest outlet of the dam and that cannot readily be withdrawn from the reservoir.

Discharge: Rate of flow or volume per unit time of water flowing along a channel or through a pipe at a given

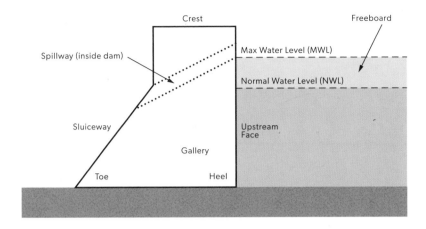

Gravity Dam

instant. In the United States, commonly measured in cubic feet per second.

Diversion dam: A dam built to divert water from a waterway or stream into a different watercourse.

Drawdown: The difference between a water level and a lower water level in a reservoir within a particular time. Used as a verb, it is the lowering of the water surface.

Earthfill dam: An embankment dam in which more than 50 percent of the total volume is formed of compacted soils. *See page 227.*

Embankment dam: Any dam constructed of excavated natural materials, such as both earthfill and rockfill dams, or of industrial waste materials, such as a tailings dam.

Fill: Man-made deposits of natural soils or the process of the depositing;

an earth or broken-rock structure or embankment.

Fish ladder: An inclined trough which carries water from above to below a dam so that fish can easily swim upstream.

Flashboards: Structural members of timber, concrete, or steel placed in channels or on the crest of a spillway to raise the reservoir water level but intended to be quickly removed, tripped, or fail in the event of a flood.

Flood plain: An area adjoining a body of water or natural stream that may be covered by floodwater. Also, the downstream area that would be inundated or otherwise affected by the failure of a dam or by large flood flows. The area of the flood plain is generally delineated by a frequency (or size) of flood.

Fluvial: Refers to streams and stream processes.

Forebay: Area of a reservoir closest to the dam.

Freeboard: Vertical distance between the reservoir surface and the top of the dam.

Gravity dam: A dam constructed of concrete and/or masonry, which relies on its weight and internal strength for stability. *See page 225.*

Groundwater: Water held in pores and crevices of the subsoil, mainly derived from rain or other water source that percolates from the surface.

Grout: A fluidized material that is injected into soil, rock, concrete, or other construction material to seal openings and to lower the permeability and/or provide additional structural strength.

Headgate: The gate that controls water flow into irrigation canals and ditches.

Impeller: Rotating wheel of a turbine; also known as a rotor.

Impoundment: A body of water formed by a dam, dike, floodgate, or other barrier for future use.

Intake: Any structure in a reservoir, dam, or river through which water can be drawn into an outlet pipe, flume, etc.

Levee: A natural or man-made earthen barrier along the edge of a stream, river, or lake to prevent the flow of water out of its channel.

Log boom: A chain of logs, drums, or pontoons secured end-to-end and floating on the surface of a reservoir so as to divert floating debris, trash, and logs.

Masonry dam: Any dam constructed mainly of stone, brick, or concrete blocks pointed with mortar. A dam having only a masonry facing should not be referred to as a masonry dam.

Maximum flood control level: The highest elevation of the flood control storage.

Mitigation: When used in the context of an environmental assessment, it refers to an action designed to offset, lessen, or reduce adverse impacts due to a dam's construction and subsequent presence.

Nonconsumptive water uses: Water uses that do not substantially deplete water supplies, including swimming, boating, waterskiing, fishing, maintenance of stream-related fish and wildlife habitat, and hydropower generation.

Peak flow: The maximum instantaneous discharge that occurs during a flood.

Penstock: A pressurized pipeline or shaft between the reservoir and hydraulic machinery.

Perennial streams: Streams which flow continuously throughout the year.

Regulating dam: A dam impounding a reservoir from which water is released to regulate the flow downstream.

Revetment: An embankment or wall of sandbags, earth, etc., constructed

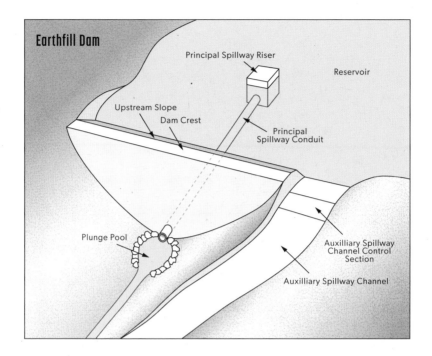

Earthfill Dam

Principal Spillway Riser

Reservoir

Upstream Slope

Dam Crest

Principal Spillway Conduit

Plunge Pool

Auxilliary Spillway Channel Control Section

Auxilliary Spillway Channel

to restrain material from being transported away. A facing of stone, cement, sandbags, etc., to protect a wall or embankment.

Riprap: A layer of large uncoursed stone, precast blocks, bags of cement, or other suitable material, generally placed on the slope of an embankment or along a watercourse as protection against wave action, erosion, or scour. Riprap is usually placed by dumping or other mechanical methods, and in some cases is hand placed. It consists of pieces of relatively large size, as distinguished from a gravel blanket.

Rockfill dam: An embankment dam in which more than 50 percent of the total volume is comprised of compacted or dumped cobbles, boulders, rock fragments, or quarried rock generally larger than three-inch size.

Rubble dam: A stone masonry dam in which the stones are unshaped or uncoursed.

Runoff: Water that drains or flows off, such as rainwater flowing off from the land or water from snow draining from a mountain range.

Sill: Horizontal overflow line of a measuring notch or spillway. Also a horizontal member on which a gate rests when closed.

Siphon: An inverted enclosed pipeline structure to convey the water under roads, drainage channels, rivers, etc.

Skimmer gate: A gate at the spillway crest whose prime purpose is to control the release of debris and logs with a limited amount of water.

Spillway: A structure over or through which flow is discharged from a reservoir. If the rate of flow is controlled by mechanical means, such as gates, it is considered a controlled spillway. If the geometry of the spillway is the only control, it is considered an uncontrolled spillway.

Tailrace: The channel into which water is discharged after passing through the outlet works or turbines.

Tailwater: The water immediately downstream from a dam. The water surface elevation varies due to fluctuations in the outflow from the structures of a dam and due to downstream influences of other dams or structures.

Toe of the dam: The junction of the downstream slope or face of a dam with the ground surface; also referred to as the downstream toe. The junction of the upstream slope with ground surface is called the heel or the upstream toe.

Trash rack: A device located in the forebay (the upstream side) of a dam to prevent floating or submerged debris from entering the intake.

Turnout: A branch in the canal for diverting water to a specific destination; where water is diverted to users.

Water table: The surface of underground, gravity-controlled water.

Watershed: The area drained by a river or river system or portion thereof. The watershed for a dam is the drainage area upstream of the dam.

Weir: A notch of regular form through which water flows.

ACRONYMS AND INITIALISMS

In addition to its own vernacular, every specialized field seems to possess its own alphabet soup of acronyms. Knowing your FONSI from your FERC before you dive into this arcane world can only help. Here are some of the most common:

BA: Biological Assessment

BLM: Bureau of Land Management

BMP: Best Management Practice

BiOp: Biological Opinion

CR: Conservation Recommendation

EA: Environmental Assessment

EFH: Essential Fish Habitat

EIS: Environmental Impact Statement

ESA: Endangered Species Act

FEMA: Federal Emergency Management Agency

FERC: Federal Energy Regulatory Commission

FONSI: Finding of No Significant Impact

IP: Individual Permit

JRFPA: Joint Removal Fill Permit Application

NEPA: National Environmental Policy Act

NOAA: National Oceanic and Atmospheric Administration

NMFS: National Marine Fisheries Service

NRCS: Natural Resources Conservation Service

NWP: Nationwide Permit

PRG: Project Review Group

RFP: Request for Proposals

RFQ: Request for Qualifications

SEF: Sediment Evaluation Framework

SLOPES: Standard Local Operating Procedures for Endangered Species

SOQ: Statement of Qualifications

SOW: Scope of Work

SWCD: Soil and Water Conservation District

USACE: US Army Corps of Engineers, also commonly referred to as "the corps"

USFS: US Forest Service

USFWS: US Fish and Wildlife Service

USGS: US Geological Survey

PATAGONIA SIN REPRESAS

Summer is ending in southern Chile, dusk creeping in, and I'm heading south on Chile's Carretera Austral, careening along the two-lane gravel road in a white crew-cab pickup. The driver, Rene, looks a little like a cheerful, copper-skinned, cigarette-smoking Prince Valiant. He speaks about six words of English, me about six of Spanish, but somehow, we've figured out we each have two kids, Donald Trump is a *pendejo*, fishing is fun, and watching birds is okay too. Rene tells me it will take five hours to get to Puerto Bertrand and the Río Baker, in northern Patagonia, where Rene works logistics, operations, and maintenance for Green Baker Lodge, a luxury fly-fishing resort. The bus takes eight hours to get to the same place. In the absence of small talk, I work on a math story problem. If the bus averages forty miles an hour for eight hours, and Rene can make the same distance in five hours, we must achieve a velocity about twenty-five miles per hour greater than the bus. And lo, as I cast a furtive glance at the speedometer, we've got that and five miles an hour to spare. Seventy on a twisting gravel road may seem excessive, based on previous experience. But I've never been here before, so previous experience need not apply.

Sacred waters. The churning confluence of the Río Baker and Río Neff, chocolate milk on one side and sapphire blue on the other. Both rivers have been threatened by proposed dams. Tehuelche ancestral lands, Patagonia, Chile. CHRIS BURKARD

Patagonia, on the Chilean side, looks like a mash-up of the biggest mountains in Colorado, Utah, Wyoming, and Montana, or a head-on collision between a fjord in Norway and a savanna in Tanzania, but mostly like a landscape you wouldn't dream of, much less begin to comprehend, unless you've been there. And that's why I'm here, to begin to comprehend. What is the name, for instance, of that most common roadside plant with leaves so large they could shelter you and a friend in a rainstorm? What masochistic fool or egotistical *alpinista* dared climb that prehistoric stone tower looming over the Río Ibáñez Valley? Why are there no grizzly bear–sized predators at the top of this food chain? And is that really the same guy in the red truck who passed us a few miles back, now stopped in the road, smiling at us, waving with one hand, while with the other holds his schlong to pee? Rene smiles and waves back, unfazed. We pass the pee-er and accelerate on the straight to Montana highway speeds. Paved Montana highway speeds.

To keep my mind off the road, I focus on the current issues and enduring questions, ones I first wondered about more than a decade ago, as bad news about more dams planned for Patagonia's rivers made international headlines. Back then, Chilean dam opponents were reeling from the loss of the Biobío, where, in spite of vocal opposition, Endesa, a Spanish subsidiary of Italian corporate giant Enel, completed the Pangue Dam (Represa Pangue) in 1996, displacing Indigenous Mapuche people, and ruining Chile's second largest river. Corporate eyeballs quickly turned next to Chile's largest river, the Baker, where

Reports of the death of the Baker proved to be premature. Four years later, it was the dams that died...

we are currently headed. A suite of large dams was slated, two for the Baker, three for its wilder neighbor, the Pascua. The dams would plug the prodigious output from the two largest ice caps outside the arctic poles, glaciers that give these rivers an outlandish shade of electric blue that looks like an imaginative film editor invented it. The blue water might remain, but on land, transmission lines would run a thousand miles to north, supported by several thousand towers each more than two hundred feet tall. A thousand miles of forest would be clear-cut to create a winding corridor nearly four hundred feet wide, bisecting sixty-four communities and fourteen protected areas. It would split endangered forests and some of Chile's most spectacular national parks.

To combat these plans, a coalition of community groups and national and international NGOs formed as the Patagonia Defense Council and launched a campaign in 2009 known as Patagonia Sin Represas (Patagonia Without Dams).

The odds of achieving the groups' namesake goal back then were slim to none. Legally and politically, all the cards were on the side of Endesa and HidroAysén, the Chilean subsidiary Endesa created. Aysén is a mostly roadless wilderness region, with around a hundred thousand people scattered about in a Northern California–sized territory, whose sheep ranching and seasonal tourist industries were of little concern to the nation's sixteen million citizens. Conventional wisdom espoused amongst the Chilean press and pundits was that Chile needed energy, and the choice was either coal-fired generation or these dams. Hydropower was hyped as greener than coal, ergo, kiss a couple wild rivers in Patagonia good-bye and embrace the fully electrified twenty-first-century future of the country. Sure, there's an environmental review document that the company is writing, but once that's done, the dams are a done deal. Right?

Reports of the death of the Baker proved to be premature. Four years later, it was the dams that died—or at least went into a deep coma. In 2014, a body called the Committee of Ministers, Chile's highest-ranking administrative power, cancelled the permits for all five dam projects in Aysén.

But as David Brower observed, all environmental victories are temporary, and all defeats permanent. Chilean activists I'd spoken with before arriving in Patagonia were ill at ease, sensing the monkey wrench they'd jammed into the dam industry's gears would soon slip, and the well-oiled political machine that wants the dams would produce some less overtly offensive version of the dams. How long would the win hold out? And how would Chile's growing antidam factions respond to a kinder, gentler proposal for dams on Aysén's rivers?

Dusk left Rene and me with a sliver of light with which to view General Carrera Lake. Though he makes the twelve-hour round trip from Coyhaique (co-yai-ke) and back to the Río Baker a couple times a month during the lodge's busy season, I can tell by the look of satisfaction on his face that he never gets tired of the view. *"¡Qué bonito!"* Rene says as he pats me on the shoulder and points beyond the truck. *"Dos horas más."*

The night inked the outlines of peaks above the lake, which is an enormous catchment basin for meltwater from the vast but shrinking ice caps of Patagonia. The Río Baker is the neck of a massive wine-bottle-shaped store of glacial meltwater. The bottom of the bottle, Lago General Carrera, flows into the narrower, smaller Lago Bertrand. This lake constricts in its downstream end, where a riot of whitewater commences—the Baker River, which flows with an average volume of about thirty thousand cubic feet per second. This unique geological arrangement was shaped in part by glacial outburst floods created when portions of Andean glaciers hanging on nearby peaks succumbed to gravity and sloughed away. These inland tsunamis gained size and speed as they ran over the surface of lakes, then squeezed into the canyon of the Río Baker. The phenomenon will likely happen again, and engineers have yet to answer questions about the wisdom of placing a large concrete backstop in the way of one of these waves. Absent the dams, the locals need to know what, if not dam development, might power a twenty-first-century economy.

The Aysén region, or what is roughly northern Patagonia on the Chilean side, is increasingly becoming an international travel destination, and fly fishing, in terms of total money, is the number one draw. The irony for advocates of preserving the native flora and fauna of this unique ecosystem is that the salmonids of Patagonia are an invasive species. They displaced the fish that evolved in Patagonian streams, but here they are now, thriving, and contributing in significant ways to the construction of an economy that presents a viable alternative to reckless resource extraction. That emerging economy belies a climate chaos–borne reality facing Chile and several other South American countries: their water supply descending from glacial meltwater is disappearing.

Doug Tompkins' Vision

A vision for sustainable development that might transcend the drier future Chile faces has been resolutely pursued for the past twenty-five years. After a rocky start, Chileans have fallen in love with their growing inventory of reserved lands and national parks—and subsequently, fueled the unlikely success of the Patagonia Sin Represas movement. Bucking an unfortunate trend of heavy-handed interventionism over the past century, two Americans can take partial credit for this emerging national love affair with a natural Patagonia.

When Kris and Doug Tompkins began buying up old sheep ranches in Patagonia, with the publicly stated goal of rehabilitating these lands and returning them to the Chilean people, few Chileans took the Tompkinses' claims at face value. The most fantastic rumors proliferated in the South American press. The Tompkinses were pro-abortion zealots. The Tompkinses were Nazis, looking for ground from which to launch a global campaign. The Tompkinses were Israelis, looking to expand the Jewish homeland into Chile. The Tompkinses were agents of the American intelligence community, scouting locales for a subterranean bunker in case of nuclear holocaust. When the Tompkinses began delivering on their promises, this effort, along with their unyielding opposition to the dams, were vital to changing the way many Chileans view their mountains, rivers, forests, and coastline. And it just so happened these initial efforts at national park creation were coming to fruition, just as the antidam factions in Chile were gaining traction over saving the Baker River.

Hernán Mladinic works for Tompkins Conservation and is the executive director of Pumalín Park. The crown jewel of the lands projects of Tompkins Conservation, Pumalín is nine hundred ninety-four

Next spread: A view of Valle Chacabuco in the heart of Chilean Patagonia. Activists, including Doug and Kris Tompkins, worked relentlessly to protect wildlands here. Tehuelche ancestral lands. BETH WALD

thousand acres that stretch from fjords on the Chilean Pacific Coast eastward through mid-elevation rain forests to glacier-capped Andean Peaks. Some two million acres in Chile and Argentina have been set aside through land purchases by foundations, an effort initiated by the Tompkinses. Twelve areas within these two countries are designated as potential national parks.

Doug Tompkins died in a sea-kayaking accident in December of 2015, and the grief felt in the wake of his passing is still palpable in the voices of his friends. "The last dream of Doug was a chain of seventeen national parks that would extend from Puerto Montt all the way to Cape Horn," recalls Mladinic wistfully. "It's a grand vision. But the campaign so far has also created a stronger regional identity for Aysén. People have a stronger sense of belonging to the land. I remember a conversation that Doug had with a stranger in a small town. This man explained how he had worked hard all his life and resented how little he had to show for it. But the man told Doug that because of Tompkins, he no longer worried as much. He said he spent more time appreciating the beautiful place he was living in, that the beauty of Aysén was part of his prosperity too."

I ask Mladinic if this deep level of locals' appreciation for the land would continue if the number of tourists visiting Aysén continues to double each year. He points out that outside the posh fly-fishing lodges, it isn't just foreigners accounting for the increase in visits. Young Chileans are climbing, backpacking, and paddling their way around Aysén in unprecedented numbers. "Douglas thought tourism and conservation could make a good strategic partnership," says Mladinic. "People in Chile are now demanding beauty, not that Patagonia be turned into batteries for the rest of the country." Mladinic explains that it has never been just the Tompkinses' money that made them effective conservationists. They weren't just the faces of the campaign, he says, they were at various times its heart, soul, and brains. "Doug was involved both with the antidam and of course with the parks movement from the very beginning," Mladinic recalls. "Doug designed a lot of the work in the antidam campaign."

David Tecklin has worked on conservation issues in Chile for twenty years. Currently he works for the Pew Charitable Trusts on forestry issues there and knows well the vital role the Tompkinses have played in raising conservation causes to the national level. "It wasn't just the money," Tecklin agrees. "Doug and Kris were also the bridge between the big, international NGOs and the small local groups. They also had access to key government contacts, and they were vital in getting all these factions to work together."

Without a doubt, the Tompkinses have played a starring role in the Sin Represas campaign. But contrary to claims made by some dam proponents, they weren't the only reason the dams haven't been built. And they weren't the first foreigners to fall in love with Patagonia and dedicate an outsized portion of a life's work to protecting the place. Multinational corporations have been trying to exploit Patagonia's resources for quite some time. For thirty-five years, a German transplant to Aysén has been there to fight these companies every step of the way.

Locals, But Not Locals Only

Coyhaique's claim to fame is that it is the seat of Chile's Aysén region, home to fifty thousand people. One of them is Peter Hartmann, a German ex-pat, activist, and architect by training who has lived in southern Chile since embarking on a bicycle tour here in the early 1970s. He's fought in all of Aysén's major environmental battles. With long graying hair and a beard, he looks a svelte, sober Jerry Garcia. We met for coffee on a crisp late summer morning at a café a block from the Plaza de Armas, the round central park that marks the center of Coyhaique's radial street layout. A steady stream of customers wave hello to Hartmann as we talk. "I've been here a long time, but I wasn't born here. And for some of the locals, that's a big difference. They call themselves 'nacidos y criados' [born and raised]. To them, I'm an outsider. But the important thing is to be in love with Aysén, and not worry if you're an insider or outsider."

For most of Chile's existence, Hartmann recounted, Aysén was treated as a colony of Chile. "It was a place for cattle, sheep, timber, and people the government didn't want in Chile," he says. "With the state incentivizing all the wrong things. So, you had transnationals in fishing, transnationals in salmon farming, and in mining." These policies invited the abuse of multiple corporate-backed resource extraction schemes. But things changed. The real beginning of the resistance to the dams was a fight against a proposed aluminum smelter in Aysén. The smelter would have been built in Chacabuco Bay, along with dams on three nearby rivers to power the project. Alumysa is the South American subsidiary of the Canadian mining giant, Noranda, and would have owned the smelter. The antismelter campaign attracted the attention of some international NGOs, initially MiningWatch of Canada, and later the Natural Resources Defense Council (NRDC).

"We won. Alumysa didn't build their smelter. And they complained about it. They said, 'You brought in all this outside influence,'" recalls Hartmann. "Now wait a minute! This is a multinational corporation. So, they say they want globalization. But they only want it for their side. We had globalized solidarity, and in their view, this was not a fair way to fight a globalized corporation." The kind of twisted logic that claims globalism is good only for global companies was applied elsewhere when the debate over dams on the Baker was reaching full pitch. "The press had it wrong. They kept framing the debate as Doug Tompkins vs. HidroAysén. And then there were HidroAysén people broadcasting interviews with local people on the banks of the river. The locals were saying 'Americans are against the interests of Chileans.' No one [from the press] was looking at how the dams would wreck the river, or which parties would gain from the power being exported to the north."

The argument for "local control" remains popular among resource-extractive industries, dam builders included. Antidam activists the world over are badgered by proponents of dams as outsiders who are just trying to keep the locals down with their citified and impractical daydreams about free-flowing, clean water. But stories like Hartmann's bring up an important counterargument: Locals with illusions that multinational corporations will look after them at the expense of profit are kidding themselves.

Hartmann has seen corporate promises evaporate like water in a desert reservoir once the corporation gets its way. "Go to Alto Biobío [where a large dam was built in the late 1990s on the Biobío River]. They were promised all the same things as people on the Baker are being promised: roads, schools, hospitals. You go there now, and it is one of the poorest places in Chile. No jobs. No hospital. High prices. High unemployment. They have a road, but no one travels on it very much." He thinks another dam proposal will eventually be made. But he doesn't have time to worry a lot about it. "There are proposals that are bad for Aysén and bad for the people of Chile that have been made, and that the government has approved," he says.

Just the evening before, he'd sat in a conference with HidroAysén officials eager to advance a smaller hydro project out on the coast, near Puerto Aysén, one that the Chilean government quietly approved in 2011. Energy executives are still making the case that Aysén needs to be exploited for the greater good of Chile. "Pinochet changed the economy," Hartmann told me, "and now we have a neoliberal economy and a neoliberal[3] government. Power concentrated among a few companies, the government, and the courts. People here read about how corrupt the government is, and they quit caring, quit voting. Just like in America, no? What you are talking about is a cultural change, and that takes time. Ten years, at least. We do need a revolution, and we all hope of course that it is a peaceful one. But until then, the water of Aysén is still there for the taking. That is the view of HidroAysén and others." Hartmann thinks implementing the Tompkinses vision of a chain of national parks might be the only way to permanently protect the rivers of Aysén. "We could block them with a National Monument,"

---

[3] "Neoliberal" is a term most Americans might vaguely recall from listening to a Noam Chomsky interview or having read in a college textbook on world history. The word "liberal" throws us off. The phrase denotes an economic and political system of "free" markets, and "limited" government (no regulation and no taxes). In international affairs, it can be associated with a US-dominated, interventionist style of economic "aid" that comes with many pro-American strings attached. Criticism of the programs of the International Monetary Fund, the World Bank, and the World Trade Organization are liberal critiques of neoliberal policies.

says Hartmann. "In the meantime, we win on one front, and they come at us on another."

Not everyone who hates dams in Aysén is enamored of national parks. There are differences amongst the players on the no-dams-for-Aysén team, though dam proponents thus far have been unable to exploit them.

The Paul Revere of the Patagonia Sin Represas movement is a slightly built, fifty-ish *gaucho* with eyes the same shade of electric blue as the Baker River. Aquilino Olivares's ranch, near the confluence of the Baker and Neff Rivers, would be underwater behind a dam if the original plans HidroAysén proposed had been implemented. In 2007, when there was little hope for stopping the dams and saving his ranch, Olivares (and his father) made headlines by hopping on their horses and riding three hundred miles to Coyhaique to protest. Soon, the ride was repeated, with many of his neighbors joining in, some of whom would have been flooded out of their homes if the dams were built. Olivares was cast as the hero who organized a cavalry of pissed off cowboys and their families. Their plight catalyzed the antidam movement, particularly among Chileans who hadn't given the issue of the dams much thought.

I met Olivares in Cochrane, six hours south of Coyhaique, where businesses and schools still shut down on weekdays for a couple hours around noon. This small-town, European-style proclivity helps facilitate the noon-hour takeover of the town square by a giant flock of large green parakeets that dive-bomb randomly selected stray dogs and the occasional pedestrian. One victim, an elderly gentleman sporting a Syracuse University sweatshirt, appears to have been driven legitimately insane by the birds, accosting passers-by with the fervor of a street evangelist. After Olivares arrives, the Syracuse man tries to interject his urgent query about the birds. Olivares dispatches the fellow with a short reply in staccato Chilean Spanish that apparently neither encourages nor offends, and the man wanders off. Olivares's deft read and response to this bird-brained fellow helped convince me of his considerable skill as a communicator. "Here in Cochrane there's still lots of wonder," he says, nodding his head toward the pine tree where the parakeets have settled.

Pioneering antidam activist Don Aquilino Olivares inspects the Neff Glacier in Patagonia. The glacier, along with Olivares's way of life, was threatened by dam construction. Tehuelche ancestral lands, Chile. PADDY SCOTT

"Here you can still live, you can breathe, you can dance, in other parts of the world, well, you breathe and dance, but your spaces are more restricted, and your dangers are very big as well. Here in the Patagonia, there is lots of wide-open space. You can converse with every person and you're safe. Life in Patagonia is a joy. My roots are all here."

All of Olivares's replies to my questions possess the quality of a cowboy poet, not in the laconic, wry-humor-laced western American tradition of that form, but as a *huaso* who somehow has channeled the spirit if not the vernacular of Pablo Neruda. What I want to ask him about is his opinion of transforming working sheep ranches into nature reserves, whose economic value relies on tourism. What would Olivares think of Peter Hartmann's call for a cultural revolution that would help save Patagonian rivers? I knew that Olivares's dual concerns were saving Patagonian culture along with its water. It was far too complex an inquiry for an interviewer that speaks little Spanish, but eventually the gist of the question was clear enough. "We lost the biggest parcel of land that we had in the Baker," says Olivares. "We lost it because it belonged to an American, Douglas Tompkins. He did create a park, which is not a bad thing. I think we should have many other parks in Patagonia. I'm ok with the things that Douglas Tompkins did, but it was very badly executed by the bureaucrats that allowed it to happen. This is a valley meant for grazing. But it was not the fault of Douglas Tompkins, it is the fault of the Chilean law."

If the valley that is now Patagonia Park is "meant" for grazing, the same rules did not apply when a Catholic foundation granted a group of ranching families, for whom Olivares was spokesman, the cash to purchase land on which they could continue to graze livestock and maintain their way of life. These families then sold this land to interests ultimately backing HidroAysén. "When that happened, Aquilino lost a lot of credibility with people involved with Sin Represas," recalls Peter Hartmann. "We were offended by what they did. But I can understand why they did it. There's no money in sheep or cows these days. There never has been much money. But there's less now than ever before. These people live pretty close to a subsistence life. But they do need a little bit of cash income. And they should have the right to graze their animals in some places—just not everywhere."

These kinds of internecine conflicts allow HidroAysén, and companies like it, to deploy the classic colonial strategy of divide and conquer, a possibility the antidam coalition hopes to avoid. That Aquilino Olivares's vision of a future Chile with more nature reserves isn't the same as Peter Hartmann's matters less than their shared opposition to a future Aysén region with more dams. "The project of the Baker and Pascua were dreams floating on foreign capital," says Olivares. "They wanted to execute these megaprojects that, in the end, are only projects for the destruction of Chilean Patagonia. Patagonia is a lung of life for the whole world, a reserve of sweet water. I think it's the only sweet, free water that is worth promoting the world over. We have a nature unlike any place else in the world." He ended with a plea: "I am asking

you, don't merely interview me. You can be a voice, one that partici-
pates and engages in the fight to protect our rights, protect our waters.
The water is not mine, it is not yours; it belongs to all Chileans, and that
is our basic but vital right."

Every movement needs its eloquent leaders, men and women like
Olivares who can inspire thousands of people to march in the streets,
to organize, to speak truth to power. But there is an equal, if not more
pressing need to keep all the paperwork straight.

Elisabeth Schindele, like Peter Hartmann, first came to the Aysén
region from Germany as nothing more than a wide-eyed tourist. She
has ash-blond hair, and is bookish and busy these days, with activism, a
farm, and a tourist business to run, all whilst raising her two kids. There
was a man she met on that initial visit who was as appealing as the scenery. Rosendo Sanchez, like Aquilino Olivares, is a horseman and farmer.
Schindele and Sanchez were quickly smitten with each other. They married. "And then we began looking for land to farm," she says, speaking
English. "And we found our paradise, maybe forty-five minutes southwest of here. We bought it in 1999. Very quickly we added sheep,
cows, chickens, dogs. . ." she laughs. "In America, you would call us a
pioneer family." Their nearest neighbor, five kilometers away, told them
of the visitors in white trucks and vans, who were always smiling, but
would never answer questions. "Everyone knew what had already happened on the Biobío. Then in 2001, we started to build a small irrigation project [that took water from the Río Baker.] And we were told we
cannot have water from the Río Baker. It belonged to HidroAysén," she
recalls. "And without water, we cannot farm."

Worst fears confirmed, Schindele became a founding member and
acting secretary of a small band of local families determined to fight for
their rights. It turned out they didn't have many. "Enel [the Italian parent
company of HidroAysén] owned all the water. What could we do?"

It became clear that the company was somewhat sensitive to public opinion. "What started out to be one giant dam, wiping out thousands of hectares of farms, ours included, became two smaller dams,"
Schindele recalls, of the company's concession to leave a token stretch

of the Baker free-flowing. "But the idea of stopping them seemed ... well I just never thought it would happen."

Not long after Schindele and Sanchez bought their farm, HidroAysén went public with their plans for five dams—two on the Baker, and three on the remote Pascua River farther south. What quickly evolved was an opposition that was, as Peter Hartmann described in the effort to beat back an aluminum plant in the 1980s, global, but also local; determined, but also nimble and flexible. "If you look at Patagonia Defense," says Hartmann of the consortium of more than seventy NGOs that took part in the Patagonia Sin Represas campaign, "those in favor of dams in Aysén will say 'the Tompkins did it.' And then they will use all the usual arguments about outsiders meddling in Aysén matters. But because of Elisabeth, Aquilino, and others like them, the campaign is really elastic. It can respond to local and national and even international concerns. That's part of what made it possible for us to succeed."

A thorough review of the legal document outlining the environmental impact of the proposed dams gave the Sin Represas campaign the means to at least delay the start of construction. But it was a PR campaign that ran the spectrum from Cochrane grassroots to Chilean television, to eventually the Italian parliament that really did the trick.

For Schindele and her family, being on the front lines did not represent any kind of strategic advantage. It simply meant that if they lost, they would lose everything. But she never wanted her activist work to be seen as merely an act of self-preservation. "We always want this work to be not just about us, but about the thousands of people of Aysén who care about the rivers. We want to make sure the government hears us. We don't want or need megaprojects. We need small solutions for small towns. And we need to not sacrifice our rivers. It's our responsibility to make these things known. To remind others," she says.

Having done just that, it still very much seemed the case as the years rolled by that the Baker would be stilled, and the Schindele-Sanchez ranch would go underwater. Then Olivares took his first politically galvanizing horseback journeys to Coyhaique starting in 2007. National and international attention on the Baker grew exponentially.

In 2011, despite growing opposition to the dams, the Chilean government gave final approval to HidroAysén for construction. "I was in Coyhaique then. It was the worst day of my life," recalls Schindele. "It started out with twenty or thirty of us, crying, chanting, drumming. From there it grew, to perhaps two thousand. But the government made enemies of the people that day. They used tear gas on us." Spontaneously, marches all over Chile sprouted. Tens of thousands in Santiago. "There were marches in Paris, Munich, Bucharest," she says.

It wasn't until 2014, however, that the Chilean government put the Baker and Pascua Dam permits into deep sleep mode. But the threat of a scaled-down version of the same project, or damming of different rivers in the region, still looms over the antidam movement in Aysén like a dark cloud over a wind-swept cordillera.

I mention to Schindele how the controversy over the actions of Aquilino Olivares—selling the land to HidroAysén interests after the same property was bought so that his way of life might continue—could be exploited by interests favoring the dam. "The worst outcome of all this, is how this has divided our community. Day after day, we have to live with the consequences of our decision. Cochrane is a small town, without very much opportunity. And so, there are many people who are just looking for someone with money to tell them what to do. This project for the moment is dead. So now we have to examine the consequences of the fight. The community is now divided. A cut will heal. But it could take years."

I ask her if, having achieved veteran status in the planet's dam wars, she has any advice or inspiration to share. *"Se puede,"* she tells me with a smile. We can.

When Antidam Activism Kills

But can we? At least in other countries in Latin America these days, it can be very hazardous to your health to be an antidam activist. Berta Cáceres, the Honduran activist who won international accolades for her grassroots fight on behalf of Indigenous Lenca people against the Agua Zarca Dam, was murdered in her home by a hitman hired by the company overseeing the construction of the dam; the hitman also had ties to the Honduran Army. As described in her book *Hard Choices*, Hillary Clinton—as the US Secretary of State—endorsed and supported new elections after a 2009 coup that ousted democratically elected Manuel Zelaya. Less than a year later, a dam-friendly, business-allied man named Porfirio "Pepe" Lobo was elected president. Lobo proceeded to declare Honduras wide open for exploitation and to crack down on dissidents. In 2015, eight environmental activists were murdered in Honduras, making it one of the most dangerous places in the

In 2020, the human rights group Global Witness tallied 227 environmental activists around the world who had been murdered for having the courage to speak their minds.

world to support clean air and water, healthy forests, or dam-free rivers. In 2020, the human rights group Global Witness tallied 227 environmental activists around the world who had been murdered for having the courage to speak their minds.

In 1997, Juan Pablo Orrego Silva won the same prestigious award that Berta Cáceres did in 2015, the Goldman Environmental Prize, for work on similar dam-prevention issues. The award, granted annually, recognizes activists for "sustained and significant efforts to protect and enhance the natural environment, often at great personal risk," according to the prize's website. Like Cáceres, Orrego was working on stopping a dam on behalf of local Indigenous people.

Orrego, with long, salt-and-pepper hair and a still-youthful visage, has never quite shed the look of a career dissident, an occupation he knows can come with a high price. "At least they aren't shooting at us," Orrego says. "At least for the time being."

I went to Santiago to talk with Juan Pablo Orrego. Before I knew who he was, he was described to me as "the John Muir of Chile." Like

Muir, some of his early efforts at preservation seemed a little kooky to the uninitiated. "When Juan Pablo was organizing the protests of the Biobío Dams," recalls Peter Hartmann, "most people thought he was just some crazy man talking about stopping dams. Now of course he is the most often quoted spokesperson for the Sin Represas campaign. That he's being taken seriously is a tribute to how far the movement has come."

Though murder for the time being is no longer a viable strategy for silencing opponents of unfettered energy development in Chile, and

[The dam] also faces competition from the rapid growth of renewable energy sources. Chile is embracing solar power.

the halting of dams on the Baker and Pascua is a landmark achievement, Orrego takes little comfort in the progress that's been made over the past twenty years. "We've stopped HidroAysén momentarily, just momentarily. In fact, the government invalidated the permits for the dams. They did not revoke them," says Orrego. "And right now there is a case making its way through the appeals courts. HidroAysén claims that those permits are an asset of the company that they should be able to recover. And they want to solve the water rights issue they've faced from the start."

"Solving" for the company involves finding a way to uphold the water law implemented by the Pinochet regime. The prospect of renewing the Baker and Pascua Dam permits comes amidst a blitz of modern problems Chile faces. Orrego describes the grim scenes of poverty and violence on the outskirts of Santiago, a stark contrast to the bright narrative of Chile as a model for sound economic development. "Chile is ... a country of appearances," says Orrego. "These [slums] are not the places where reporters are sent, or politicians go to make speeches. There are thousands in Santiago who are caged in their own homes at night. They are afraid to go outside. We have become a country of haves and have-nots. In some ways like the United States, in other ways much worse." The part that's worse, according to Orrego, is that the degradation of the environment and the erosion of human rights are intertwined in parts of Chile in a way that makes injustice more painfully obvious. "The villages around the mines. The towns around Alto Biobío. These are sacrifice areas where people just get used to living badly. They no longer see alternatives."

In the long term, perhaps the largest trouble Chile, and for that matter, the entire western coast of South America will face is the loss of freshwater access and declining river flows due to the receding of glaciers. To Orrego, this fact alone makes any megadam proposal in his country—and there are others already permitted in the Aysén region—untenable. "We create climate change then compound the problem by destroying watersheds and rivers. We're making it worse and worse with these patchwork solutions. Climate change is affecting Chile in a strong way. Desertification is happening in the North. What we should do is be working backward to make ecosystems whole again, restoring watersheds and restoring rivers. Instead, Aysén is once again in the crosshairs of the government."

Beyond Aysén, a suite of new hydropower projects, most of which would work to the benefit of the copper mining industry in the North and the detriment of everyone else, has Orrego scrambling to help opposition movements organize. Among the most urgent is a diversion tunnel already under construction in the mountains, just an hour east of Santiago, in the valley of the Río Maipo. "It's taking water from high up in the watershed, snow and glacial melt, and putting it into a seventy-four-kilometer-long, six meters in diameter, tunnel. The power generated would go to a mine two hundred kilometers north of Santiago. We find in the newspaper this week that disturbing the watershed in this way is putting arsenic in the river. And this is the watershed for the seven million people of Santiago. It's crazy," says Orrego.

Nearly complete in mid-2021, the 531-megawatt hydroelectric project is faced with reduced capacity because of the region's ongoing drought. It also faces competition from the rapid growth of renewable energy sources. Chile is embracing solar power.

The new hydro project amounts to an old brand of socialism for the rich. The hydropower tunnel is financed by at least nine banks from all over the world, including three American banks designated to underwrite projects in developing countries. Yet 85 percent of the power generated by this project would go to power a copper mine owned by the Luksic Group.

Andrónico Luksic Abaroa was the Chilean son of a Croatian immigrant. He built a fortune in mines, banks, and the beverage industry. He died in 2005, leaving a fortune to his wife and children, estimated in 2011 to be worth over $19 billion. While Chile is apparently in need of further economic development, the Luksic Group is about as economically developed as any business should be. "The lies that sell projects like this one get sold to the public before the banks get involved," says Orrego. "At the height of the Sin Represas campaign, the opposition was running ads showing a hospital room with a team of doctors in surgery when the power goes out. Another showed the lights going out in a stadium during a football match. But recently we've learned that Chile is producing 140 percent of the electricity it needs, and the talk has turned to exporting energy."

The rationale for these new energy projects, as Orrego notes, is not clear; and their ambiguous purpose seems to have infected their financing. AES Gener, a Chilean utility company that became AES Andes in 2021, announced in late July of 2017 that it had defaulted on over $600 million of debt amid cost overruns. A year before, in August 2016, AES Gener ominously warned Alto Maipo would go over budget due to construction difficulties. And in early 2017, Chilean mining company Antofagasta, which held a 40 percent minority stake in Alto Maipo, bade a quiet *adiós* to the project.

Demonstrations against the Alto Maipo project have taken place regularly in Santiago, staged by the thousands of Chileans who flock to the Maipo Valley to hike, climb, ski, and float the river to get away from the pollution, heat, concrete, and crowds of the city. Images of these

A hanging glacier and waterfalls in a land where the rivers still run wild.
Cascada de Ventisquero Colgante, Queulat National Park, Tehuelche
and Chono ancestral lands, Chile. AP IMAGES / OLIVER GERHARD

recent civil demonstrations remind me, I tell Orrego, of the pictures that made international news in the spring of 2011, when sixty thousand people marched in the streets of Santiago, in protest of the government's approval of the Baker and Pascua River dams, numbers that must have seemed impossible when the work Orrego started twenty-five years ago seemed to everyone else to be "a little kooky."

What advice does he have for the leaders of the latest fights against water exploitation? "Work in networks. Know that industry works in really long-term strategies, so you have to be prepared to do the same. Pool your talents. You need people like Peter Hartmann, who has the ability to wade through thousands of pages of documents. You need people that can attract the attention of the media, like Aquilino Olivares. You need students, who have the energy to take to the streets. But you also need to be disciplined with your information. Have faith that monsters can be stopped."

Stomping on a monster's foot takes a certain variety of courage, but also requires faith in higher ideals. For Orrego, encouraging the defense of beauty is as important as the practical directives he issues about the nuances of networking. "The defense of beauty is behind everything we do," says Orrego. "When you bring up the idea of beauty with industry people, they tend to get very sarcastic. If you ask, 'Why do you want to destroy such a beautiful thing?' They'll accuse you of sentimentality, of having emotional problems. But I'm an ecologist. And I've been thinking about these kinds of rebukes. The fact is when you see an ecosystem, because it's complex, because it's diverse, somehow beauty is an external manifestation of ecosystem health and integrity. But beauty also is an important part of human mental health. We need beauty to be really healthy internally."

The notion of beauty, Orrego contends, ought not to be limited to the mountains, flowers, nature poems, or moving water. He sees beauty in the relationships forged among allies. One unlikely coup forged amongst this network occurred when the Catholic Bishop of Aysén Region, Luis Infanti della Mora, who is Italian, was so moved by the pending doom of the rivers in his archdiocese that he flew home to

Italy to scold HidroAysén's parent company, Enel, in its annual share-holder's meeting. Enel is one-quarter owned by the Italian government. "It's beautiful when the Catholic Bishop of Aysén Region goes back to Italy to speak in front of their parliament in his native language about the beauty of Aysén," contends Orrego. "He talks about the 'hydroma-fia' in Chile and the theft of sovereignty, and challenges his audience to think about how all the tiny countries of Europe have been able to live lives so rich in natural resources for so many centuries. And the execu-tives of Enel are listening in shock."

Bishop della Mora, for his part, was unequivocal when I asked him why he made the trip back to Italy, in addition to penning a Pastoral Letter pointing out the ethical breaches and spiritual lapses of any plan to build dams. "You have been to Patagonia Park," he told me as we sat in the dining room of his house back in Coyhaique. "And at the cemetery, where I understand they held a memorial service for Doug Tompkins, there is a sign: 'Beauty is the foremost expression of God.' The land belongs to God. We are part of the land. The suffering of the over-exploited land carries along the suffering of people that are as well exploited with the land."

I relate this story to Orrego, and he drifts into a reverie for a moment. "Douglas—and I like to talk about him in the present tense, because I be-lieve he is still with us—he's a pilot," says Orrego of his departed friend Doug Tompkins. "He has that macro-view. And he had a pilot's eye for the whole picture," Orrego says, letting himself lapse into the past tense. "He was a traveler. He went to Africa. He went to Chernobyl. He wanted to see with his own eyes what was happening all over the world. He's always trying to see the big picture. He wanted you to really see what it is you are looking at. Really study it. And if you really learn to see, it's a di-saster. But Douglas was not pessimistic," Orrego tells me. "He was lucid. If he was pessimistic, he would have just gone into hiding and built a bun-ker somewhere. Everything he did was about transcending the disasters we've made. And the bigger ones we might not be able to avoid."

Orrego is possessed of a buoyant, infectious enthusiasm that he nur-tures in conversation as well as speeches, and sensing that he ended the interview with a downer prognostication about unavoidable disasters was something he wouldn't settle for. "This country is awakening—but they change little things, and the old model is still fouling us. But if we put our minds and bodies and hearts to work," says Orrego, "if we work like Douglas did, and like Berta did—we have to do it ourselves: what a world we could have, man! A world of beauty and intelligence. Paradise. It's still just a minute shift away. We're really still so close to it."

Orrego's vision of a still-attainable earthly paradise is worth contemplating. Places that by luck or design have stayed out of the way of industrial development might be viewed as much more than a mere refuge. If they exist by design, if the human history of their defense is taken into consideration, they could double as blueprints for the rebuilding of a better world, a map for the way out of the ruins. It's possible.

But even in the worst-case scenario, as only a stay of execution, specific little sweet spots like Elisabeth Schindele and Rosendo Sanchez's farm represent the most miraculous victories in the here and now.

I dwell on this after leaving Orrego's Santiago office. I shuttle to the airport through Los Ángeles—the capital of the Biobío Province—amid dense traffic and smog, the Mapocho River running brown, hemmed in its straightened concrete banks, past slums, then fallow, parched fields. Not long after, in a sky the color of a bruise, I'm on a plane headed for Dallas. I sleep almost the whole way, waking over Texas in the inky blackness just before dawn.

Then, I'm thinking of Schindele and Sanchez at their kitchen table, far from any city. The chickens, cows, sheep, dogs, their children are all there. Dawn has blushed the eastern Patagonian sky. Steam rises from two full mugs. A harmonizing sigh before the chores of the day begin. The quick squeeze of hands across the table. The low whisper of lovers who've spent thousands of mornings together.

The rhythmic soft clomp of boots on a wooden floor. A front door opens, then shuts. The exhalations of every mammalian creature vaporize in the cool autumn air, which smells like smoke and honey. There's work to be done, familiar work done with hands and feet and strong backs, familiar enough that it's possible to pause, and watch the sun illuminate the snowcapped peaks above the river valley. To track the sun as it pulls the curtain of night back to the valley floor, and finally, into the river, whereupon, just as the swift shadow recedes to the far bank, the neon blue of the glacier-fed stream gets switched on as instantly as a stage light.

Sunrise catches Texas as the plane descends, hanging in the balance between the world we could have, and the world we have.

THE BLUE HEART OF EUROPE

Continental Europe, with its more than seven hundred million souls, cosmopolitan cities, cathedrals and castles, its autobahns and museums and centers of international trade and finance, its coffee houses and haute cuisine all coming out of its hairy old ears, is not generally lauded for its wild places, unless an all-night bacchanal in Barcelona is your kind of thing. The other kind of wild, as that term applies to untrammeled nature, is in short supply, especially where wild rivers are concerned. Except for one place that the twentieth century overlooked.

East from Italy across the Adriatic, a suite of storybook small and relatively sparsely populated countries harbors the last wild rivers in Europe. Albania, Bosnia, Serbia, Croatia, Montenegro, Macedonia, and Kosovo cover the territory north of Greece, roughly in the shape and angle of an umbrella at a sidewalk café in Athens. Activists hoping to preserve this mountainous, river-bejeweled territory are calling it the Blue Heart of Europe.

Wars, dictators, and oppressive Soviet-era regimes spared wide swaths of these nations from the development bug that ruined

The river time forgot, at least in the twentieth century. The Blue Heart of Europe includes the Vjosa River as it flows unimpeded through Albania.
THOMAS HADINGER

thousands of rivers via worldwide dam building. The oversight left this region known as the Balkans with thousands of miles of streams cut into deep canyons and surrounded by thick forests. The living pieces of this ecosystem are something to marvel at as well. The water itself is remarkably healthy. Of some thirty-five thousand kilometers of streams surveyed by conservation groups in the Balkans, 50 percent were found to be in good condition, and another 30 percent were deemed pristine. Sixty-nine species of fish are endemic to the rivers of the region, including several species of trout found nowhere else in the world.

Globe-trotting trout fishers take note: species of caddis, may, and stoneflies extirpated virtually everywhere else in Europe are thriving here. Higher up the food chain, the fish express their gratitude. The Danube salmon, known locally as the huchen, grows up to one and a half meters in length. A panoply of birds, bugs, turtles, and even a few toothy mammals are still roaming the hills and swimming the waters of the wild Balkans. Cursory biological surveys never before performed in any of these watersheds have yielded a host of previously undocumented organisms. If history is any indication, scientists had better work faster: There are thirty-four hundred dams planned or already under construction in the Blue Heart of Europe.

Ulrich (Uli) Eichelmann grew up in Austria, just in time to watch the rivers of the Bavarian Heart of Europe croak. "I grew up along a river, catching fish with my bare hands, building forts, and fell in love with them then. But I also watched the rivers of my childhood die," he says. The bittersweet upbringing led him to a career in fighting dams, beginning with the World Wildlife Fund in the 1980s. As the specter of climate change crept into conservationists' consciousness, Eichelmann noticed a profound change that's still largely unacknowledged in the world of conservation work. "We used to travel around, looking at the ground," he recalls. "Now everyone is looking up. Land and water, that's where the fight took place. Details about the flora and fauna, that's where you'd find the means to stop a dam or a mine, or the logging of a forest," Eichelmann explains. "But in the 1990s the fight of the largest NGOs became about greenhouse gas emissions, and ways to cut them."

This meant finding alternate means of producing energy. Hydropower still means "green" energy to much of the conservation world. "There's so much money in dam building that for much of its history, if there's a problem, a dam is the answer," says Eichelmann. "Water supply, flood control, power, irrigation, and for a while, fighting global warming. But it's really the same old road of growing the economy by destroying nature." While science continues to disabuse dam promoters of the idea that dams are net greenhouse gas reducers, Eichelmann long ago bailed out of the large NGO nest to continue looking at the water rather than the sky.

> # Hydropower still means "green" energy to much of the conservation world. ... "Water supply, flood control, power, irrigation, and for a while, fighting global warming. But it's really the same old road of growing the economy by destroying nature," [Eichelmann says.]

Alliances have shifted in the dam-busting world, but one constant has been the shady financing of such projects. Public banks—World Bank–style financial institutions designed to catalyze huge infrastructure projects in developing countries, underwritten with taxpayer money—have lavished cash on contractors willing to plug up the Balkans. According to Bankwatch, out of 142 hydropower projects investigated on Balkan Rivers, seventy-five are financed by international financial institutions. Thirty are in protected areas, set aside to preserve biodiversity, rare species, and natural beauty. "There are laws and policies in place that should prevent the banks from dam building in a national park. There are good laws. [But] there is no incentive to enforce," Eichelmann says, adding that the amount of public money going into private contractors' hands is much higher than the Bankwatch study indicates, since private banks are often subsidized with public bank money to undertake dam projects, and are not obliged to report how this money is spent. Eichelmann points out the majority of the planned projects are tiny compared to the megaprojects made famous in China and the United States. "Most of these are not typical dams with a huge reservoir, but rather, because of the limitations of the topography of the area, small diversion projects that will dry up some small streams completely. Everything downstream is decimated. And the benefits go to the company that builds the project, who gets subsidies, and the seller of the power, who gets a thirty-five-year price guaranteed contract, regardless of what happens in the market." This pattern of limited benefit but widespread cost is consistent with dam projects around the globe.

A study by Bent Flyvbjerg, former chair of Major Programme Management at Oxford University's Saïd Business School, analyzed 245 large dam projects in sixty-five countries. He found construction costs run, on average, 96 percent over their budgets, which the study authors point out is a conservative estimate and does not take into account environmental costs or the volatility of currency in developing nations.

Saving the Blue Heart: A Strategy in Two Parts

To stop the damming of the Blue Heart of Europe, Eichelmann is employing a two-pronged strategy. "We have to convince officials in this country and the international community that this jewel is something very special worth saving. And we have to go after the violations, the corruption that is allowing these projects to proceed," he says. On the latter front, Eichelmann coordinates with a battery of attorneys who are scrutinizing everything from the seamy underbelly of hydropower financing to applicable environmental laws. But to draw attention to the otherworldly loveliness of this "jewel," Eichelmann deployed a flock of scientists.

For their initial investigation at Eichelmann's behest, they gathered in the spring of 2017 on the Vjosa River, which runs nearly undammed from its source in the Pindus Mountains in Greece, then bisects Albania on its way to the Adriatic Sea. Albania has been obsessed with dams in the post-Soviet era, permitting 435 hydro projects from 2007 to 2013. Two large dams were given the green light on the Vjosa. The hydrologists, entomologists, and ecologists spent a week in the field, sampling, weighing, measuring, observing, and describing the flora, fauna, and flow of the Vjosa. The results were even more impressive than the scientists were expecting. They identified species of mayfly and stonefly cataloged nowhere else in Europe that week on the Vjosa. They photographed a plant-hopping insect new to the annals of entomology for the first time. They found so much undocumented life along the last large, undammed river in Europe, that the scientists decided the discoveries merit their own book. Beyond the bugs, they found species of amphibians, birds, and fish that are rare or altogether missing for decades from the rest of the continent's rivers. These experts also took the time to put their heads together and make some general prognostications about what would be lost should either of the two dams proposed for the area be built. The short list of consequences includes:

- deterioration of groundwater resources;
- development of toxic algal blooms due to the flooding of fertile agricultural areas;
- endangering of rare habitat;
- increased coastal erosion due to the drastic reduction of sediment transport by the river;
- loss of livelihood for the residents in the affected area, as their agricultural fields are to be drowned in the projected dam reservoir; and
- considerable reduction of energy production within a period of about thirty years, as the dam reservoir fills up with the high sediment load of the river.

Science week on the Vjosa was strategically planned to closely precede a critical court date. The legal team defending the Vjosa would argue that dam proponents didn't do their homework, and that the

Next spread: Kalivac dam site on the Vjosa River in Albania. The dam project had an inadequate environmental report, protestors rallied against it, and the project was abandoned in 2021. ANDREW BURR

required Environmental Impact Assessment (EIA) as well as the public consultation process were legally insufficient. In May of 2017, judges on the Albanian Administrative Court in Tirana announced their decision that dam builders had not followed the law well enough, and a minimum three-year delay on breaking ground at the proposed dam site was also granted, so that a proper EIA could be performed. The Ministry of the Environment rejected the project in 2020. Uli Eichelmann, while thrilled at the temporary reprieve, views it only as a stepping stone to saving more rivers in the Blue Heart. "You've got to have a good strategy. You've got to find ways to motivate others," he says. "Most of us value beauty, and that will be part of our appeal. We need to keep repeating our message. You want to see a real living river? Go to the Balkans."

A huchen (*Hucho hucho*). Also known as the Danube salmon or redfish, it's endemic to the waters of the Blue Heart of Europe and grows to five feet (1.5 m) long. HERBERT FREI

DRAIN POWELL FIRST

Don't ask for what is reasonable. Ask for what is right.
– Martin Litton, legendary Grand Canyon River guide

It was wrong. – Stewart Udall, US Secretary of the Interior who oversaw the Bureau of Reclamation during the construction of Glen Canyon Dam, commenting in a PBS interview on the decision to build the dam.

One October day in 1776, two Franciscan priests, Father Francisco Atanasio Domínguez and Father Silvestre Vélez de Escalante, got good and lost in what is now southern Utah. They were trekking with eight others, having set out months earlier from their Catholic mission home in Santa Fe, New Mexico. They were hoping to establish an overland route to the missions in California. For twelve days they searched with increasing desperation for a way to cross the Colorado River, finally finding a suitable ford on November 7, 1776. Having crossed to safety, the good Fathers decided that they'd seen enough and humped it back to

Glen Canyon Dam and Reservoir Powell. The dam drowned the canyon that was the traditional home of the Navajo, Hopi, and Southern Piaute people. Arizona. GIANFRANCO VIVI

Santa Fe. The canyon where they must have contemplated what salvation would look like if they could not find their way was named by Father Escalante: Sal Si Puedes (Get Out If You Can). The place they crossed the Colorado now lies under a few hundred feet of water in Padre Bay, on Reservoir Powell, the impoundment behind Glen Canyon Dam.

Roughly 240 years later, three of us latter-day explorers are traveling a portion of Escalante's road in an enormous white rental SUV, headed into the hinterlands on a washboard BLM road. This, too, is a mission, though more fact-finding than route-finding. Eric Balken is executive director of the Glen Canyon Institute, founded in 1996 with what was then a radical goal: making clear to the public that Glen Canyon Dam is expensive and unnecessary. Reservoir Powell is drying up, and portions of Glen Canyon have re-emerged. Will the place where the fathers crossed be un-drowned someday soon? We will walk along the stretches of Father Escalante's namesake river, as part of the ongoing work to answer these questions. That's assuming the early spring rain and snow will cease, and the long dirt road to the trailhead doesn't turn to gumbo. *Entra si puedes*. Get in if you can.

The weather holds, skies clearing as we park just in time for sundown. Yet solitude in Utah's canyon country isn't what it used to be back in the padres' day. It's March, and there are a dozen other cars at the end of the road. You can't blame anyone for wanting to be here. Balken fills a small rucksack full of beers, and we head west on foot into the slickrock, it's cartoonish landforms and gargantuan expanses of earth and sky beckoning. Cairns mark the way toward the canyon. Atop the sienna-colored nose of a fifteen-hundred-foot-tall cliff face, we peer down into the Escalante. "There's Stevens Arch," Balken points out. "The reservoir used to back up the Escalante all the way to it. Tomorrow, you'll be able to see where the river's running again."

Fill Mead First: The Reasoning Behind Letting a Damned Dam Stand

In the gloaming at the edge of the cliff, it occurs to me that we're here to witness the early signs of a protracted emergency. The Colorado River is drying up. Its flow has been reduced dramatically by climate change already, and in another century, may be as little as half of twentieth-century normal. But normal was overestimated in the first place.

Seven states, thirty First Nations, and Mexico all ascribe to the Colorado River Compact. That agreement, signed in 1922, overestimated the amount of water the river annually delivers. In the early 1940s, the agreement was amended so that at least a trickle of the river would make it into Mexico. But farther north, a different and far more arbitrary border became an excuse to build Glen Canyon Dam. The seven states in the Compact are divided north and south: Colorado, Wyoming, New Mexico, and Utah comprise the upper-basin states, while Arizona, Nevada, and California form the lower-basin contingent. The Compact estimated wrongly that fifteen million acre-feet could be put to use for domestic, industrial, and agricultural purposes. But in reality, only ten to thirteen million have historically been available. Despite the overestimated flow, under the terms of the Compact, upper-basin states must maintain the capability to deliver half of those fifteen million acre-feet to the lower basin in years of average water conditions. The border between the upper and lower basin is the Utah and Arizona state line. In 1936, Hoover Dam and Reservoir Mead, 250 river miles south of that border, started to provide adequate storage for the lower basin. But in the 1950s, when BuRec was coming up with as many different rationales to build a dam as possible, the notion was floated that water storage was needed at the basin's mid-point to ensure that the upper basin could guarantee water to the lower basin. Never mind that for the first forty-one years of the Compact gravity alone delivered the water across the basin's middle border to the lower basin without any help from BuRec. Glen Canyon Dam and Reservoir Powell were never a necessity and are increasingly looking like an outdated redundancy.

In late 2021, the elevation of Reservoir Mead dipped below 1,075 feet (above sea level), 40 percent of total capacity. (When full, the elevation of Mead is over twelve hundred feet. Since 1999, the last year it was close to full, the reservoir has lost 125 feet of water, lending it the white "bathtub" ring effect that continues to grow each year.) As I write this, Mead—the largest reservoir in the United States, supplying water to twenty-five million people, has dropped to 1,067 feet, 35 percent of capacity. Another forty-five feet worth of drop and the delivery of hydropower is threatened. Another 120 feet below that, and Reservoir Mead is at "dead pool," meaning all the services it was designed to provide will no longer be possible. Yet 250 miles upstream lies another reservoir, Powell, that is at less than a quarter of "full pool."

A quorum of conservation groups, the Glen Canyon Institute among them, have posed a logical question: Why operate and maintain two huge reservoirs each less than half full? "We're not advocating for dam removal. Complete removal of Glen Canyon Dam is too expensive anyway," Balken tells me as we roll out our sleeping bags and pads in the windbreak between two cars. "We're advocating for filling Mead first." The concept is simple enough. It's an argument based on efficiency. Sacrifice Reservoir Powell. Drain it to its bypass tunnels in the forebay. Reconfigure the tunnels to facilitate easier draining of the reservoir and let the wilderness garden that once blossomed in Glen Canyon restore itself. "The drought is doing our work for us." It's a catchphrase I've heard from several advocates of Fill Mead First. It merits further scrutiny.

Many stakeholders, including some major river conservation groups, oppose Fill Mead First. They believe, despite the overwhelming evidence to the contrary, in an incremental effort to keep both Reservoirs Powell and Mead operational. The Metropolitan Water District of Southern California, Central Arizona Water Conservation District, Denver Water, and the Southern Nevada Water Authority are pooling millions of dollars to pay upper-basin farmers to fallow fields and let their allotted water flow all the way to Reservoir Mead.

A host of minor changes—some helpful, some of dubious benefit—have been proposed to "save" the Colorado by saving Glen Canyon Dam. In December of 2015, The US Department of the Interior announced what the media called its "moonshot for water" initiative. The fine print reveals just a few wrinkles in a dreadfully familiar game plan: public/private partnerships investing in more diversions and storage projects, and a streamlined regulatory process to speed construction. An emphasis on innovation is relegated to plumbing: new pipes, better sprinklers, and an emphasis on water efficiency and re-use. But these plans don't so much divert water as they do the public's attention. The real trouble isn't with the water pipes.

Federal government-built dams on the Colorado River already deliver water in lavish proportion to farms in the basin. About 70 percent of the water diverted into reservoirs is used to supply agriculture and related interests. The number one crop in the Colorado Basin is alfalfa, a water sucking, low-value grass that cows devour on their way to becoming cheeseburgers. Much of this forage for cattle is being exported (in the empty returning containers)—to China, Japan, and Saudi Arabia,

Las Vegas is building a $1.4 billion dollar drainpipe into the bottom of Reservoir Mead, so that, when it reaches dead pool, the fountains at the Bellagio will keep on pumping.

to feed the cheeseburgers of the Middle and Far East. Export forage in the state of Utah alone is now a $124 million a year business. The new market has increased the amount of acreage devoted to alfalfa in the Colorado Basin, even as total farm acreage has dropped. More water to meet market demand is being called for.

The Bureau of Reclamation has approved a large new controversial diversion of water out of the Upper Colorado River, pushed forward the permitting process for a controversial new diversion in New Mexico, and stayed silent on a massive new diversion in Wyoming. In Utah and Colorado, large new dams proposed by other federal agencies await permits. Two permits for dams were granted by the Trump administration, with an eye toward fast-tracking more. Farmers aren't the only thirsty party.

Las Vegas is building a $1.4 billion dollar drainpipe into the bottom of Reservoir Mead, so that, when it reaches dead pool, the fountains at the Bellagio will keep on pumping. Not to be outdone, development

Next spread: Reservoir Powell in 2022. As water levels recede, it becomes possible to explore on foot the re-emerging wonders of Glen Canyon in tributaries around the Escalante River. Navajo, Hopi, and Southern Paiute ancestral lands, Utah. PETE MCBRIDE PHOTOGRAPHY

boosters in Utah are pushing for yet another straw to be installed in Reservoir Powell, this one a 139-mile-long pipeline headed south that would deliver twenty-eight billion gallons of water a year to Saint George so that the city can continue its exponential growth.

The federal moonshot for water initiative would improve efficiency, but put no limits on use. Efficiency, in the federal western water control world, is dedicated not to saving a reservoir or river, but to "total use for greater wealth," that telling turn of phrase deployed by the Bureau at the peak of its mid-twentieth century dam-building powers. Efficiency is simply a more expedient means by which a few people can turn water into money. This is still, in spite of the myriad climate chaos–driven calamities in plain view of anyone who lives in the American Southwest, the main purpose of the United States Bureau of Reclamation.

Yet to advocates of a free-flowing Colorado River, what's happening in the basin is a catastrophe with a very tangible silver lining. The goal the Glen Canyon Institute was created to achieve has been partially won by a prolonged drought. Evidence gathered from tree-ring surveys indicate the drought currently plaguing the Colorado is the worst in at least a thousand years. The proper term for this prolonged dry spell is aridification. The word connotes permanent dryness, at least in human time scales.

Some historical droughts have lasted for a quarter century, including the one that may have played a role in driving the Indigenous Anasazi people out of the canyon country in Utah, New Mexico, and Arizona. These long droughts occurred before humans unlocked the warming power of millions of years of stored carbon. How long a drought driven by dinosaur juice might last is anyone's guess. In the meantime, water use has exceeded the ability of the snowpack and rainfall to recharge reservoirs in every year since 2000. Big reservoirs are quickly shrinking.

The Hazards of Not Removing Glen Canyon Dam

Back at the Escalante, we settle in for the night, but a rhetorical query keeps me from shutting my eyes: To what extent is the notion of "drought doing the work of conservationists" simply the flip side of devil-may-care attitudes about other climate-induced calamities? After all, a long dry spell could mean the mothballing of Glen Canyon Dam. And yet: outside the realm of ancient myth, it seems justice as a function of the weather is a rare occurrence.

Nature, as we're reminded in the platitudes of bumper-sticker lore, bats last. The return of perennially parched conditions in the Colorado Basin has precipitated the partial return of a wilderness lost when the gates at Glen Canyon Dam were closed in 1963. This paradise re-revealed has also rekindled some previously dormant questions about the future of water and civilization along the length of the Colorado. The more Glen Canyon dries out, the more grottoes, slot canyons, and hanging flower gardens return, the more its admirers seem to remember the river once had a purpose other than watering field and town. As Balken pointed out on our evening walk, the Escalante River is free-flowing as it passes along in its canyon adjacent Stevens Arch. Other notable landmarks, the Anasazi ruins at Moqui Canyon and Cathedral in the Desert, have also re-emerged. These days, it's a boat ride and a hike to witness Rainbow Bridge, when before at full pool you could have floated your boat beneath that same iconic arch.

Attempting to drift off to sleep, I snicker at the absurdity of three environmentalists using a behemoth SUV as a windbreak. And as if in defiance of my conception of the weather as an inscrutable force, the wind kicks up, swirls beneath the cavernous underside of the rental rig, and blows a fine sandstone powder into every orifice on my head. The work of expelling it from my ears, eyes, nose, and throat keeps me up, and after that I'm too awake to sleep. I flip on my headlamp and read some of my scrawled notes, landing on a lament from Ed Abbey on the drowning of Glen Canyon. "There was a time," he wrote, "when, in my search for essences, I concluded that the canyonland country has no heart. I was wrong. The canyonlands did have a heart, a living heart, and that heart was Glen Canyon and the golden, flowing Colorado River." I pull the hood on my sleeping bag up over my head, turn off my headlamp, and wonder if conservation strategies based solely on the

A sandstone maze in the heart of Escalante Canyon country. Navajo,
Hopi, and Southern Paiute ancestral lands, Utah. ELIOT PORTER /
AMON CARTER MUSEUM OF AMERICAN ART (See note on page 321)

rationale of efficiency are a worthy defense of any place with a heart.
And does Glen Canyon still have one? Tomorrow we'll get to see if we
can detect a pulse.

Early the next morning, we follow those same cairns back to the edge
of the canyon and find the path down into the Escalante. We arrive at

the crux of the downhill portion of the hike. The entrance to the canyon squeezes through a narrow slot not two feet wide called Crack in the Rock. Getting to the upper end of the crack requires a mild scramble, then a sideways shuffle between the canyon wall and a massive slab of sandstone that calved from high off the wall above. It's tight. We watch from above as a party of six, led by a professional guide, struggles through the crack. The largest fellow in the contingent, a graybeard well over six feet tall with a protruding beer belly, nearly gets stuck. To his credit, he doesn't panic, taking the wisecracks of his companions with good humor as he coaxes his considerable mass through the constriction. The group emerges dusty and sweaty, but totally elated. "Where the lake used to be," one woman chortles, "it's like God made a whole new little bit of beautiful earth."

The morning chill burns off. We hop down through a boulder-strewn willow thicket and greet the free-flowing Escalante. Back at the rim, I thought the description the woman at Crack in the Rock offered was exaggerated. It wasn't.

For several miles downstream of Stevens Arch, the Escalante, once again flowing on the oxygen side of the Earth's crust after a relatively brief hiatus beneath the slack water of Reservoir Powell, is rapidly recolonizing its little niche. Here and there along the banks, at the mouth of side-canyon creeks, appearing like randomly segmented remnants of some ancient fortification, crumbling walls of sand line the Escalante's banks. This is what's left of the mind-boggling load of sediment that so rapidly clogged the ancient path of the Escalante River during the first forty years of its Glen Canyon–dammed existence. "What amazes me is how fast the river moved all the sediment out of the way," says Balken as we examine the cobbled riverbed. "Back down to its original level." Right now, the sediment can't move far enough. Where the reservoir begins, sediment transfer ends.

Canyon country tends to be a place where parties spread out, seeking a healthy distance from each other. Balken and I separate, perhaps a quarter mile between the two of us. There's too much to look at, see, and feel. Millions of years are visible in canyon walls. Space and time stretch in this stone-walled vault with its cobalt sky as a lid. Among the initial treats in this visual and aural feast of revitalized river, of water over rock, of birdsong, and of bug life: a copse of thirty-foot-tall willows looms over a windblown pile of remnant sediment, the amorphous windrow reminiscent of the ruins of a sand castle after the ravage of high tide. I stop to admire a complex of springs spilling out of the canyon wall, covering one house-sized boulder in a perfect, clear skin of flowing water, a feature as finely wrought as in any zen garden.

A flaw in the Fill Mead First plan is that this could all go under again. The re-emerged portion of the Escalante, its tall new willows, its flowing springs, its chattering birds, and a hundred other places like it, will never be safe from repeated inundation if, as some advocates of draining the reservoir claim, they will concede that the Glen Canyon Dam should remain in place. The most glaring fault with leaving a dam like Glen Canyon intact will be the temptation for future politicians and water bureaucrats to once again close the floodgates, presumably during years of high water, but also at the behest of the same short-sighted practices that got the Colorado in so much trouble to begin with. The hazards of leaving the dam intact have yet to be parsed by advocates of the plan. Here are a few of the most obvious ones:

- Repeated flooding and draining of Reservoir Powell would simply create an attractive nuisance for wildlife that would recolonize the revegetating reservoir area when it is refilled periodically. This would force expanding terrestrial wildlife populations out of the reservoir area as it fills and cause adjacent competition, predation, and displacement. Periodic flooding would prevent restoration and revegetation from occurring effectively or completely.

- Often forgotten in the lament over the drowning of Glen Canyon has been the biological impoverishment Glen Canyon Dam has caused to the Grand Canyon immediately downstream. Depriving the Grand of river-born sediment and nutrients has negatively altered the ecosystem of one of the world's most revered places. It helped cause the extinction of a number of species of native fish of the Colorado, and the endangered status of several others. Deprived of sediment, beaches for boaters and, more importantly, a healthy riparian eco-system in the Grand have both dwindled since Glen Canyon Dam was built. A Fill Mead First–scenario would not replenish missing sediment downstream of Glen Canyon Dam.

- Periodic refilling of Reservoir Powell would increase, or at the very least, continue methane emissions as new vegetation grows, dies, then decomposes underwater. Studies show that reservoir emissions are particularly high when reservoir levels are ramped up and down for hydropower or irrigation operations.

- Ongoing drain-and-fill cycles in wet and dry years would add insult to injury amongst the half dozen tribes with sacred ties to holy places like Rainbow Bridge. Drowning and resuscitating sacred places must feel to these tribes a little like waterboarding Pope Francis would feel to good Catholics.

- The largest recreational benefit of restoring Glen Canyon, both economically and aesthetically, is to restore multi-week adventures. Fill Mead First, with the monolith of Glen Canyon Dam still in place, would prevent boaters from passing through what should be the erstwhile site of the dam. A buzzkill trap-and-truck operation for recreational floaters would be required, and a cordoned-off river, replete with official warning signs to stay away from the gargantuan bypass tunnels, and a human collection area just upstream would remain, solely to drive people and boats up and around the dam to relaunch downstream.

- Any Fill Mead First plan would require ongoing operations and maintenance budgets, and a line item in congressional appropriations, all for the purpose of keeping an ill-conceived and outdated project on federal life support. It won't be cheap to maintain a fleeting hope that the project will somehow pencil out. At least one Fill Mead First proposal includes maintaining new hydropower turbines in the bypass tunnels, which would meet two vital criteria for wasteful government spending: 1) wildly expensive; and 2) impossible to put to good enough use to recover a reasonable portion of the expense or to provide adequate public benefit.

Beauty Compels Us Toward a Moral Obligation

So yes, like some conservationists, I'm skeptical of Fill Mead First. But not in the name of timid incrementalism, or as a sop to powerful interests some of these skeptical conservationists seem obliged to accommodate. Certainly not to save Glen Canyon Dam. This absurd position reflects some of the more vexing challenges of the modern conservation movement.

The kind of work environmentalists used to do—think of Edward Abbey and company unraveling the long black plastic "crack" down the face of Glen Canyon Dam, or the Sierra Club's 1966 national ad campaign comparing a proposed Colorado dam to flooding the Sistine Chapel—has fallen out of favor. In its place, a new, more sophisticated and generally improved generation of activists, highly qualified professionals, working for a myriad of sizes and shapes of nonprofit organizations, frequently possessing advanced degrees in law, communications, and science, are doing the lion's share of environmental work. Many of these greenies-gone-pro are friends of mine. They are doing difficult work. Some of them are doing their jobs well enough that they have earned the wrath of powerful enemies. Concurrently, criticism of this model of environmental advocacy is not lacking, and some of it, not without merit.

One of the more significant obstacles to generating momentum for removal of Glen Canyon Dam is that one of the main sources of funding for Colorado Basin conservation work, a large foundation created by the founders of Walmart, works actively against the idea. Why? The reasons are speculative.

Some recipients of this corporate-derived largesse forbear the option to enter litigation over violations of environmental law, creating a bizarre scenario where environmental groups meet payroll by agreeing to not uphold environmental laws. These groups also agree that communication on any given issue that pops up will be coordinated to achieve standardized messaging. Recipients of this funding are thus subject to a quandary. The money they receive has strings attached to the way the funder, tacitly or not, wishes to see business done. With office space to rent and employee retirement accounts to match, the temptation for some nonprofits to settle on what appears as a reasonable solution has eclipsed the dogged pursuit of what's right, which in turn displaces the consideration of what ought to be. The notion that Glen Canyon can be rescued by leaving in place the dam that destroyed it is morally troublesome. The technical issues are secondary.

The fight over the fate of the Colorado in the 1950s and '60s was part of a fight over the soul of the country. It wasn't the only conflict of that

The notion that Glen Canyon can be rescued by leaving in place the dam that destroyed it is morally troublesome.

turbulent era, and far from the most important one. And yet it shared the rhetoric of morality, conscience, and consciousness that was deployed in ultimately successful campaigns to set aside wilderness, to protect air and water, and to preserve biodiversity. The necessary economic and scientific arguments had a seat on that bus but did not drive it.

Fill Mead First has technical issues, but its lack of heart is its fatal flaw. Matters of the heart cannot be effectively addressed via arguments steeped solely in statistics or the strict adherence to efficiency as an unconditional highest virtue. Skeptics may scoff at the notion that justice is central to the issues surrounding Glen Canyon Dam, but the first conservationists to protest its destruction gave defiant witness to what they saw as a grave injustice, a horrific tragedy that occurred when the gates of the dam were closed.

David Brower led the fight that saved portions of the Grand Canyon from dams, yet in negotiating the deal that saved the Grand, he acquiesced to the condition that he not contest BuRec's plans for damming Glen Canyon, a deal he almost immediately regretted and continued to lament for the rest of his life. In the preface to *The Place No One Knew*, photographer Eliot Porter's stunning tribute to the loss of Glen Canyon,

Brower wrote: "Glen Canyon died in 1963, and I was partly responsible for its needless death. So were you. Neither you nor I, nor anyone else, knew it well enough to insist that at all costs it should endure. ... So a steel gate dropped, choking off the flow in the canyon's carotid artery, and from that moment the canyon's life force ebbed quickly. ... At this writing the rising waters are destined to blot out everything of beauty which this book records."

Brower goes on to outline the moral issue at stake,

> "The best of the canyon is going or gone. Some second-best beauty remains along the Colorado, but much of its meaning vanished when Glen Canyon died. The rest will go the way Glen Canyon did unless enough people begin to feel uneasy about the current interpretation of what progress consists of—unless they are willing to ask if progress has really served good purpose if it wipes so many of the things that make life worthwhile.
>
> Evolution demonstrates the value of learning from mistakes; so perhaps we can evolve a subservient technology—one that follows man rather than leading him. The closing of Glen Canyon Dam in our time was a major mistake to learn from.
>
> Good men, who have plans for the Colorado River whereby 'a natural menace becomes a natural resource' would argue tirelessly that the Colorado must be controlled, that its energy should be tapped and sold to finance agricultural development in the arid West. But our point is that for all their good intentions these men had too insular a notion of what man's relation to his environment should be, and it is a tragedy that their insularity was heeded. The natural Colorado—what is left of it—is a miracle, not a menace. The menace is more likely the notion that growth and progress are the same, and that the gross national product is the measure of the good life."

Social critic as much as environmentalist, Brower challenged the staid, prissy politics of a toothless conservation movement. It simply would not do to have a few polite couch liberals negotiate to save a flower or two while a vast garden belonging to the American public was drowned. That he became more outspoken, more controversial, more embittered, and more influential as he aged suggests his own expanding awareness that the stakes in the battle in which the nascent conservation movement intervened would prove to be as great as any humanity has faced.

Environmentalists, including those now working in the Colorado Basin, revere what Brower did. They know better than Brower could how profoundly the fate of humanity and the fate of nature are intertwined. It is a point still frequently evoked in conservation circles too, that this common fate creates in people of conscience a moral imperative to protect and restore the wonders of the Earth. "Our politics and science," writes Wendell Berry, "have never mastered the fact that people need more than to understand their obligation to one another and to the Earth; they need also the feeling of such obligation, and the feeling can only come within patterns of familiarity. A nation of urban nomads, such as we have become, may simply be unable to be enough disturbed by the destruction of the ecological health of the land, because the people's dependence on the land, though it has been expounded to them over and over again in general terms, is not immediate to their feelings."

One vital purpose of national parks, of wilderness, of any untrammeled half-acre on Earth, must be to rekindle this affinity for the good earth, to make its riot of life once again immediate to our feelings, if for no other reason, that we might rise more indignantly and compassionately to its, and our own, defense. That wild places affirm our kinship with land and water and with each other and can therefore be a place where not only evolution, but revolution begins, helps to explain why so many authoritarian interests hate the idea of any quadrant of the planet left undrilled or unplowed.

The kind of feelings Brower had—ones that he allowed to inform his opinions, and to permeate his eloquent writing—also helped formulate

Next spread: A trio of hikers are dwarfed by the scale of the stone in a re-emerging canyon upstream of a shrinking Reservoir Powell. Glen Canyon, Navajo, Hopi, and Southern Paiute ancestral lands, Utah. TAD NICHOLS

his sharp distinctions between growth and progress, and of offense at the notion of a river as a menace. The moral code he followed may be as simple as the one Aldo Leopold was so concise about in composing his land ethic: "A thing is right when it tends to preserve the integrity, stability, and beauty of the biotic community. A thing is wrong when it tends not to." It was, and still is, this well-defined sense of right and wrong that makes those lucky enough to have known Glen Canyon when it was free flowing speak of the loss as they might the death of a loved one. Just as palpable is their rage at having suffered the loss of what all who saw it agree was one of the most beautiful places on Earth.

... Glen Canyon Dam should be reduced to rubble as soon as possible. Sound logic, legal, economic, and scientific arguments have already been built around this simple proclamation.

If Brower's introduction was tinged with the pain of inconsolable re-gret, photographer Eliot Porter seemed to be determined to leave his record of Glen Canyon not as a eulogy, but as a promise: "We shall seek a renewed stirring of love for the Earth," he wrote in the epilogue to *The Place No One Knew*. "We shall urge that what man is capable of doing to the Earth is not always what he ought to do, and we shall plead that all Americans, here, now, determine that a wide spacious untrammeled freedom shall remain in the midst of the American earth as living testi-mony that this generation, our own, had love for the next."

Sitting next to re-emerged springs spilling out of a canyon wall that was buried under Reservoir Powell for most of my lifetime, listening to the subtle, joyous music moving water makes, it's possible to sense that the love Porter described may yet come to fruition. The drought is not doing our work for us but is reminding us that the work is still possible, still desirable, and still needs to be done. "Never forget that justice is what love looks like in public," advises philosopher Cornel West. Glen Canyon restored, as a "wide, spacious untrammeled freedom in the midst of the American earth," as the Sierra Club envisioned it, would be among the nation's finest public monuments to justice, to beauty, and to the love that beauty inspires. It would, on the other hand, be a travesty if, in another forty years, this place was once again buried under water for no good reason. Justice would be truncated if the work the drought has begun is not finished by those who care enough to do it.

For the sake of the health of the Colorado River, for the love this generation has for the next, for justice that was denied when that gate dropped some sixty years ago, choking the life out of the river, Glen Canyon Dam should be reduced to rubble as soon as possible. Sound logic, legal, economic, and scientific arguments have already been built around this simple proclamation. All that's needed is the patience and determination to carry it out.

Remove Glen Canyon Dam First. We'll remove Hoover Dam later.

For the Love of the Good Earth

I proceed on. My good hosts from the Glen Canyon Institute are now completely out of sight. I could use a good map, though I am not worried about getting lost. I just want a little help visualizing the surrounding country, a vulture's-eye view of the territory. I rest for a moment, sip water, and drink in the scenery. My water-logged running shoe rests on a round rock, and when I pick it up, I see it's an odd little crosscut section of petrified wood. As if some ancient Anasazi with a mesquite-powered chop saw was cutting little round medallions of wood upon which summer camp enrollees could emblazon their names. Maybe it was a piece of bristlecone pine trunk from high up on Boulder Mountain, the headwaters of the Escalante. Probably it was already petrified when Father Silvestre Vélez de Escalante himself happened by it one autumn afternoon in 1776, despondent after nearly two weeks of searching for a way to cross the Colorado. Did he catch the same glint off the old wood cookie as I did, turn it over in his palm, and chuck it back in the creek after deciding it was too heavy to cart around in his holy rucksack?

I carry the rock like some sort of talisman as I slog downriver, musing about how many times explorers laying out the course of the western American empire misconstrued the country and got lost. Sal Si Puedes, the good father christened his crossing, with more than a hint in that naming of a sentiment of good riddance.

If patterns of familiarity are, as Wendell Berry suggests, necessary ground for cultivating an emotional, and therefore ethical loyalty to a place, Father Escalante failed, as most of the rest of our colonial culture has, to be sufficiently observant about what those patterns might look like here. It's not so much that he lost his way. His expedition may have been the first group of white people to experience both Glen Canyon and the Grand Canyon. Escalante's reaction to both natural wonders is underwhelming. What so occupied his mind that he could dismiss this place? You wouldn't expect him to be as perspicacious as that more ebullient outdoor supplicant, John Muir, who correctly and uncannily guesstimated the driving forces behind the shape of Yosemite. The good father would not have been able to differentiate between Wingate and Navajo sandstone no matter how long or hard he contemplated the canyon. But you might reasonably expect him to figure out there was no need to starve to death. However, that didn't happen. Escalante's focus was elsewhere. Whether he had his eyes on the prize of glorifying God full-time as he'd been trained to do, or earning a reputation as an explorer by establishing a road to California, or just couldn't get his mind off hot soup and a warm bed back at the Mission in Santa Fe, we'll never know.

Escalante can be forgiven for not appreciating Glen Canyon for the natural wonder it is. He needn't be held accountable for not singing more lofty praises of the scenery with his very survival at stake. But his failures of perception, and the subsequent disdain, however mild, for terra incognita that could be both menacing and heart-wrenchingly beautiful represent a missed opportunity.

It was almost a century later that John Wesley Powell, starting out with nine men and four boats ill-equipped for whitewater travel, spent the summer of 1869 exploring the length of the Colorado. Powell's journals record the tribulations of a ragged bunch, always wet, frequently nearly drowned, sometimes starving, and occasionally enthralled by what they saw. Powell and his crew took time to describe, label, and name places, always carefully, sometimes poetically. "On the walls, and back many miles into the country, numbers of the monument-shaped buttes are observed," wrote Powell that summer. "So, we have a curious ensemble of wonderful features. Carved walls, royal arches, glens, alcove gulches, mounds, and monuments. From which of these shall we select a name? We decided to call it Glen Canyon."

Sixty-eight years later, Buzz Holmstrom, a gas station attendant from the tiny Oregon logging town of Coquille, floated through Glen Canyon in the fall of 1937, the only solo traverse ever taken of more than a thousand miles of the free-flowing Green and Colorado Rivers. Repeating the journey is no longer possible because of dams. He built the lapstrake-hulled wooden dory he rowed, and after greasing Grand Canyon on his own, rowed through flatwater on Reservoir Mead for four days to symbolically thump the bow of his homemade boat against the crest of the newly completed Hoover Dam. Holmstrom's journal too, relates the impressions of an ordinary man taking on extraordinary hardship just for fun—for the reward of letting himself be utterly beguiled by the landscape.

This feeling—what E.O. Wilson later identified as "biophilia," the instinctive bond between human beings and other living systems—was, and still is, a palpable force in Glen Canyon, one of those great nerve centers of the Earth, a place where the land and water seem to be on the verge of a sacred offering if only we would pay close enough attention to hear it. And yet from the time of Escalante to the day Holmstrom bumped his boat against the backside of Hoover Dam, few white people—Powell and his crew and Holmstrom are the only of which I'm aware—were able to describe or at least allude to feeling any affinity for this place.

Among the milestones the conservation movement has achieved, it has become as acceptable to talk about one's personal biophilia as it is to campaign to protect and to defend the places where it's most

Next spread: Experts say the western "megadrought" is the worst in twelve hundred years, and predictions forecast Reservoir Powell dropping so low, the Glen Canyon Dam turbines would not be able to function. Navajo, Hopi, and Southern Paiute ancestral lands, Arizona. PETE MCBRIDE PHOTOGRAPHY

possible to nurture this feeling. The previous geographic isolation that Brower identified as the curse of the canyon, that "neither you nor I, nor anyone else, knew it well enough to insist that at all costs it should endure," is no longer the issue. Plenty of people know and love this place. The question now, as Berry suggests, is whether acts of political determination, commensurate with the affinity for this river, will be enough to recover it, and ourselves, from a time of considerable ignorance.

Because of explorers like Powell and Holmstrom, because of visionary activists like David Brower, river guides like Martin Litton, artists like Eliot Porter, and writers like Edward Abbey, we remember Glen Canyon. As long as we remember, we keep alive the possibility that our mistakes need not define us. And though there is always more complexity to any river, any landscape, than what we can imagine, we might imagine that we still have a chance to get things right, this time by honoring the simple promise Porter offers.

"It is reflection that imparts magic to the waters of the Glen Canyon and its tributaries. Every pool and rill, every sheet of flowing water, every wet rock and seep—these mirror with enameled luster the world about. In narrow chasms streams of melted gems flow over purple sand past banks of verdant willow. Small puddles, like shining eyes, fuse the color of pink rocks and cerulean sky, and wet ripples of mud may do the same thing. In the changing light nothing remains the same from year to year or hour to hour. Flood and drought, heat and cold, life and death alter the finer details incessantly, but they leave unchanged the grand plan and enchanting quality of the Colorado's masterwork."

- - -

I finally catch up with Balken, finding him basking in the warm sun on a broad sandy bench above the river. The canyon has opened, and Balken tells me it remains more valley than cliff walls until the Escalante joins the Colorado several miles downstream. I ask him where the river succumbs to the slack water of the reservoir. "Not sure," he replies. "It varies from year to year, but every year since about 2005, everything

from just a little way back upstream of here has been free-flowing."
After a moment's pause, he ventures, "I should get down here more.
And I should get people like you down here more. It's part of what GCI
should be doing. But besides that, it just feels great down here." We
nod quietly. We peel oranges and try to identify an unseen bird by the
sound of its song. The intervals of silence between the bird's calls are
filled with bright possibility. We're smiling. Still smiling as we stand on
the banks of a miraculous river returned from the dead and begin the
slog back upstream.

> To put the world and yourself at the same time in a valid
> perspective, you must remove yourself from the demands
> of both. The world's demands fade the faster, but none-
> theless surely your own will shrink to acceptable propor-
> tions and cannot sally forth to attack you. In the wilder-
> ness of Glen Canyon you do not assail yourself. You glide
> on into the day, unusurped, living, as all good river travel-
> ers should, in the present. — Eliot Porter

WHAT SPIRITS MIGHT WEAR IN 2050

Let me assure you that we have only begun to fight, and we are not going to rest until we have established the principle "that our National Parks shall be held forever inviolate," and until we have demonstrated to the satisfaction of everyone that the American people stand for that principle. We are going to keep up the good fight without fear or favor, "if it shall take until doomsday."
— William E. Colby, Sierra Club Secretary, in a 1909 letter to Gifford Pinchot

It would appear that John Muir failed in his bid to save Hetch Hetchy Valley. "One of nature's most rare and precious mountain temples," as Muir described it, was buried in 1923 by O'Shaughnessy Dam to provide water for a growing San Francisco Bay Area population. Before this happened, there were two Yosemites: the one visited in the past decade by four million people a year, and its twin, the Hetch Hetchy Valley, which no living person has seen. John Muir saw it and loved it as

The Hetch Hetchy Dam receives the bulk of its water from the Sierra snowpack miles above the reservoir. The Hetch Hetchy water system supplies the entire city of San Francisco. Southern Sierra Miwuk ancestral lands, California. MICHAEL MACOR much as any place on Earth. The drowning of Hetch Hetchy broke Muir's heart, and perhaps hastened his death. A century later, calls persist for the tomb of Muir's most favored mountain temple to be exhumed.

O'Shaughnessy Dam, which blocks the Tuolumne River at the foot of the now drowned valley, is nearly a century old, and yet the controversy it engendered has not aged much since Muir's dying day. Like the dams recently removed from the Elwha River in Washington State, O'Shaughnessy Dam was built inside the boundaries of a national park. The Raker Act, signed by President Wilson in 1913, allowed for the exception. Back then, two hundred newspapers around the country editorialized that Hetch Hetchy should not be drowned, that it was a violation of the spirit, if not the letter of the law that created Yosemite. Congressional opposition to damming the valley was considerable, so much so that another law, the Organic Act, which created the National Park Service and stipulated that dams were required to receive a permit to be built within national parks, was passed in 1916.

I'm standing on a wooden footbridge, spanning a gap three-quarters of the way down majestic Wapama Falls, to see for myself if sunlight should again illuminate the once verdant meadows of the Hetch Hetchy Valley; to determine whether Muir's campaign to save a "precious mountain temple," begun more than a century ago, is work worthy of completion. From this vantage point, all appears tranquil: O'Shaughnessy Dam lies across the valley, watched over by its ancient massive granitic sentinels. Beyond the horizon line of the dam lies the Grand Canyon of the Tuolumne.

The bridge I'm standing on sits at the foot of the eleven-hundred-foot falls, which is, technically speaking, fourteen-hundred-foot Wapama Falls. O'Shaughnessy drowned the lower portions of it. Fixing my gaze upward, toward the point of origin from where the water descends, I imagine, as Muir did in his description of these falls, "the flowing white gossamer gown of a very tall, whisper-thin goddess, emerging miraculously via some mysterious alchemical reaction out of the angled slabs of schist above, bejeweled in sunlight from head to knee." From there on down, shins to toes, she's cemented into the sawed-off half of an old moldy refrigerator—the quieted waters of the Tuolumne River. We can no longer see what Muir did, what drove him to so passionately defend the valley he called "Yosemite's twin."

"After my first visit, in the autumn of 1871, I have always called it the Tuolumne Yosemite, for it is a wonderfully exact counterpart of the great Yosemite, not only in its crystal river and sublime rocks and waterfalls, but in the gardens, groves, and meadows of its flower park-like floor. The floor of Yosemite is about 4,000 feet above the sea, the Hetch Hetchy floor is about 3,700; the walls of both are of gray granite, rise abruptly out of the flowery grass and groves are sculptured in the same style, and in both every rock is a glacial monument." So yes, it appears to me, at least, that Muir's work should be completed. By all means, free that figurative goddess from her slack-water shackles. But it will probably take the diligent effort of someone who isn't spending his time conjuring up metaphorical waterfall mythologies. Someone who's head isn't so often in the clouds. Someone like Spreck Rosekrans.

"I'm a heavily quantitative guy," he says. "Some environmentalists will say 'live with less,' but I'm just as inclined to see if we can't give people the same thing in another way." Rosekrans, a computer programmer by training, a career conservationist whom David Brower once asked to calculate the hydrological feasibility of removing Glen Canyon Dam, is an obsessive analyst of water delivery systems. He's also the executive director of Restore Hetch Hetchy, a nonprofit that aims to give America the other half of its Yosemite National Park back by removing O'Shaughnessy Dam.

What Rosekrans is measuring is the water supply in and around north-central California, and there doesn't seem to be any reason for regional citizens here to equate the restoration of Hetch Hetchy with a water-impaired future. According to research compiled by the meticulous Rosekrans, water supply improvements in California over the last twenty-five years have accounted for more than seventeen times the storage volume of Hetch Hetchy Reservoir, which provides three hundred sixty thousand acre-feet. California's ongoing megadrought has helped spur development of additional water supply

Next spread: The future site of the Hetch Hetchy Reservoir. Southern Sierra Miwuk ancestral lands, California. MICHAEL MACOR / THE SAN FRANCISCO CHRONICLE / GETTY IMAGES

4727

HETCH HETCHY

storage. Since 1990, more than 5.5 million acre-feet of storage have been added.

Two of these projects, Los Vaqueros and Diamond Valley Reservoirs, are surface reservoirs. The rest are groundwater aquifers that have been developed either to serve local communities or to use as "banks" that exchange ground and surface supplies, using California's vast network of pump canals. In another instance of the Golden State pursuing policy goals the rest of the world would do well to emulate, a lot of new water storage is underground, where infrastructure has been put in place to replenish and access depleted aquifers—and where water doesn't evaporate. This is, in any kind of sane future in arid western American climates, how water will be stored. The potential for groundwater storage is vast: between 850 million and 1.3 billion acre-feet, according to California's Department of Water Resources. By contrast, the state's surface reservoirs store less than fifty million acre-feet.

Some communities have invested in their own groundwater, and others have entered into banking contracts with agencies hundreds of miles away. Santa Clara Valley Water District's contract with Semitropic Water Storage District includes storage capacity of three hundred fifty thousand acre-feet—almost identical to the storage capacity of Hetch Hetchy Reservoir.

The power lost by the decommissioning of Hetch Hetchy is negligible in light of California's renewables portfolio law. All new forms of renewable energy in California are slated to produce almost two hundred times the power O'Shaughnessy Dam makes, which is roughly one-half of 1 percent of California's last nuclear power plant, Diablo Canyon, which will close in 2025. It produces enough power to supply 1.7 million homes, yet state and utility industry officials are unconcerned that shuttering the plant will deter the Golden State from its renewable energy goals, much less cause an energy shortage.

Safe, Sane, and Sensible: Daylighting Yosemite Valley's Twin

Water supply capacity and flexibility need not be sacrificed, and might even improve, if the dam that plugs Hetch Hetchy Valley is torn down.

Eight other reservoirs can be tapped by the City of San Francisco for municipal water, four of them on the Tuolumne. One of these reservoirs alone, Don Pedro, has six times the capacity of Hetch Hetchy Reservoir. "San Francisco has poor drought-year water rights," says Rosekrans. "If Hetch Hetchy were restored, it could also create an opportunity for the city to acquire drought flexibility." The senior water rights owned by the City of San Francisco would not be diminished if the Tuolumne River had just one less storage point. Those water rights, enough to hydrate 2.7 million Bay Area homes, could be stored elsewhere in the system, and "banked" for use in drought years.

Other projects, Rosekrans points out, including the controversial Bay Delta plan that affects the whole state of California, will require water system improvements and volumes of water far greater than the restoration of Hetch Hetchy Valley would require of San Francisco.

While Hetch Hetchy Reservoir's storage capacity is a minuscule part of the region's water storage array, it's the quality of the water stored there that San Franciscans rightfully cling to. San Francisco is just one of a handful of larger municipalities in the country whose water is still clean enough to forgo expensive filtration. But the dedication to un-adulterated purity may not last anyway. Portland, Oregon's, water was similarly unfiltered, but after sampling in their Bull Run Reservoir revealed a persistent bout of *Cryptosporidium*, an $800 million filtration system was designed.

But Rosekrans doesn't think quality or quantity will suffer—he knows that under any viable plan to restore the valley, good water must be a guarantee. "Any proposal to restore Hetch Hetchy Valley must assure that the San Francisco Public Utilities Commission (SFPUC) system can still deliver ample, reliable, high-quality water to its customers in San Francisco and other Bay Area communities," says Rosekrans. "Likewise, it is essential that San Francisco's modified system be operated to fully protect the Turlock and Modesto Irrigation Districts, which also rely on the Tuolumne River." There are, Rosekrans points out, multiple ways to ensure Bay Area residents that their water remains among the purest in the country. But they cost money, a fair bit of it. Estimates for restoring

Previous spread: Hetch Hetchy Reservoir lies within the boundaries of Yosemite, one of the United States' most visited national parks. Southern Sierra Miwuk ancestral lands, California. GIUSEPPE DI ROCCO

Hetch Hetchy Valley range from $3 billion to $10 billion dollars. Which seems like a fortune, until you consider that the budget for the City of San Francisco in 2021–22 was $13.1 billion. Or that the California state budget for the same year is $286.4 billion—complemented by a $21.4 billion surplus. Assuming dam removal costs $10 billion, for a fraction of the annual state budget, Hetch Hetchy could be brought back to life. Much of the capital expense of large public works projects is secondary to what a critical mass of citizens would like to see happen. Alas, San Franciscans are not down with doubling their Yosemite just yet.

"Beyond that, we need to do it, for our children and their children. They will need to know they don't need to live with the mistakes of the past," [Rosekrans says.]

A 2012 local ballot proposition, Proposition F, the "Water and Environment Plan," proposed to have the City of San Francisco prepare a two-phase study that would evaluate how to drain the Hetch Hetchy Reservoir and identify replacement water and power sources. It was soundly defeated by San Francisco voters. Proponents of the plan were outspent by a ratio of ten to one. Courts of law have proven as recalcitrant as the court of public opinion.

In 2016, attorneys for Restore Hetch Hetchy argued in state court that the location of the dam and reservoir, which flooded a valley in the park after construction in 1923, violates standards under the California constitution outlining rational water use. But a state appeals court in Fresno ruled that Congress had superseded state laws when it authorized construction of the dam. In late 2018, the state's high court unanimously denied an appeal by Restore Hetch Hetchy.

The campaign sits at something of a low ebb. At one time in the late 1990s, the campaign was supported by major environmental groups like the Environmental Defense Fund and the Sierra Club. The loss of support from the Sierra Club is a source of consternation for Rosekrans, as is the dearth of major NGO allies in what's routinely perceived as one of America's most progressive cities. But Rosekrans remains optimistic. "I hope people aren't viewing what we're working toward as quixotic," he says. "The fact of the matter is, it's feasible in terms of policy, in terms of water management and economics, to restore Hetch Hetchy. Beyond that, we need to do it, for our children and their children. They will need to know they don't need to live with the mistakes of the past."

Nevertheless, We Persisted

The milieu of the Restore Hetch Hetchy campaign seems apropos of the state of many dam removal campaigns around the country: the science and economics are on the side of free rivers. But politics, even in one of the bastions of progressive urban living in America, are not always conducive to heeding science, economics, and established law. This impasse, between compelling rational facts and data and the motivation to take wise action in light of what is known, is a frustrating component of many activists' work. Rosekrans has dealt with it his entire career. "So I did finish that report that David Brower asked me to do on what the Colorado would look like in terms of power and water supply without Glen Canyon Dam," recalls Rosekrans. "Even before the onset of the big drought, assuming even conditions of better water supply, the research I did back in the 1990s indicated you could lose Glen Canyon and have an equal or better river system in place."

Just as it has long been known that Glen Canyon is not necessary, practical, or justifiable, it has been widely and loudly protested that a place of such stunning beauty like Hetch Hetchy was drowned for a municipal water project. Spreck Rosekrans, it occurs to me as we wrap up our conversation, has contributed his exacting quantitative analysis to two of the most heart-wrenching dam removal campaigns in the nation. In his voice, I could detect something of the dejected state that all activists also must confront all too frequently. Brower felt it, along with an outsized case of existential regret after his acquiescence to Glen Canyon Dam. True confessions: I feel the way Rosekrans sounds all too often myself, in my own attempts to defend a couple rivers I love.

The facts, vital as they are, it occurs to me have not generally provided enough motivation for people to make healthy choices. Perhaps it's just the opposite: Reckoning with the facts of our increasingly precarious existence may well cause lots of people to obsessively and compulsively drink, smoke, crassly consume, take up religion or yoga or Facebooking or scrapbooking—anything from dwelling too long on reality, which, given the various modern crises we face, looks daunting to say the least.

Another nugget of wisdom from poet Wendell Berry goes like this: "Be joyful, though you have considered all the facts."

The context in which the dam removal movement has so quickly grown perhaps illustrates what this somewhat cryptic platitude intends. The facts don't look good. The daily litany of bad news can make it hard to move past coffee first thing in the morning. So, when you click on that message in your inbox and read, to give but one example, that according to a report from the World Wildlife Fund, freshwater species in North America have declined by 83 percent since 1970, that fact in isolation would seem to make a state of joyousness a proclivity of only the most far-gone bliss-ninny.

Rivers Returned

But in the broader context of the reaction to this disaster, O joy begin: eighteen hundred dams removed in the United States are part of a larger movement to fix what's been broken. Be joyful, though you have considered all the facts: O'Shaughnessy Dam is still plugging up the Tuolumne River in Yosemite National Park, but dams illegally ensconced inside another national park, the Olympic National Park, are gone. Halfway between the Bay Area and Portland, nine dams have come out on the Rogue River Basin, three good-sized ones on the mainstem. The Rogue's fall Chinook run is 99 percent wild and has increased five-fold in the past decade, even as other dammed and hatchery-reliant fish on major river systems up and down the West Coast have tanked.

Californians, or at least some Californians, recognize the cost-benefit ratio to removing obsolete, fish-killing dams, and it's likely just a matter of time before a few perspicacious legislators and agency administrators see a similar benefit in getting rid of one dam that's killed half a national park. Joyful fact: Spreck Rosekrans estimates a restored Hetch Hetchy Valley would be worth $8 to $9 billion a year.

On the other side of the country, eastern seaboard rivers, plagued by dams for centuries, are increasingly running free. The trout-fishing around New York City is picking up. River herring, at the base of the nearshore Atlantic aquatic food chain, are swimming up the Kennebec, the Penobscot, and the Sebasticook Rivers in the millions. Lobstermen reap the benefits, and shad and Atlantic salmon suddenly have a fighting chance. Waterways straightened and strangled by industrialization and urbanization are revitalizing Columbus and many other towns in economic and ecological metrics that make them rich in more ways than one. Dam removal works. It just needs to work more, and faster. Globally, although far too many megadams are under construction or otherwise in the works, the true cost of ruining a river with a dam has been made plain to a growing number of citizens. Though being a dam dissident will still get you killed in some countries, a "free-river revolt" spanning the globe from Chile to Myanmar to Albania and Croatia has grown. More and more people want to keep their remaining wild rivers wild.

There is opportunity in calamity, another fact British journalist George Monbiot had well in mind when he described what kinds of actions are not only desirable, but necessary in this window of opportunity. Of political as well as biological fortunes, Monbiot observes, "Things can change quickly. Only shifts commensurate with the scale of our existential crises have any prospect of averting them. Softer aims may be politically realistic, but they are physically unrealistic."

The pace and scale of freeing rivers not only in the United States, but around the world, ought to increase exponentially. The good that is done will be done in just the nick of time. We'll have to fly by the seats of our pants—keeping in our back pockets something like the advice that Franklin Delano Roosevelt gave during a cabinet meeting as the country seemed to be falling apart. "Try something," FDR said. "And if that doesn't work, try something else."

Something along the lines of this maxim was the motivation behind a creative and highly effective legal campaign by the Māori people, long-time citizens of the Whanganui River, New Zealand's third longest, flowing down the south end of the north island there.

Existentially threatened by the destruction of their home waters, these Māori, the Whanganui iwi, sought protection under the law, starting off with an intriguing legal thought riddle: If a corporation can legally be granted the same rights as an individual, why couldn't a natural system like a river have the same rights? After all, the well-being of the river could be directly correlated to the well-being of Whanganui iwi. And in 2017, in New Zealand at least, Fluvial Personhood is a thing. "In the eyes of the law," said Chris Finlayson, New Zealand's Treaty Negotiations Minister, "there will be no difference between harming the river and harming the Tribe. The river will now be seen the same way that some companies are also seen as legal persons. It will have guaranteed rights like a natural person, or human beings. It will grant the river the right of natural expression and protection under the law." The joyousness factor was so high in that New Zealand courtroom on the day the Whanganui iwi's river came to legal life, they broke into song right there on the spot. In their native tongue, they sang together, many of them with tears of joy streaming down their faces, one of their old standards: "As the river flows from the mountains to the sea, I am the river, the river is me."

This contingent of Indigenous river protectors are worth emulating. River activists might eagerly adapt the ontological position of these fine people, the Whanganui iwi: You, too, are a river. Not just any river. Think of yourself as your favorite river. How can your life be improved? What do you need most? What's required now are some tangible goals. What do you want to look like in thirty years? Who will you be?

If you're the Colorado, by 2050, Glen Canyon Dam should be cut out of your body like the cancer it is. You're tickled by the thousands plying your waters, many escaping the triple-digit heat in Phoenix and Las Vegas. In Glen Canyon, there's music again in Music Temple. In Page, the former offices of the defunct Bureau of Reclamation have been converted into a combination honky-tonk, hotel, and yoga retreat center called The Place No One Knew, where intrepid explorers, some of them attempting to repeat much of the thousand-mile journey that John Wesley Powell did 180 years earlier, can enjoy a night or two of cold beer, a warm downward dog, and loud local music before floating through your Grand Canyon.

Maybe you're the Snake River. After sixty years of being slowly asphyxiated by four dams down by your ankles in eastern Washington, you were freed in 2032. Your muscle memory of being a conduit for millions of salmon vaulted back into your consciousness. A few of the charming little towns along your lower reaches, drowned out when your currents were stilled and pools swollen, are now peopled by grape growers, peach orchardists, solar power entrepreneurs, river boat men and women, including employees of a Nez Percé guide service called The New Medicine that will take you from Stanley, Idaho, to Pasco, Washington, in a leisurely thirty-day journey down the Middle Fork Salmon, Main Salmon, and Snake Rivers.

Or maybe you're the Tuolumne. The people who undammed you in Yosemite National Park were partially inspired by the ending of a book published in 2023 about the dam removal movement in its early adolescence, whose author pointed out in the last few pages that John Muir did not fail to free the Hetch Hetchy Valley, he just did not quite succeed in his lifetime. It is unfinished business, the author wrote, up to those who saw the beauty Muir saw, and wanted to pass it along like a vast inheritance to their own children. Back then the author wrote that the "divine repose" Muir saw before Hetch Hetchy was drowned is the rightful ecological inheritance of every American, not merely the water-users of one municipality or the power brokers of a single corporation. In the meantime, thanks to the prose of John Muir, that valley may be drowned, but is not quite dead, composed as it is of the stuff that "spirits might wear" as Muir described it,

> Imagine yourself in Hetch Hetchy on a sunny day in June, standing waist-deep in grass and flowers (as I have often stood), while the great pines sway dreamily with scarcely perceptible motion. Looking northward across the valley you see a plain, gray granite cliff rising abruptly out of the gardens and groves to a height of 1,800 feet, and in front of it Tueeulala's silvery scarf burning with irised sun-fire. In the first white outburst of the stream at the head of the fall there is abundance of visible energy, but it is speedily hushed and concealed in divine repose, and its tranquil progress to the base of the cliff is like that of downy feathers in a still room. Now observe the fineness and marvelous distinctness of the various sun-illumined fabrics into which the water is woven; they sift and float from form to form down the face of that grand gray rock in so leisurely and unconfused a manner that you can examine their texture, and patterns and tones of color as you would a piece of embroidery held in the hand. Near the head of the fall you see groups of booming, comet-like masses, their solid, white heads separate, their tails like combed silk interlacing among delicate shadows, ever forming and dissolving, worn out by friction in their rush through the air. Most of these vanish a few hundred feet below the summit, changing to varied forms of cloud-like drapery. Near the bottom the width of the fall has increased from about twenty-five feet to a hundred feet. Here it is composed of yet finer tissues, and is still without a trace of disorder—air, water, and sunlight woven into stuff that spirits might wear.

That eighty-year-old author and Spreck Rosekrans and a few thousand of the old farts come back to Hetch Hetchy every year now, kids and grandkids in tow, watching the restoration as it proceeds on pretty much the way David Brower suggested it should back in 1990,

Watch the process. Record it with word and sketch, as John Muir would have done, or with your video camera, so that you can report nature's progress to others before the day is over.

I lived in Yosemite Valley for three years and have been visiting it for seventy. I have a rough idea of what might be brought to Hetch Hetchy Valley if people are too impatient to wait for nature.

Here is my list. Reintroduce oaks, maples, dogwood, mistletoe of course, azaleas, Douglas fir, ponderosa pine, incense cedar, yew, a lodgepole or two, and plant them in random order, not in regimented rows. Add frogs, crickets, and coyotes for night music. Daytime birds are welcome, especially canyon wrens. Squirrels too, gray squirrels preferred, because Muir liked them best. Foxes, raccoons, and bears, but a limited visa for bears that have become addicted to human dietary habits. Add an eager throng of tourists, and all the wise owls you can get.

To the voices of all the wise owls, amen. To all creatures great and small displaced by dams, we will welcome you back.

To all who love living water: You are a river. Keep flowing home.

Next spread: The Bright Angel Trail descends 4,380 feet from the South Rim of the Grand Canyon through the million-year-old Kaibab Formation to the 1.6 billion-year-old Zoroaster Granite at the river. Navajo, Hopi, and Southern Paiute ancestral lands, Utah. PETE MCBRIDE PHOTOGRAPHY

INDEX

Pages 32/33, additional note: Photographs in the Carol M. Highsmith Archive, Library of Congress, Prints and Photographs Division.

Page 276, additional note: Eliot Porter, *Ruess Arch and Amphitheater, Davis Gulch, Escalante Basin, Lake Powell, Utah, May 12, 1965*, dye imbibition print, Amon Carter Museum of American Art, Fort Worth, Texas, Bequest of the artist, P1990.61.1.52.1, © 1990 Amon Carter Museum of American Art

Next spread: Adult Chinook salmon hit the end of the river in a pool below the Elwha Dam, which blocked their passage upstream. The dam was removed in fall 2012. Lower Elwha Klallam ancestral lands, Washington. STEVE RINGMAN / SEATTLE TIMES